ST MARTIN'S

TRUE CRIME
CLASSICS

ST. MARTIN'S PAPERBACKS TITLES BY CLIFFORD L. LINEDECKER

THE MAN WHO KILLED BOYS

NIGHT STALKER

KILLER KIDS

MASSACRE AT WACO, TEXAS

DEADLY WHITE FEMALE

POISONED VOWS

DEATH OF A MODEL

SMOOTH OPERATOR

THE VAMPIRE KILLERS

BABYFACE KILLERS

BLOOD IN THE SAND

THE MAN WHO KILLED BOYS

CLIFFORD L. LINEDECKER

St. Martin's Paperbacks

THE MAN WHO KILLED BOYS

Copyright © 1980 by Clifford L. Linedecker.

Cover photograph of Gacy courtesy AP/Wide World; cover photograph of house courtesy Bettmann/Corbis.

ISBN: 0-312-95228-7

Printed in the United States of America

St. Martin's Paperbacks edition / February 1986

St. Martin's Paperbacks are published by St. Martin's Press, 175 Fifth Avenue, New York, NY 10010.

10 9 8 7 6

Contents

Introduction

A President is shot down before thousands of witnesses, a school bus loaded with children is kidnapped, a religious fanatic forces hundreds of his followers to drink poison, and an individual known for his industry, generosity, and neighborliness is arrested in the sex-slayings of thirty-three young men and boys.

The incidents capture our attention for a while until some new horror occurs to eclipse the old. For a time there is shock and grief, but hardly any surprise. Politics by assassination, terrorism, and mass murder have become too commonplace. The perpetrators in some ways are like the professional gunmen of the Old West who reigned as the "fastest gun" until, inevitably, they were replaced by someone new.

The chain of atrocities in my own lifetime has seen a succession of American mass killers, all reaping successively higher tolls, that has included Howard Unruh, Charles J. Whitman, Richard Speck, Juan V. Corona, and the team of Dean Corll and Elmer Wayne Henley.

Now John Wayne Gacy, Jr., has been accused of eclipsing the toll of twenty-seven dead in the Houston slayings of Corll and Henley. But I have no doubt that some day even the grisly record of dead attributed to Gacy, that rotund amateur clown who reputedly used his contracting business to attract young male victims for sadistic torture, homosexual rape, and murder, it will also be eclipsed.

But it will be difficult to overshadow or even match the grisly ruthlessness of the murders that occurred in suburban Chicago. The murders are personally significant to me because I live in such close proximity to where they originated and occurred. My home is in the center of New Town, and almost every day I pass the clubs, discos, and street corners where many of the victims were apparently picked up by their killer. I know the street people, and I know people who have been friends, business associates, and neighbors of the man accused of some of the most horrifying crimes of the century.

I will also remember the murders because they so eloquently illustrate some of the serious flaws in our criminal justice system, which make anyone a potential victim of violent crime. The slayings expose both the worst of the system, and—thanks to the work of a relatively small but well-trained and dedicated suburban police department—the best.

A court order enjoining authorities and others from discussing the case prevented me from obtaining interviews with several policemen and others close to the investigation. Dozens of other people were available and cooperative, however. They were of immense help in compiling information for the book. Thanks to their consideration, it was possible, though difficult, to complete the research. It was necessary to work harder and dig more industriously, but the information was there to be minded.

Among individuals and organizations who gave of their time or facilities to assist in the book were: Jack Hovelson, of the Waterloo Bureau of the *Des Moines Register;* Chris Baum and Carolyn Lenz, of the *Times Home* newspapers, Division of *Lerner Newspapers,* Chicago; Barbara Buell, of the *State Journal Register* of Springfield, Illinois; Tim Dahlberg of the *Las Vegas Review-Journal;* Leslie Griffin, police reporter for the *Kalamazoo Gazette;* Don N. Jensen of the *Kenosha News;* Micki Winfield; Richard Crowe; Mary Benninghoff; Kathy Gunther; former friends, neighbors, and business associates of John Wayne Gacy, and parents of victims who willingly talked to me, as well as others related to the case in a more official capacity who cannot be named.

My thanks also go to the friendly people in the Black Hawk County Courthouse in Waterloo; the County

Clerk's Office in the criminal courts complex in Chicago; and to the staffs of the public libraries in both Chicago and Waterloo.

Finally, it should be noted that the names of Donald and Lydia Czarna and of their son-in-law, Gregory Katelanos, are aliases, in accordance with their wishes, as is "Kotowski," the maiden name of John Gacy's second wife, and James Tullery, Mark Miller, and Dwight Andersson.

Cliff Linedecker

Prologue:
Blood and a Euchre
Deck

Christmas-tree lights were already twinkling from the windows of the neatly kept single-story brick homes in Norwood Park township, an unincorporated area just outside the northwest boundaries of Chicago.

A biting wind swept across the tidy lawns, and twenty-nine-degree cold frosted the windows of the cars and pickup trucks parked on freshly plowed driveways and along snowy curbs.

By December 2, Chicagoans have accepted the arrival of cold, snowy winter weather and they plan their activities accordingly. In Norwood Park that means that many people had merely moved their weekend parties from backyards outfitted with picnic tables and barbecue pits, indoors to dens and living rooms or to basement recreation areas where guests could perch on stools in front of bars and relax in the snug comfort of sofas and easy chairs.

The families in Norwood Park, like those in the nearby communities of Norridge, Des Plaines, Niles, and in the far northwest side of Chicago, are made up of people who work in area printing shops, chemical laboratories, and factories that produce everything from screws and machine tools to surgical instruments and cutlery. They had long ago grown accustomed to ear-shattering blasts of noise from the engines of jets skimming low over their houses on their way to or from busy Chicago O'Hare International Airport.

The approach of the holiday season was making itself known in increased traffic at O'Hare, already the world's busiest air terminal, as travelers rushed to beat the almost impossible crush anticipated in a few weeks. It was also the busiest time of the year for Florence Branson, a one-time Iowa farm girl who had worked in her daddy's restaurants near Des Moines and Grinnell as a teenager before riding a bus to Chicago with a girl friend during World War II.

Widowed after eighteen years of marriage, during which she and her printer husband had moved to the northwest suburb of Rolling Meadows, she had taught herself to make a good living as a psychic and card reader.

Her system was unusual. She used a twenty-four card euchre deck, and, as she had been taught by a gypsy friend, relied on not only the pattern of the cards as they were dealt face up, but also on the psychic impressions that they stimulated.

She coined a professional name for herself by dropping the "n" from "Florence," and became well-enough known locally to obtain regular work as a reader four nights a week at a popular Italian restaurant and lounge at the far northwestern edge of Chicago. She also built up a private clientele who consulted her in an office she set aside in her home, and she regularly read at house parties.

Donald and Lydia Czarna, clients and close personal friends, asked her to read for about a dozen people, at a house party on December 2, 1978. Seated at a wooden card table set up in a small utility room used as an office near the kitchen of the bungalow, Florece had read for a half dozen guests, some of whom she remembered from previous parties, when the door opened and a big-bellied man she had never seen before walked in.

His cheeks were soft, with jowls that slumped wearily into a double chin, brushed blue black by dark but recently shaven whiskers. A Charlie Chaplin moustache, darker than his carefully styled, gray-flecked brown hair, helped dispel what might otherwise have been an almost cherubic appearance. Despite his bulk and obvious exhaustion, he wore his clothes well. The checkered gray-and-brown sport jacket, vivid red-striped tie, white shirt, and brown trousers gave his bulky frame the appearance of strength rather than flab.

But it wasn't the way he wore his clothes that impressed the reader. It was the uneasy foreboding of danger that seemed to follow him into the room. Her initial uneasy psychic impression was intensified when she half stood in her chair and leaned forward to shake his hand.

There was just time to brush his fingers and feel the moistness before he pulled his hand away. He nodded and muttered his name as he stared at her with unblinking, blue eyes that were rimmed with dirty yellow. He then eased warily into the straight-back chair across from her.

When Florece reads, she hands the cards to her client to shuffle. Then she takes them back, lays the deck on the table, and asks for a three-way cut. That's the last time the client touches the cards. Working from the left, she begins turning them up, arranging them one at a time into a three-tiered pattern of four cards each.

Taking the deck from the reader, the man balanced the ends of the cards on the fat inside ridges of his wide palms and quickly riffled them three times, then slapped the deck back on the table, still not taking his eyes off her. Diamonds on a ring that encircled a chubby left-hand finger glimmered as they winked at the light.

Florece's thoughts flashed to the image of a gigantic grizzly as she watched his hands. They were huge and powerful with stubby, fat fingers and nails that had been trimmed or bitten to the quick. A tiny scar stood out as a crescent of white flesh on one of his little fingers. Unusually broad palms made his hands look blocky. Florece studied hands closely. She was not a palmist, but the shape and condition of hands can provide valuable clues to the personality, occupation, and emotional state of the owner.

When she asked him to cut, he lifted the top cards with the thumb and forefinger of his right hand, and dropped two stacks next to those he had left untouched. Florece began turning up the cards. As they were flipped face-up, she talked of their significance, disclosed by the pattern forming on the tabletop as well as by her psychic impressions.

Her initial discomfort increased as the ace of hearts was placed on the table, surrounded by jacks, which in turn were separated by spades. Most disturbing was the inverted ace of spades, a certain indicator of danger or tragedy.

To the reader's trained eye and psychically attuned mind, the jacks represented young men grouped around the house card. They were surrounded by darkness.

"You have boyfriends," she ventured, posing the remark as a half question.

Although the reader shifted in her chair from time to time, the solidly built man seated across from her never moved. He never changed expression or moved his ham-like hands from his knees. His stare was as unemotional as warm milk.

"You mean friends, people I drink with?" he asked.

"No, I mean young men you have a . . . a different interest in. You're attracted to them romantically."

The uneasiness bothering Florece was growing. She had read for homosexuals before, and although she was personally repelled by what her Iowa farm upbringing had taught her was sinful and perverse, it was more than that. It wasn't his homosexuality that bothered her. The man was evil.

"That's just something I fantasize about," he murmured without animation. "It's one of those things you wonder about sometimes." His eyes remained locked, unblinking, on Florece's. His responses to her comments and questions were defensive, as if he were in a contest with her. He was curious, yet protective and jealous of his privacy.

His lack of emotion and movement was upsetting. He moved hardly at all, interrupting his passivity only once when he reached one hand to his face and brushed lightly at his cheek as if to smooth away the tiredness and the tension with a touch of his fingertips.

When Florece said she saw a young woman in his house, he corrected her. He was divorced, he said, and there was no woman in his life. He was argumentative. "I see some work being done by a woman. She's a woman with light hair. Housework. She's at your doorstep," the reader persisted, her finger tracing the outline of the queen of diamonds, which she had just placed in the next to last open space near the ace of hearts.

"I don't have a house," the man insisted. "I live in a condominium."

The reader knew better. She realized when he continued to insist that he had no house of his own that he was deliberately attempting to mislead her.

"But I see some work being done by the woman. Housework," Florece reiterated.

"I have a lady in to clean sometimes."

Florece abandoned the subject of the woman, which was obviously better left alone, and dropped the next card into the last position around the ace of hearts. It was the ace of clubs, an authority card—which, because of its position in relation to the others, indicated a jail experience in the man's past and serious trouble in the near future.

She kept her face as expressionless as possible and the conversation light. If the stocky man sitting across from her hadn't wanted to discuss a woman in his house, it was certain that he would balk at talking about a jail experience or trouble with the police. As quickly as possible she turned other cards, moving on to other events. "I see some problems with your family?" she ventured.

"I don't have a family," he grumbled.

"Do you mean to tell me you have no family?" she asked. This time Florece made no attempt to mask her disbelief.

"Well . . . I was married twice," he conceded, speaking hesitantly, through dry lips. "But my first wife ran off with my children and they've been gone for years. I hate my children anyway." His voice lowered and his brows knotted into a frown over his heavy lidded eyes. "I never want to see them. I don't want to talk about them."

Florece ignored the presence of still another woman in his house, which was indicated by the queen of clubs. He was doing his best to turn and twist facts and hide information. The reading was unpleasant, and she was anxious to get it over with. The discomfort was becoming physical and her stomach was beginning to emit warning signals.

After the last of the cards had been turned face up in neat rows of four and examined, she collected them again, shuffled them, and fanned them out, face down over the checkerboard pattern on the table. "Now, do you have any questions of the cards?" she asked. His question took her off guard, jarring her with its inanity.

"Do you think I can make out with the cleaning lady?"

As ludicrous as the question was, it was the first admission that the woman the cards had divined did indeed exist. Florece knew that the question was not sincere, and that it was obviously coined to convince her that her client was not homosexual.

"Oh, maybe if you work hard on it," the reader suggested, "then you might be able to date her."

He appeared to be satisfied that his love life had been put in order. Next, he wanted to know if a business proposition he was considering would be consummated and make him rich. The cards and Florece's psychic impressions showed that he was a capable businessman, with a good sense of organization and an ability to use others. There was no indication of riches in his future, although the cards showed signs of involvement in an important undertaking with another man.

Florece wanted to end the reading. She couldn't tune out the message of the cards or her own psychic impressions warning of danger to young men who were somehow connected with her client. The impressions hovered over the table like a shroud. She knew that she had to get the man out of the room.

"Yes, yes," she said. "You can be very successful. There may be a partner. I see a partner. Someone working closely with you."

He was satisfied. Thanking her for the reading, he arose from the chair and walked out the door. Florece gathered up the cards, slipped them into an empty box, and took a new deck from her purse. She would never use the cards for another reading. She had just spent one of the longest twenty-minute periods of her life.

She finished the rest of the readings mechanically, fighting the nausea that swelled within her. Five of the readings were for friends of the man whose presence had so upset her, and were paid for by him. David Cram, a young man who sometimes worked construction jobs, and his date, were two of those he treated.

When the other guests had left and it was the turn of the hostess, Florece told her of rushing through the reading of the uncommunicative, chunky man. "I was afraid of him," she admitted. "He's perverted and violent."

That couldn't be right, the hostess said. He had been a friend of the family for at least six years, she insisted, and was a thoughtful, generous, and gentle person.

Driving to her home that night, Florece Branson stopped her car along the highway, staggered outside, and vomited.

1

Murder City

Perhaps the most auspicious aspect of the birth twenty-nine minutes after midnight, Central War Time, March 17, 1942, was the date itself. It was St. Patrick's Day, traditionally one of the most widely celebrated ethnic holidays in Chicago.

The thoughts of Chicagoans and of all Americans on that day were on other things, however. Barely three months earlier the nation had been plunged into a savage and destructive world war, and American soldiers were dying in an unremitting series of demoralizing defeats in the Pacific.

Yet, at Edgewater Hospital in the city's far north side, thoughts were on life, not death and defeat. It made no difference that the parents of the St. Patrick's Day baby traced their heritage not to Ireland, but to Poland and Denmark. And it made no difference that the baby was born into a tempestuous time and into a city more known for the violent and venal ways of its citizens than for its positive accomplishments.

Chicago and the world welcomed the lusty, squalling baby boy. His parents named him John Wayne Gacy, Jr.

Beginning with its earliest days as a settlement, the history of Chicago has been solidly engraved with violence. Chicago has spawned and sheltered some of the country's most unscrupulous and rapacious politicians and most infamous and ferocious killers.

As the gateway to the West, Chicago had always

offered fortunes to be made by those who were strong enough and bold enough to take them. Every kind of vice and corrupt scam that man could think of existed in Chicago. Even the great fire that roared through the city in 1871 failed to cleanse or slow the villainy. From the Haymarket Riot in 1886, to the St. Valentine's Day Massacre in 1929, through the Democratic Convention riots in 1968, Chicago has been identified with acts of violence.

"Chicago is unique," once observed Professor Charles E. Merriam, University of Chicago political scientist and civic reformer. "It is the only completely corrupt city in America."[1]

But Chicagoans refuse to live in grief and loss for the past any more than they are willing to live in terror of the future. Some citizens, in fact, take a rather perverse pride in their city's violent and shifty reputation. There is never a February 14 when the media fails to commemorate the St. Valentine's Day Massacre with nostalgic stories of the mad days of Prohibition.

The Chicago Convention and Tourism Bureau would undoubtedly prefer that the city achieve its fame for landmarks like Navy Pier, the 1,468-foot Sears Tower, and Buckingham Fountain, or for such aspects of human achievement as its part in splitting the atom and opening the atomic age, or for the great men and women who lived and worked there, such as Clarence Darrow, Jane Addams, George Ade, and Richard J. Daley.

Unfortunately, too many events in Chicago history that should have been remembered with pride and satisfaction have been marred by violence. Events like the World's Columbian Exposition of 1893–94 commemorating Christopher Columbus' landing in the New World. While 21 million people were paying admission to the World's Fair along the lakefront, a little man with the prosaic name of Herman W. Mudgett was filling a charnel house on the south side with the bodies of murder victims and laying claim to the very unprosaic title

---

[1] *Playboy's Illustrated History of Organized Crime* by Richard Hammer, Playboy Press, 1975, p. 56.

of most industrious mass murderer in the history of the United States.

Mudgett, who used various aliases but preferred the name of Harry Howard Holmes or H. H. Holmes, was believed responsible for the murders of as many as two hundred victims, a large number of them unsophisticated young women and small children. Although he was linked to murders occurring as far away from his home base in Chicago as Toronto, and was eventually hanged for slaying a business partner and coconspirator in an insurance-fraud scheme in Philadelphia, investigators believed that he found many of his victims at the Columbian Exposition.

Although Mudgett eventually admitted to only twenty-seven murders and was officially credited with twelve, workmen and investigators who dug up the cellar under his murder castle found so many bones, teeth, and other fragmentary remains that it was estimated that he had killed hundreds.

There have been other celebrated crimes in Chicago since the days of Mudgett's horror castle. Child slayings like the ruthless thrill killing of fourteen-year-old Bobby Franks in 1924; six-year-old Suzanne Degnan, whose dismembered body was pulled from sewers in 1946; the triple murder of John and Anton Schussler, thirteen- and eleven-year-old brothers, and their fourteen-year-old friend Robert Peterson in 1955; and the puzzling deaths of the Grimes sisters, fifteen-year-old Barbara and thirteen-year-old Patricia, in 1956.

The child killings were dreadful, but it was 1966 before a mass murder occurred within walking distance of the Lake Michigan beachfront near the South Chicago Community Hospital that was so sudden and savage that it horrified people throughout the world. Mudgett's grisly deeds had been exposed nearly three quarters of a century before. The torture castle had been demolished and long since forgotten. Chicago was ready for a new horror.

It was just after 6 A.M. on a warm, humid July Thursday when Patrolman Daniel R. Kelly braked his squad car to a stop outside a building in the 2300 block of East 100th Street. A young woman he later learned was twenty-three-year-old Filipino nursing trainee Corazon Amurao, was standing on a ledge ten feet above the sidewalk screaming: "Help me. Help me. They're all dead. I'm the last one alive."

Drawing his Smith & Wesson .38, Kelly clattered up a half dozen steps and through an open rear door, moving quickly past the kitchen and into the living room. He stopped abruptly. The naked body of a young woman was lying face down on a divan. By a bizarre twist of fate, he recognized the victim as Gloria Jean Davy, a pretty twenty-three-year-old nursing student he had dated. A strip of torn linen that had been used to strangle her was still stretched around her neck.

It is not unusual for a policeman to date or marry a nurse. Their jobs bring them in frequent contact. And city policemen learn to find their way around hospital emergency rooms as quickly as they learn to travel with a partner.

Kelly's partner was Patrolman Lennie Ponne. As Ponne coaxed the shrieking young woman from the ledge back into the building, Kelly moved past the body on the divan and climbed the stairs to the second floor. He was met by a hideous scene. The mutilated bodies of seven more student nurses were scattered like limp and broken dolls throughout the apartment. Their wrists were bound with linen strips. Their mouths were gagged. They were all dead.

When Miss Amurao, the lone survivor of the slaughter, had quieted enough to be questioned, she explained that she had let the killer into the building at about eleven o'clock the night before.

Six of the girls were in their rooms, she said, when someone knocked on the door downstairs. Assuming it was one of the nurses who had forgotten her key, she went downstairs and opened the door. A slender young man confronted her. He was dressed in dark trousers and a jacket that opened over a white T-shirt. He held a long, gleaming knife in one hand and a revolver in the other.

"I'm not going to hurt you. I need your money to get to New Orleans," he said, attempting to make his voice soothing and reassuring. "I'm not going to hurt you. I just want your money." The unmistakable sweet odor of whiskey followed him as she led him upstairs, the gun trained on her back.

The girls were quickly assembled in a single room and forced to lie face down on the floor as the gunman tied their hands and gagged them with strips of linen he tore from a sheet. Three other girls were professionally tied with good strong square knots and gagged as they returned to the house during the next forty-five minutes.

All of them submitted without struggling. The Filipino nurses suggested at the last moment that they all try to overpower the armed intruder, but were overruled by some of the American girls who, calling on their knowledge of classroom psychology, believed it would be better to cooperate and avoid doing anything to make him angry.

With their last opportunity to resist gone, the young women listened in eye-bulging dread as the man rummaged through their rooms. One by one he then led them from the front room. Miss Davy was first. She was taken downstairs. He returned alone nearly a half hour later and led away one of the Filipino girls.

The quiet was terrifying. The more time that passed, the hollower his promises not to hurt anyone began to sound. The young women were helpless and in the power of a man who was a thief, had been drinking, and was armed with terrifying weapons capable of dealing death or horrifying injury. There was little about the situation to inspire confidence in his good intentions. Wriggling and squirming, Miss Amurao rolled over to one of the bunk beds and squeezed underneath, pressing her body against a wall.

She remained there, her frightened brown eyes wide open as the remaining girls were led away. After the last girl left, there was total silence. At 5 A.M., the shrill peal of an alarm clock shattered the funereal quiet. The young nurse began to struggle free of her bonds, and thirty minutes later she was on the window ledge screaming for help.

The mass murder had been carried out with almost unbelievable ferocity. Cook County Coroner Dr. Andrew J. Toman, working with a half dozen pathologists and investigators manning a mobile crime laboratory, quickly determined that Miss Davy had been strangled. All the other victims had been stabbed. Some had been both stabbed and strangled. One nurse's throat was slit. Another had been stabbed in the back, neck, and eye. Newspapers described the massacre as the most bestial crime in Chicago's history.

Three days later, concluding one of the biggest manhunts ever mounted in Chicago, police picked up a Texas drifter who drank too much alcohol and shot too much dope and charged him with the crime.

A sketch by a police artist made from a description provided by Miss Amurao, and a tattoo, "Born to Raise Hell," on the left arm, led to his capture. Richard Speck, a sometime maritime worker who had been trying to book working passage to New Orleans, was arrested after he had slashed his wrists in a skid-row hotel and was recognized by a doctor at Cook County Hospital. The doctor had seen the police sketch and read of the tattoo in a newspaper, just before being called to the emergency room to work on Speck.

A young lawyer with the State's Attorney's office, Louis B. Garippo, handled the administrative details of the trial, which was moved from Chicago to Peoria, Illinois in an effort to dilute the circuslike shenanigans and the effect of publicity to ensure a fair trial for the defendant.

One of the most difficult aspects of the task was accommodating the unruly horde of reporters who fought each other for seats, while still managing to keep a few spots for other members of the public. But Garippo, whose deceptive easy-going manner and meticulous workmanship were honed during three years in Army intelligence, calmly did his best. Before the judge and jury were halfway to a finding of guilty, and sentences for Speck totaling from 400 to 1,200 years in prison, there were empty seats in the courtroom almost every day. Even the shock of murders coming eight at a time can pale after a few months, especially if they occur in Chicago, where hundreds of people die violently every year.

John Wayne Gacy, Jr., was born twenty-four years before the butchery committed by Richard Speck. He was the offspring of a forty-one-year-old machinist, John Wayne Gacy, Sr., a Chicago native, and his thirty-three-year-old wife, born Marion Elaine Robinson, in Racine, Wisconsin.

The father-to-be checked his wife into Edgewater Hospital at about 9:30 P.M. on March 16. Barely three hours later their first and only son was delivered by their physician, Dr. David S. Levy. Dr. Levy would periodically continue to provide medical care for members of the family, including the healthy baby boy, for more than thirty-five years.

The baby was a Pisces, with the same birth date as Rudolf Nureyev and the same astrological sign as George Washington, Albert Einstein, and Charley Pride. On the birth certificate, his mother's profession was listed as "housewife." It was an occupation she had followed for more than three years after a depression-year wedding in 1938.

When the new baby was taken home a few days later, it was to a family that already included a two-year-old sister, Joanne. Two years later the third and last child, Karen, completed the family.

The world of war and urban violence seemed far away from that of young Johnny Gacy as he grew up on the north side. His mother had inherited a Danish respect for cleanliness from her Scandinavian ancestors, and he lived in a neatly kept home, attending neighborhood Catholic schools with his sisters until he was eleven.

The family moved at about that time and he transferred to public schools, earning a reputation as a student ranging from good to indifferent. He was a well-behaved child and got along well with his teachers. He had a newspaper route and worked part-time in a grocery store after school hours. Everywhere the family lived, his relationship with his neighbors was good. He was a typical neighborhood boy who joined the Boy Scouts, romped with his dog, and played stickball and other street games with his friends.

He hit his head on a playground swing when he was eleven, and suffered occasional blackouts until he was about sixteen, when the trouble was diagnosed as a blood clot on the brain. The clot was dissolved with medication and the blackouts stopped.

There were other encounters with the medical profession, however. The boy was hospitalized for five days to have his appendix removed when he was fifteen, and in 1958 he began taking medication for a heart ailment.

But his health was probably as good or better than many of the youngsters he went to school with. Perhaps the most significant aspect of his school experience was the fact that he attended four high schools and never completed his senior year.

The first was Carl Schurz, a huge coeducational high school on the far north side. At Schurz, Johnny Gacy was no more and no less noticeable than any other student. He was never one of the popular boys. Nevertheless, he made friends and he got along well enough with his schoolmates to earn a reputation as a generally easygoing young man, although years later he told his first wife that he was taken out of school in a straitjacket a couple of times after flying into uncontrollable rages.

His grades could have been better, but those of many of his schoolmates were worse. If there was anything outstanding about him during his student years, it may have been his neatness. Many of the other boys his age were careless about their dress. He wasn't. His clothes weren't expensive, but they were always neat and carefully chosen.

His manner of dressing was one of the things about him that most impressed a girlfriend of his sisters, Carole Kotowski. Carole was petite and perky, with a kind of vanilla-ice-cream beauty, and she giggled with John's sisters about the fact that he kept his room cleaner and neater than theirs.

Even though they dated only once, when they were both sixteen, she remembered his neatness. She was a student at Schurz, and he had just transferred from there to Providence St. Mel High School.

As a high school student, he did better in some classes than in others. He made better grades in English and science than in print and auto shop. Soon after his date with Carole, he transferred again, this time to Cooley Vocational High, and signed up for business courses. But a year later he had again changed schools and enrolled at Charles A. Prosser Vocational. His enthusiasm for classes changed along with the shift of schools. At Prosser his attendance was spotty, and after a couple of months he dropped out. The restlessness that had been growing within John Gacy until it culminated in his leaving school led him to a brief separation from his family. It was perhaps overdue.

The singlemost blight in his life was his relationship with his father. The entire family suffered from the elder Gacy's nightly drinking bouts and drunken brutality. The head of the household beat his wife, terrorized his daughters, and repeatedly abused and belittled his only son. Yet, John loved his father, and constantly, and vainly, attempted to earn his praise. In later years the son talked sadly of his love for his father and his disappointment that they weren't better friends. The teenager was closer to his mother and sisters. The bond between the young man and his mother was particularly strong, and she affectionately called him "Johnny."

The day finally came when Johnny Gacy, still a teenager, left home. He headed west and eventually wound up nearly broke and alone for the first time in his life without family or close friends nearby. He landed in Las Vegas, where newcomers are appreciated more if they arrive with money than without. Jobs weren't easy to find for a teenager without so much as a high school diploma, but he finally found part-time work as a janitor, cleaning up at the Palm Mortuary.

Twenty years later, funeral director George Wycoski recalled that Gacy was a good worker, who cleaned about two hours a night when he showed up. "He was trying to get money to get back East," said Wycoski. "That's all there is to it. He was just a transient."[2]

Gacy saved enough money within a few months to pay for his transportation, and a couple of nights later he was at home with his family, being fussed over by his sisters and eating his mother's cooking.

His parents would have been pleased if he had returned to high school to earn a diploma. Although he had not graduated, he enrolled at Northwestern Business Col-

[2]*Las Vegas Review-Journal,* January 10, 1979.

lege. This time he applied himself to his lessons, and on graduation day he celebrated on campus by posing with his parents for pictures.

If there was any trouble ahead for the young man, it seemed that it would involve his health. He was developing a weight problem, and the heart condition that had intruded into his life was still bothering him. In one period of three years he was doctored or hospitalized several times with heart trouble. In 1961 he spent twenty-three days in the hospital with a spine injury.

Nevertheless, his future looked rosy, and he left business college optimistically looking forward to carving out a place for himself in the business world. A position in the sales profession was perfect for him. He loved to talk. Words spilled topsy-turvy from his mouth, and few people listened closely enough to realize how little meaning the motley collection of words and phrases often had. He was articulate and ingratiating. Those qualities, along with his natural gregariousness, made him a good salesman.

So it wasn't long after his graduation from business school that he went to work for the Nunn-Bush Shoe Company as a management trainee for sixty-five dollars per week. He did so well that by 1964, just before his twenty-second birthday, he was transferred to Springfield, Illinois, to manage the company's retail outlet at Roberts Brothers, a leading men's clothing store.

The March 8, 1964, *State Journal Register* in Springfield reported that Gacy was with Nunn-Bush several years in the Chicago area, where he attended school. The new manager of the shoe store held a degree in accounting and business management, the article said, and "... up and until his transfer (he was) very active in youth work and young adult clubs, of which he is a member of the board for the Catholic Inter-Club Council and membership chairman for the Chi Rho Club."

The article added that Gacy was an officer of the Holy Name Society, served for three years as commanding captain for the Chicago Civil Defense, and was a member of the federal Civil Defense for Illinois. The introductory spiel concluded by saying that Gacy was living in Springfield's Sherwood subdivision with an uncle and an aunt.

Springfield was good to the young shoe salesman. He worked there only a few months before he had met, courted, charmed and—in September 1964—married a pretty co-worker, Marlynn Myers, in a Catholic Church ceremony. Short, stocky, and pudgy-faced, Gacy was nothing special to look at. He made up for what he lacked in good looks with personality and generosity. The young woman whom he married was an only child and was impressed by the big spender from the city who talked of being so amazingly well traveled and accomplished, despite his tender years.

Marlynn felt a personal pride when she watched him charm customers. He sold shoes as spiritedly as he sold himself. It was important to him and he applied himself to the task with the same charm, persistence, and roguish bluster that he had brought to his romance.

Fortune smiled on the young couple when Marlynn's parents purchased a string of Kentucky Fried Chicken franchises in Waterloo, Iowa, and moved there. The family home was left for the newlyweds.

Springfield offered more than a bride to the dynamic young Chicago native. It was in Springfield that he discovered the Junior Chamber of Commerce, and joined the local group of energetic young business and professional men working to make their community a better place to live in by carrying out a never-ending series of activities.

As devoted to improving their communities as Jaycees may be, they also believe in publicizing their accomplishments. Jaycees are not known for their modesty, and for every public-spirited project they are involved in, it seems that there is also a dinner or awards banquet where members are publicly and profusely thanked, recognized, and rewarded for their various achievements.

The Jaycees was the kind of organization that Gacy could relate to. By dedicating himself to club activities, he found that he could win recognition and acclaim as one of the up-and-coming bright young men in the state capital and manufacturing center of ninety-six thousand. Instead of being a faceless shoe salesman in Chicago, through commitment and strict attention to club politics he could acquire the recognition as a Jaycee that was so important to him. He worked hard, and the recognition came to him. Only weeks after his arrival in Springfield, he was chosen as the Jaycee Key Man for April for helping plan the annual boss's night banquet and in recognition of his work on a project promoting purchase of U.S. savings bonds.

In 1965, only a year after arriving in Springfield, he was elected first vice-president and the chapter's outstanding man of the year. Jim Selinger, chapter president in 1965, considered Gacy to be a devoted Roman Catholic who took his marriage vows seriously, and the most energetic, ambitious, and outgoing of the three vice-presidents then serving.

Sometimes it appeared that the ambitious shoe salesman worked almost too hard. Friends kidded that he was becoming a borderline workaholic. The jokes were not considered so funny when he was hospitalized for three days with nerve problems.

Years later, Ed McCreight, one of Gacy's fellow Springfield Jaycees, recalled that he was bright, a rapid talker, and a good family man with a firm handshake. They were all qualities valued by Jaycees. McCreight thought that Gacy looked so much like Eddie Bracken that he could have been the actor's double.

The only incident involving Gacy that McCreight could recall as being at all unusual occurred when the former Chicagoan put a flashing red light on the dashboard of his car while they were working on a parade route. McCreight asked him why he was installing the light. Gacy replied that he had a card authorizing him to use the device, which is normally reserved for police agencies, the military, or emergency vehicles. McCreight told him to take it off. He might be entitled to use it in Chicago, McCreight said, but that didn't mean it could be used in Springfield.

The red light on his car, like the Jaycees, helped set him apart from other people, marking him, if ever so slightly, as someone different. He was someone who was going places.

Gacy liked the limelight. He liked to be seen with important people, doing important things, and he insisted

on being noticed. His driving reflected his need for attention, and although he was presumably a responsible married man, he drove like he was a teenager. He liked to burn
rubber. He wanted other drivers to notice him, and he
could be impatient when he had to stop at intersections or
was caught behind slow-moving vehicles.

He once cut into a funeral procession and joined the
mourners as he was driving to work. Police gave him a
ticket. He was ticketed for speeding the same year. Prior
to that he had picked up a pair of tickets in Chicago for
ignoring stop signs. His wife said later that he had a habit
of doing "crazy things" every once in a while.

The troubles with traffic violations were only minor
missteps, and they went virtually unnoticed among the
more rewarding fruits of his labor with Nunn-Bush and
the Jaycees. He had a job he was good at, and he was
earning recognition in his community. It looked like John
Gacy was building a good future for himself in Springfield.

Then his father-in-law, Fred W. Myers, offered him
a job with the fried-chicken franchise in Waterloo. John
and Marlynn Gacy packed up and moved to Iowa.

2...

Waterloo

The early months in Waterloo added further luster to the promising life of John Wayne Gacy, Jr.

The young couple settled into a pleasant bungalow on Fairlane Street in a newer, middle-class area of the west side. It was quiet and there was ample room for Gacy to putter with his hobbies of woodworking and gardening in the spare moments he could sneak from other activities.

From all appearances, the Gacys were developing into a perfect nuclear family. Marlynn Gacy had presented her husband with first a son, then a daughter. The boy's middle name was the same as his father's and grandfather's first names, John. The girl's middle name was the same as that of her father's beloved mother, Elaine.[1]

The life of the Gacys was almost storybook idyllic. Gacy appeared to be happy with his marriage, his work, and his social activities. Even his health was good. There was no more serious trouble with his heart, and no blackouts such as those he had told Marlynn about. Marlynn too was happy. She had two healthy children she loved, a pleasant home, and an industrious husband who was good to her. They fought no more than any other married couple, and he had never hit her.

John and Marlynn Gacy quickly found that Waterloo was a nice place to live. Situated along the Cedar River in

[1]The full names of the children, who have been adopted by their stepfather, have not been used to protect them from embarrassment.

the middle of flat Iowa corn country 108 miles northeast of the state capital of Des Moines, it is the governmental seat of Black Hawk County, a mere seven miles from Cedar Falls, the home of the University of Northern Iowa.

The people of Black Hawk County are midwestern friendly, helpful to newcomers, and hard workers. Like other Americans, they are good customers for the people who make it their business to sell fast food, such as Colonel Sanders' Kentucky Fried Chicken.

Being married to the boss's daughter may have helped Gacy obtain his job with the fried-chicken outlets in Waterloo and Cedar Falls, but it didn't mean that he would step immediately into a management position that would permit him to loaf while others did the work. He began learning the business from the ground up, sweeping floors, cleaning machinery, and cooking and packaging the fried chicken. The young man became an efficient manager, working on salary and commission. Twelve- to fourteen-hour days were not uncommon for him. Yet he still found time to join the Jaycees again, and quickly plunged headlong into club activities.

His fellow Jaycees in Waterloo, like those in Springfield, were impressed by his enthusiasm and tireless energy. The new Waterloo Jaycee sent buckets of fried chicken to the local boy's club. He built sandboxes to raise money for the Jaycees. He was one of the first to volunteer to shop for Christmas presents for underprivileged children. And he hosted big parties at home for his Jaycee friends.

Spending as much time with the club as he did, most of his close friendships were formed from among its members. Gacy didn't believe in waiting months to gradually insinuate himself into the confidence and companionship of others. He attacked head-on, with florid compliments, gifts, and invitations to parties. In the Jaycees, where work went hand in hand with recognition and where almost everyone could win an award of some kind, he glowed. He reveled in the comradeship and excitement the club brought to him.

"He was always working on some project and he was devoted to the Jaycees. The club was his whole life," fellow Jaycee Charlie Hill later recalled. "He wanted to be very successful and he wanted to be recognized by his peers. But that never bothered me. We all wanted to be successful."

Steve Pottinger was to remember his onetime fellow Jaycee as having "a hell of a big man complex."[2] Even in a community as friendly as Waterloo, the obsession turned some of his associates against him. But those Jaycees who didn't particularly like Gacy respected him, Pottinger insisted. "John worked his brains out, working for his father-in-law at those chicken places from early in the morning until ten or eleven at night," he said.[3]

Another Jaycee, attorney Peter Burk, considered Gacy's obsession with braggadocio and lying to be disturbing. It irritated him when Gacy bragged of having been influential politically or of having been appointed to important committees by the governor of Illinois. It was obvious that many, perhaps most of the stories told by the fried-chicken entrepreneur were lies.

Most upsetting of all to Gacy's comrades in the Jaycees was the fact that it didn't appear to bother him when he was caught in a lie. He just manufactured another. Even his wife Marlynn had realized that her husband constantly stretched the truth.

Nevertheless, Gacy continued to do his best to ingratiate himself with almost everyone he met. When Jaycees were working into the night on a project, he frequently nudged open a door with his knee at ten or eleven o'clock, announced that "Colonel John Gacy" was there, and walked in with his arms loaded with fried chicken. As the others dug into the chicken, Gacy dug into the work, even though he may have already put in nearly two normal workdays. Most of the young men appreciated the late-night snacks, but others were suspicious of his continuous attempts to buy friends.

They also bristled at the price they had to pay—listening to his stories of the years he had spent as a

[2] *Waterloo Courier*, December 24, 1978.
[3] *Ibid.*

Marine, and of his experiences driving an ambulance in Las Vegas. They would have been especially dubious of his claims to having been a professional driver if they had known of his local driving record. He never had a reputation for patience behind the wheel, and picked up a handful of citations in the Waterloo-Cedar Falls area for speeding and other traffic violations.

A look at his powerful five-foot eight-inch, 210-pound frame helped make his claims to having been a Marine somewhat more believable. He was strong, full of energy, and a man who was fascinated with the paramilitary trappings of police work. The flashing red lights and siren on his station wagon were instruments that helped satisfy that fascination, and they also helped him to stand out among his peers. They demanded notice.

Some of his Jaycee acquaintances were repelled at the policeman playacting, however, and remembered that he always became extremely upset whenever one of his fried-chicken outlets was robbed. Gacy considered it to be a personal insult that a bandit would be crass and reckless enough to rob a business he was involved in.

When the Jaycees weren't busy on projects, Gacy and one or two of his other club brothers frequently dropped in after work at the Clayton House Motel where Charlie Hill was manager; there they could relax and smoke a good cigar and share a few drinks. For Gacy, that meant a couple of shots of J&B Scotch, on the rocks or with a splash of water. He rarely had more than three or four.

These were good times for Gacy, and the only indication of unpleasantness in his life surfaced with occasional grousing about his father-in-law making him work too hard. He was also treated at a local hospital a few times, once for the flu, and twice after being involved in auto accidents—one seven-day period with whiplash and as an outpatient for bruised ribs.

Sometimes when Gacy dropped in early enough to see his friend at the motel, he brought his children with him. He was an attentive father and never stayed too long if the preschoolers were along. At other times, when Gacy parked his station wagon or later his new Oldsmobile Vista Cruiser in the motel lot, Hill noticed that a teenage boy was waiting inside the car. That wasn't surprising because the fried-chicken outlets employed many teenage boys and girls, and it seemed natural that Gacy would occasionally give one of the youngsters a ride home.

Some of the young employees were beginning to find it unusual, however. The best-looking boys most often got the offers of rides. And not all the boys would accept.

Fast-food outlets are traditionally planned to make the most efficient use of the smallest amount of space possible, and those that Gacy was helping to manage in Waterloo and nearby Cedar Falls were no exception. It was unavoidable that while working around stoves and hot grease employees would occasionally suffer a minor burn.

Employees soon began to notice that boys who turned down rides with Gacy walked especially carefully around him when he was cooking chicken or fries. Somehow they, more than other employees, were likely to be splattered with hot grease.

Other, uglier rumors eventually began reaching adults in the community, including some of the Jaycees. A few of the club members, mostly those who were already repelled by his boastfulness, began to make even greater efforts to avoid him.

Others, like his friend Hill, who had become club president, either didn't hear the rumors or didn't believe them. There was nothing about Gacy's behavior around the Jaycees to indicate that his sexual habits were any different than anyone else's. He was an entertaining companion who enjoyed the company of other men, but if the subject of homosexuals ever came up he was among the first to sneer and belittle them.

There were enough Jaycees who believed in Gacy to name him both chaplain of the Waterloo chapter and chairman of the group's first city-wide prayer breakfast. He capped his accomplishments with the club that year when he was named outstanding vice-president for 1967, and was honored as the best Jaycee club chaplain in the state of Iowa. He was ready to succeed his friend Charlie Hill as club president.

He wasn't the only one who had his eye on the job.

Peter Burk, who was one of the Jaycees whose suspicions of Gacy bordered on dislike, also aspired to the club leadership. Even Burk was aware, however, that Gacy had a persuasive personality that drew people to him.

Gacy had meticulously constructed his political fences. He was a member of Hill's executive board, and, buoyed by the close friendship of men like Hill, Pottinger, and several others, he looked like the favorite in the contest. Life was still smiling on him. He had even given notice to his father-in-law that he was going to quit the fried-chicken franchises and go in business for himself.

So on that spring night in 1968 when he got up from a chair in the front room to answer a knock on the door, neither he nor his wife suspected that their lives were about to be drastically changed. A policeman was waiting on the porch when Gacy opened the door.

A Black Hawk County grand jury had indicted Gacy on May 10 for allegedly committing sodomy with a teenage boy, the policeman informed him. Producing a search warrant, officers confiscated five rolls of obscene movie film and an envelope containing advertisements for pornographic literature.

Marlynn Gacy was stunned. There had never been anything in their marriage to indicate that her husband harbored a sexual preference for boys. He had been a good father and a good husband who worked hard and always applied himself wholeheartedly to whatever task he was faced with. If he was guilty of molesting boys, he had fooled his wife.

Nonetheless, two boys had told the grand jury that on separate occasions he either lured or attempted to coerce them into sexual encounters with him.

James Tullery, a student at East High School in Waterloo, told investigators that when he was sixteen and working at one of the fried-chicken outlets in August 1967, Gacy invited him to his home for a drink, to play pool and to watch stag movies. Gacy's wife and the children were visiting in Springfield. According to the story as it was reconstructed by Tullery, the restaurant was closed at about 11 P.M., and he and his boss drove to Gacy's house. Gacy mixed him a drink and they began shooting pool. Just before the last game, Gacy suggested that the loser perform oral sex on the winner. The whiskey had begun to warm the boy's blood, but he wasn't drunk. Win or lose, he told the man he wasn't interested.

Gacy laughed and treated the incident as a joke. After the game, he invited the boy to fix himself another drink. In the meantime, Gacy set up a screen and loaded a stag film into the projector.

Sipping at the whiskey, the man and boy stared at the images of men, women, and animals coupling with each other on the screen. There were more drinks, and after a second film was shown, Gacy suggested that the boy walk upstairs. Gacy said he would join him a few minutes later.

Tullery jerked in a spasm of alarm when Gacy walked into the room and leveled a kitchen knife at him. By that time, the boy was unsteady and sluggish from the effects of the alcohol he had consumed, and the knife was nothing to fool with even if he had been more alert. Slowly he allowed himself to be backed into a bedroom, and stopped only when the back of his legs brushed against the bed.

Gacy lunged at him and the boy sprawled backward on the bed with Gacy on top of him. Tullery struggled to push the man off and the knife nicked him on the left arm. Blood poured from the cut, spreading over his arm and onto the bedspread. Tullery yelled.

Apparently sobered by the blood and the scream, Gacy rolled off him and stood up, helping the boy to his feet. They were both panting. Gacy put down the knife. Dabbing at the blood with a paper tissue, Tullery stumbled dazedly from the bedroom and with the older man made his way shakily downstairs.

His employer was acting as if he were oblivious to the events that had occurred a few minutes earlier. The chunky businessman was already boasting that he had taken several courses in sex education and was so knowledgeable that he had written a book on the subject. Some people, he confided, were sexually stimulated by bondage, being tied with ropes and manacles of various types.

Gacy offered to demonstrate. He explained that Tullery could better understand about bondage if he permitted himself to be chained. Unresisting, the boy put his hands behind his back and allowed Gacy to chain them together. Once his hands were securely manacled behind his back, Gacy pushed him onto a chair, then unsteadily climbed astraddle of him. Alarmed, Tullery jerked backward and Gacy toppled off.

The boy said that he remembered being lifted roughly from the chair and half-carried, half-pushed up the stairs and back into the bedroom. Again he was shoved violently onto the bed, and from somewhere chains were produced and fastened around his legs.

Moments later, Gacy's hands were around his neck, choking him. Tullery struggled momentarily, then slumped. As Gacy felt the body become limp under him, he removed his hands from around the youth's neck, lifted himself up, and unshackled his victim. Tullery left the house a few minutes later.

Gacy was not charged with attacking the boy. The sodomy charge involved Mark Miller, another youth—who, according to court records, committed different deviate sex acts with Gacy in the late summer of 1967.

Gacy denied to his wife that he had engaged in sexual relationships with boys. At one point, a court official said Gacy insisted on taking a lie detector test to prove his innocence. He failed it. Eventually he admitted to authorities that he had submitted to acts of oral sex with Miller, a sixteen-year-old West High School sophomore. Not surprisingly, Gacy's recollection of the incident differed from that of the boy.

Gacy said he was driving with Miller in his car one day when he remarked that he had heard that the boy was known to perform fellatio. Miller admitted that he had, and offered to take care of Gacy for forty dollars. Gacy objected that the price was too high. They finally agreed to five dollars as a reasonable fee. He was nervous. Despite the boy's efforts, he couldn't maintain an erection and was unable to reach a climax. The youth was understanding and agreed to try again later for the same price.

A few days later, Gacy told investigators, the boy came to his home on a Saturday morning and again performed fellatio. More comfortable in his home surroundings, this time Gacy was easily brought to a climax. He had oral sex with the boy once more the following month, Gacy said. He claimed that the youth approached him for a loan and at Gacy's suggestion again agreed to perform fellatio for five dollars.

In another statement to authorities, Gacy described the offense as an experimental situation only, an act that happened only three times. Gacy said that he and his wife practiced mutual oral sex during their marriage. Attempts to talk with Mrs. Gacy and obtain either confirmation or denial "met with stiff resistance and no cooperation from the woman or her parents," Parole and Probation Officer Jack D. Harker reported to the court.

Miller told the grand jury that he was forced to perform oral sex. Much later his statement mysteriously disappeared from the court files, although Tullery's statement was untouched.

Regardless of whose version of the incidents police and the courts believed, Gacy was in serious trouble. At home, his heretofore solid marriage was wrecked. Newspaper stories and gossip about his troubles had shattered his reputation in the community, although a few loyal friends refused to believe the reports.

Some of his friends accepted his claims that the accusations of the boys were part of a plot to defeat him in his campaign for the presidency of the Jaycees. Miller was the son of a man who was prominent in state politics and was previously thought to be unfriendly to Gacy.

Incredibly, Gacy was still thought by some to have a good chance of winning the club presidency after his arrest. He had never before been in trouble with the law for anything more serious than a traffic ticket and he certainly didn't fit the popular image of a homosexual. It was hard to believe that the burly fellow who boasted of his appeal to women was not sexually straight.

He insisted that he was being framed and had been set up to keep him from leading the Jaycees. He remained in contention for the presidency right up to the late May election meeting in the Isaac Walton League Clubhouse in the nearby town of Washburn.

Hill recalled that his friend waited until he was nominated to face Burk for the presidency. Then he stood up and, in an emotion-filled voice, announced that he was withdrawing "in the interests of the organization and my family."

"I think he didn't withdraw sooner because he always liked a contest, a race," Hill surmised. "And he always felt the charges would be dropped, that he would be cleared of that thing." Hill believed that Gacy would have easily walked off with the election if he hadn't gotten into trouble.

Burk became the new president and responded by describing the Waterloo Jaycees as one of the leading chapters in Iowa, and announcing that the local unit would host the next state convention. The new officers were dedicating themselves to attracting new members and to keeping those who were already active, he added.

Gacy was an exception to the effort to retain existing members. At the July meeting, Gacy was one of four Jaycees, including Burk, who received Key Man awards. But his troubles were burgeoning and bringing unwelcome publicity to the service club. Even Pottinger had to admit that the sexual nature of the charges made them especially difficult to contend with. "If he'd been caught embezzling, nobody would have said anything," he observed. Unfortunately, Gacy was accused of seducing or otherwise inducing one or more of the community's sons to commit homosexual acts. That was an offense that even the friendly and charitable people of Black Hawk County found difficult to tolerate.

"And of course," said David Dutton, the first assistant county attorney who was selected to spearhead prosecution of the case, "it wasn't just one incident. It was going on for some time, a few months before it was brought to our attention."

There was more trouble on the way, and it would become increasingly difficult for Gacy's friends to maintain their faith in him. In September, approximately four months after his initial arrest, Gacy's friends were dismayed to learn that new charges had been filed accusing him of hiring an eighteen-year-old boy to beat up Miller.

Filed by Black Hawk County Attorney Roger Peterson, the new charges accused Gacy of going armed with intent, malicious threats to extort, and attempting to suborn perjury. He was freed from custody after posting a one-thousand-dollar cash bond in Black Hawk County District Court.

Still dazed over the newest charges, Gacy's friends were further distressed three days later when an additional count of breaking and entering was filed against him. This time he was accused of breaking into the Brown Lumber Company in Raymond, a town about five or six miles east of Waterloo along U.S. Road 20, while he was free on bail on the sodomy charges.

Gacy went to jail, and when he couldn't raise bail, he was kept there. The burglary charge was apparently unrelated to the sodomy offense and stemmed from an incident involving his work in a merchant security operation. The job gave him a perfect excuse to outfit his station wagon with spotlights and to play policeman. The trouble at the lumberyard was not nearly as disturbing to Gacy's friends as the other alleged offenses.

First Deputy Black Hawk County Sheriff Robert Aldrich told local newsmen that Gacy had hired eighteen-year-old Dwight Andersson of Waterloo to beat up Miller. The motive behind the attack, Aldrich drawled, was Miller's involvement in the sodomy case. According to the story pieced together by Andersson, Miller, and Aldrich, Gacy gave the tough eighteen-year-old ten dollars and promised to pay off a three-hundred-dollar lien on his car if he would carry out the beating.

The new semester had just begun at West High School and it was one of those fragrant late-summer days that make students tarry outside on campus until the last minute before capitulating to the responsibilities of the real world and going inside for classes. New to the high school, Miller was pleased when Andersson approached him after classes and explained that he had been selected to act as Miller's big brother for the first few days of the new term. Andersson said it was school policy for upperclassmen to show incoming sophomores around the campus.

Miller eagerly accepted when Andersson asked if he

would like to take a ride with him. Not many eighteen-year-olds were willing to take younger students for rides in their cars unless the passenger was a girl, and the flattered sophomore chattered animatedly with his new friend as the car carried them past chartreuse fields of corn and forests of trees that were swelling with healthy color in the late summer sun.

He hardly noticed where they were headed until Andersson slowed the car and pulled it to a stop in Access Acre Park, a remote wooded area near the town of Hudson. Miller, his eyes squinting into the bright sun as he slid from the car seat, joined his companion, still talking as they walked together into the woods.

At that point, the stories told by the two boys conflict. Miller said he was told that Andersson had been paid ten dollars to kill him. Andersson said he told Miller he was paid ten dollars to beat him up.

The next moment, Miller said, Andersson produced a can of mace and squirted him in the eyes. Mace is a disabling chemical spray used by police and the military to disable unruly crowds and rioters. As Miller lifted his hands to dig at his smarting eyes, fists began crashing into his head and body.

Miller screamed and struggled furiously to get away. He was kicking and swinging wildly when he landed a fist on Andersson's nose, causing the older youth to fall back. Miller broke away and plunged through the trees. He left his shoes, shirt, and sweater behind. His glasses, which were hanging lopsided on his face, also dropped to the ground. Miller didn't stop to look for his glasses or at Andersson, who was holding a hand to his nose and trying to stop the blood that was seeping between his fingers.

Breaking through the copse of trees, the frightened boy scurried into a field of sturdy Iowa corn that towered two feet over his head and quickly hid himself behind its heavy green stalks and broad leaves. In a few weeks, the cornfield would be a silent plain of rust-colored stubs marching row after row across the field like ragged tombstones. But for the time being, the plants were full and thick and provided ample cover for Miller to hide, rabbit-like, from the older boy.

He cowered there for long minutes, until he heard the sound of the car starting up and moving away. When he felt it was safe, he ventured out and waded into a river to wash the chemical from his smarting eyes. Then he walked to a farmhouse, where he knocked on the door and told the people who lived there that he had just been beaten up.

The occupants of the house called the Hudson police and the Black Hawk County Sheriff's Department. Andersson was picked up and booked for assault with intent to commit great bodily injury. Then he was released to the custody of his parents.

By now just about everyone except Hill and Pottinger was ready to give up on Gacy. His protestations that he was innocent of the new charges, just as he was innocent of the earlier accusation of sodomy, went virtually unheeded.

"I am guilty of none of these," Gacy told the court of the newer charges, "except for making a verbal threat to Miller when he came to me in December of 1967 and wanted me to give (sic) an amplifier or else he would tell his father about this offense."

Time was running out. Dutton, who was later to move up and replace Peterson as county attorney, was committed to obtaining a conviction on the sodomy charge.

In September and again in October, Gacy was referred by order of Judge George C. Heath, of the Tenth Judicial District Court of Iowa in Black Hawk County, to psychiatrists for evaluation of his mental health. Copies of their reports would be provided for both the attorneys for the defense and for the prosecution.

The chunky businessman was first sent to the State Mental Health Institute at Independence in adjacent Buchanan County. A month later he was transported to the Psychiatric Hospital at the State University of Iowa in Iowa City, about eighty miles southeast of Waterloo.

The prognosis was not very favorable to the defendant. Although Dr. Leonard L. Heston, assistant professor of psychiatry at the State Psychopathic Hospital, and Dr. L. D. Amick concurred in finding Gacy mentally competent to stand trial, it was recommended that he receive firm and consistent external controls.

"We regard Mr. Gacy as an antisocial personality, a diagnostic term reserved for individuals who are basically unsocialized and whose behavior pattern brings them repeatedly into conflict with society," the psychiatrists wrote in a letter to Judge Heath. "Persons with this personality structure do not learn from experience and are unlikely to benefit from known medical treatment."

At the request of the judge, Heston later elaborated that "Predicting the future behavior of an individual must be based on the known performance of other persons similar to him." Individuals similar to Gacy, Heston added, appear to do best "where there are firm, consistent external controls on their behavior. Intensive parole supervision might accomplish this end as well as any other method."

Gacy was described by the psychiatrist as apparently a bisexual, and based on his personality, a person whose behavior "is usually regarded as thrill-seeking or explorative and not as an absolute fixation on abnormal sexual objects."

Dutton had been conferring with Gacy's attorney, D. A. Frerichs, and going over the charges and evidence against the defendant. On November 7, 1968, in an appearance before Judge Peter Van Metre in the Tenth Judicial District Court of Iowa, Gacy waived formal arraignment and entered a guilty plea to the charge of sodomy. The other charges were dismissed a few weeks later.

A guilty plea to one charge in return for dismissal of others is not unusual in the nation's courts. Nor is pleading guilty to a charge that has been trimmed from a more serious offense, such as a reduction from murder to manslaughter. The process is called plea bargaining.

Overworked prosecutors, struggling to keep their heads above the jam-up of cases overcrowding criminal court dockets everywhere, may find it convenient and appropriate to accept a finding of guilty to charges that are less serious than those originally filed in order to avoid long drawn-out court battles. There can be other reasons as well. A prosecutor may be unsure that evidence will support a guilty finding if a case goes to trial. Or an agreement may be reached to avoid calling a witness whose safety or activities as an informant or law enforcement officer would be jeopardized by being identified in open court.

Defense attorneys may advise their clients to plead guilty to a single offense if their case is weak, or if they fear conviction and sentencing on a series of charges. In the matter of the charges against Gacy, discomfort to the boys and to their families could be avoided if the youths did not have to appear in open court and recount potentially embarrassing testimony.

There is nothing illegal or unethical about plea bargaining. It is a device that has become increasingly necessary and prevalent in the criminal courts. It should not include agreement on sentencing. Sentencing is another matter.

Judge Van Metre, who was selected to preside over the Gacy case, is today a boyish-looking, unassuming veteran of twenty years on the bench. His father once presided over the same court, and the son moved up to the job some six years after graduating from law school at the University of Iowa.

Judge Van Metre takes the traditional image of the scales seriously and strives to temper the justice he metes out with mercy. A number of times during his career as a jurist he has lost sleep and agonized over the sentencing of a defendant, particularly young first offenders, when he was caught in the dilemma of deciding between a suspended or deferred sentence and attempt at rehabilitation, or imprisonment for the protection of the public. At times, prosecutors have grumbled that he tempers his judgments with too much mercy.

That is understandable to the judge, who concedes that he is not punitive. "My reputation is the other way around," he says. "I've run afoul of the law-enforcement people for being too lenient."

Consequently, it was mildly surprising when he rejected the recommendation of Harker, whom he had directed to make a pre-sentence investigation. Harker recommended probation on the sodomy charge, pointing out that Gacy had said he planned to return to Illinois and resume his old occupation, selling shoes.

"It appears to this agent that this is a valid plan if the

State of Illinois will accept him, as he apparently has written confirmation of a job and home situation there," Harker wrote. "What psychiatric help is available for this type of offender could be obtained there as well as in Iowa."

In the report, prepared on November 14, 1968, Harker pointed out that Gacy came from a strong family where the father was "considered a strict disciplinarian, but fair." Gacy was pictured as being assiduous with good work-performance, although he had indicated there was some conflict with his father-in-law, whom he considered to be too dictatorial in their business relationship.

Frerichs also pleaded eloquently for his client, reminding the court that Gacy was a married man, father of two children, and a citizen whose deportment and employment record were excellent until his recent "bizarre behavior."

The attorney insisted that probation would restore his client to society as a better person, while prison would return him to society "worse than when he went in. He would be exposed to many problems by a term in prison," Frerichs argued. "He will be taken back into the safekeeping of his family if given probation, and he is assured of employment."

Solemn and judicially imposing in his black robes, Van Metre listened attentively. Combined with Harker's request and the observation by Dr. Heston that Gacy might respond well to close supervision, a compelling argument had been constructed for probation.

When it was his turn to speak, Dutton reminded the court of the seriousness of the offense. "This defendant gained the confidence of many young people and abused their trust to gratify his desires," said the prosecutor. He recommended that Gacy be given the maximum sentence.

Dutton was convinced that Gacy would be a continuous threat, even on probation or supervision. Consequently, it would have been improper to recommend that the defendant receive less that the full sentence of the law.

Judge Van Metre pronounced a sentence of ten years at the Iowa State Reformatory for Men at Anamosa. It was the maximum allowable at that time for the offense.

It would be another decade before the criminal code of Iowa was revised so that under certain circumstances a similar offense could be prosecuted as a form of sexual abuse carrying a maximum penalty of twenty-five years in prison.

"The particular pattern you seem to have chosen is to seek out teenage boys and get them involved in sexual misbehavior," Van Metre said. Although prison would be unsatisfactory for Gacy, the judge remarked it would at least "ensure that for some period of time you cannot seek out teenage boys to solicit them for immoral behavior of any kind. It may possibly serve as a deterrent and a warning to others who might engage in the same kind of activity." Gacy stood impassively beside his attorney as the sentence was pronounced. He showed no surprise and no emotion.

Gacy was given credit on the sentence for eighty-four days already served in the Black Hawk County Jail. Appeal bond was set at twenty thousand dollars.

A week later, unable to raise the bond and with credit for another seven days in jail, he was transported to prison. John Wayne Gacy, Jr. was twenty-six years old when he made the transition from a life of backyard barbecues, house parties, good cigars, and relaxing drinks with friends to existence as denim-clad prisoner number 26526 in a barred cell. In the new life, other men decided what he would have for meals, when he would exercise, what time he would get up in the morning, whom he could write to and visit with.

He was also about to make the transition from husband and father of two children who shared his last name. His wife filed for divorce on the same day and in the same court building where he was sentenced. The marriage was irretrievably shattered by the arrest, disclosure of bisexuality, and criminal conviction.

Marlynn Gacy petitioned for a divorce on grounds that her husband was guilty of cruel and inhuman treatment that endangered her life and health in violation of the couple's marriage vows. Marlynn told the court that she had conducted herself as a loving and dutiful wife at all times during the marriage. She asked for alimony, property, including the car, attorney fees, court costs, and a reasonable division of other possessions. The divorce action was not unexpected. Gacy concentrated on the task of learning to live as a convict. Like every other undertaking he approached, he applied himself and worked hard at it.

A routine psychological examination he took while being processed into the prison system gave no indication that his emotional or sexual problems were so serious that they could not be solved, despite the earlier conclusions of psychiatrists.

Gacy's behavior appeared to bear out the more optimistic determination. He reacted well to the disciplined life of a convict. His reaction was typical of many people who somehow take to a prison environment where they are relieved of the pressures of decision making and earning a living. As Van Metre observed, Gacy was an individual who "behaves himself when people are watching him and he is under the gun."

Gacy settled into the routine amazingly quickly and launched himself into prison society with the same industriousness and earnest concentration he had exhibited when he moved first to Springfield and then to Waterloo as a young businessman. He avoided known homosexuals, and selected most of his prison friends from among other first-time offenders, seeking out those who were not convicted of violent crimes. One of Gacy's close friends in prison said that Gacy showed absolute scorn for homosexuals. He ignored them like the plague. All prisoners maintain some kind of false front, another inmate observed. Exhibiting a hatred for homosexuals may have been Gacy's.

Ray Cornell, who served time with Gacy and later became an Iowa prison ombudsman, witnessed the former Waterloo businessman's professed dislike for homosexuals. Cornell was one of those who knew that Gacy had asked another prisoner for protection because he was afraid he was going to be homosexually attacked.

Homosexual rape is a fact of life in prison, and it is a constant threat, particularly to young inmates. Many young prisoners, menaced with psychologically devastating mass rape by a half dozen inmates or more at a time, accept the protection of an older, stronger man and become his property. Much, perhaps most of the swift, brutal fighting in prisons, the knifings and beatings, is over soft, young first-timers.

Inmate number 26526 appeared to be uninterested in homosexual activities in prison. He impressed his convict friends as being more interested in material success. One of his friends said the John Gacy he knew in prison appeared to be always after money and was almost overly ambitious. He never missed a day of reading *The Wall Street Journal* if he could help it. And he talked animatedly of the luxurious restaurant he was going to open after he was freed, and bragged about his prosperous business investments.

To most people he felt were entitled to an explanation of why he was in prison, Gacy confided that he was doing time for showing pornographic films to teenage girls. One of his friends who knew the real reason convinced himself that Gacy must have gotten drunk and didn't know what he was doing. It was hard to believe that John Gacy was a homosexual.

On January 7, 1969, Gacy filed for a court-appointed attorney to assist him in appealing the conviction and sentence. Gacy said he was broke and without funds to employ counsel. He could not even pay for the transcription of the court proceedings and other costs.

Judge Van Metre appointed Attorney Henry Cutler to represent Gacy, but a week later Cutler was permitted to withdraw. He was replaced by Richard Knock, a Cedar Falls lawyer.

Dutton, who moved from first assistant in the Black Hawk County Prosecutor's office to the job of prosecutor while Gacy was in prison, vigorously opposed the appeal. He cited two reasons.

"One is the pattern of behavior that got him in trouble with us in the first place, involving his enticing of young boys into compromising sexual relationships," he said. "That's bad and frequently can cause irreparable harm to the young men involved. This was not just gentle persuasion, but also involved force and the use of restraining devices and weapons. I felt it involved a serious threat to young people.

"Second, this man was involved in the type of thing that is not likely to be cured but only restrained for a period of time. Since he had used weapons in the past, I felt it was just a matter of time until he harmed someone." Dutton was unimpressed by a promise of Gacy's to leave the state. A move to Chicago might solve the problem for Iowa, the county attorney realized, but it would not make the convicted sex offender less dangerous.

Dutton considered incarceration to be the only appropriate means of handling Gacy at that time. Jail or probation were the only choices available to deal with a person like Gacy. If therapy of any kind was to be involved, the prevailing theory held that state correctional professionals were more knowledgeable and better equipped to select the proper treatment programs. There was no appreciable attempt to provide therapy for Gacy. On August 28, 1969, the Supreme Court of Iowa dismissed the appeal. The conviction stood.

Accepting the fact that he was in prison for a while, Gacy set about impressing his fellow convicts and the corrections staff alike with his industriousness. He worked excessively hard, even on Sundays. With his background in the fast-food business, he was assigned to the prison kitchen as a cook and salad man. It was a job he could relate to, and he went about it with spirit.

Virgil Martin, Gacy's supervisor and food-services coordinator at Anamosa, was pleased with the enthusiasm that Gacy brought to the job. The chunky cook was a model prisoner, and the only criticism of him that Martin could think of was that Gacy had to be cooled off sometimes and reminded that he wasn't the boss.

There was a more pleasant surprise for the new inmate than assignment to the prison kitchen. Anamosa boasted a fledgling Jaycee chapter, one of the first organized in an American prison, for Gacy to become involved with. He threw himself back into the work of the service club with the same fervor, dedication, and headlong intensity that he had shown previously in Springfield and Waterloo.

On one Jaycee project alone, he worked 370 hours helping to install a donated miniature golf course inside the prison grounds. He helped with the inmates' annual Christmas drive to recondition toys for poor children. But he was best known for preparing Jaycee banquets, which were so popular that other inmates competed for the opportunity to work on them.

He impressed those around him with his business and organizational ability, as much as with his cooking.

Even in prison he managed to satisfy his need for attention and praise. He earned the Jaycee Sound Citizens Award and other honors. His work with the service club was so outstanding that he was featured in an Iowa newspaper article which brought him statewide publicity. But all other recognition was eclipsed when he finally realized his goal of leading a chapter of the Jaycees. He was elected president at Anamosa.

Gacy had been in prison for nearly a year when his divorce was scheduled for a final hearing. On September 18, 1969, he was back in the Black Hawk County Criminal Courts Building before Judge George C. Heath. The judge was no stranger to Gacy. It was Heath who had ordered the psychiatric examination before Gacy's guilty plea on the sodomy charge. This time, as attorney Donald H. Canning stood by for Gacy and attorney Frederick G. White stood by Gacy's wife, Judge Heath issued a decree of absolute divorce. The judge stipulated that neither the husband nor the wife would be allowed to remarry for one year.

Marlynn Gacy was awarded custody of the children and property, including the house, car, and most of the furniture. When her husband went to prison he left a mortgage on the house and an unpaid loan on the Oldsmobile in favor of the Waterloo Savings Bank. Gacy was also directed to pay $350 for his wife's attorney's fees.

Property awarded to Gacy included his movie camera, projector, screen and other film equipment, still camera, record albums, adding machine, typewriter, card table, file cabinets, golf clubs, fishing equipment, men's jewelry, portable radio, clothing, personal books, papers, awards, cookbooks and food-service books and Jaycee items.

Gacy said that the pornographic films confiscated from his home belonged to other Jaycees. They were not claimed.

Marlynn Gacy agreed to provide her former husband with photographs of the children twice yearly at his expense. He never contacted her or sent money for photos, however, and no photos were mailed to him. Heath deferred determination of visiting rights and establishment of the amount of child support until Gacy was released from prison.

The woman returned with her children to the comfort and security of Springfield, and obtained her old job back at the store. She told a neighbor that she had been unable to hold her marriage together because her husband was a homosexual and abused the children.

On his ride back to Anamosa, morosely peering out the windows of the police car at the ocher-smeared cornfields and dairy farms of rural Iowa, Gacy must have pondered the changes in his life and the role played by a couple of talkative teenagers. When he told his friends that he had done no wrong, it must have been easy to blame the boys for the problems that were leading him back to a convict's cell and away from Waterloo, where he had been a respected businessman and master of his home.

Gacy had lost his position in his community, his home, his wife, and his children, but he hadn't lost all his friends. Charlie Hill and a handful of other chums still believed in Gacy. Hill was still his friend and he wasn't afraid to say so. He believed unabashedly in Gacy's story that he had been framed and was set up by political enemies.

Hill figured that he knew Gacy about as well as anyone. They had been close friends who worked on club projects together and partied together almost from the day Gacy arrived in Waterloo, and Hill had never seen anything that would make him believe that Gacy was the kind of man who would molest young boys. In fact, Gacy projected an image that was just about as macho as it could be. So Hill accepted Gacy's explanation of why he was in trouble. "Somebody," Hill was convinced, "had to believe in the poor guy."

When Gacy was transferred to the prison release center at Newton, the minimum security institution where he was to spend the last few months of his sentence, it was Charlie Hill who showed up to see him on family day. On family day at Newton prisoners were given furloughs of a few hours outside the gates. Gacy qualified, and his friend Charlie Hill drove him thirty miles west to Des Moines for a steak-and-baked-potato dinner. Gacy ate two.

His friend watched, pleased and only mildly surprised as the burly convict dug into the double meal. He was a man who enjoyed eating good food as well as preparing it. It had been months since Gacy had sat down to a similar meal.

That night, as Charlie Hill drove on the long trip back to Waterloo, he felt better about his friend than he had in a long time. Gacy had been a model prisoner, and he was sure to win final approval for early parole.

He had stayed out of trouble, avoided bad companions as best he could, and never missed attending Mass on Sunday. He was so well-behaved and nonviolent that when a quarrel flared and another inmate punched him in the face, he didn't even strike back. John Prenosil, who worked in the kitchen with him and later became an Iowa state corrections officer, watched as Gacy shrugged his beefy shoulders, then turned and walked away, his eye already puffy and turning black and blue. Gacy had no intention of dying in prison with a piece of sharpened mattress spring or a filed-down spoon handle jammed between his generous ribs. And he didn't intend to lose good time by getting into a no-win fight with another inmate. The better he held his temper in check, the sooner he would be a free man again.

Gacy's parole was approved eighteen months after he had begun serving time in the Black Hawk County Jail.

No one consulted judge or prosecutor about the parole. The court's jurisdiction over a felon ends once he or she is sentenced. There are no provisions for the sentencing judge or prosecutor to continue their involvement in the fate of a convicted criminal. The convict's immediate fate is in the hands of the Department of Corrections and the Board of Parole.

"Even if Gacy hadn't been paroled after eighteen months," Judge Van Metre pointed out, "he would have been out in less than five years." The Iowa Department of Corrections has a "good-time" formula, similar to those in most other states, that permits a well-behaved convict to compile slightly more than five years credit off a ten-year sentence.

When Gacy left Newton on June 18, 1970, he was a passenger in a car driven by his friend, Charlie Hill. Momentarily at least, Gacy's enthusiasm for life was dampened. He admitted to his friend that he was depressed by his experience in prison and by the way he had been mistreated and framed on the sodomy charge.

He was also bitter because while he was in prison, his father had died—during the Christmas holidays—and state corrections officials refused to permit him to return to Chicago and attend the funeral. Gacy had told court investigators before he was sentenced that his father had a history of heart trouble.

His mood changed as they neared Waterloo. Gacy began talking passionately about getting a new job there and putting his life back in order. But first, he said, he planned to go to Chicago and visit his mother.

Less than twenty-four hours after his return to Waterloo, Gacy walked into Hill's office and told him he was leaving for Chicago and would see him again in a few days. Gacy never returned.

3

A Model
Neighbor

The bright splash of freshly cut flowers catching and re-
flecting the warm rays of the midsummer sun contrasted
with the pathetic, hunched figure at the grave. The
heavy body was shaking with sobs, causing tears to well
from the puffy eyes and slide slowly over fat ruddy
cheeks, as the head bowed and the thick neck shrank
into sturdy shoulders.

To someone who knew John Wayne Gacy, Jr., it may
have seemed strange. During his father's lifetime there
were harsh words and hurt feelings. Now that the elder
Gacy was in his grave, one among thousands at the Maryhill Cenetery in northwest suburban Niles, the old hurts
were engraved into the relationship between father and
son forever. There could be no more explanations, no
apologies. The misunderstandings could not be changed.
Yet, it appeared that in death Gacy's father was closer to
him than in life.

Gacy was deeply grieved that he had not been able
to attend his father's funeral. He was hurt that, as the
last of the remaining males in the immediate family, he
could not have been there to comfort his mother and
sisters. It also distressed him that he could not pay his
final respects to his father, whom he loved despite their
misunderstandings.

Gacy visited the sprawling cemetery that covers about one tenth of the land area of the attractive Chicago suburb many times during the years after his father's death. Most often he stopped there when he was troubled, bringing fresh flowers to place on the grave.

He always visited the grave on Christmas. Holidays were important to Gacy, and Christmas was the most important of all. It meant good food, gifts, and the warmth of a family that was close and loving. Now the Christmas period marked the anniversary of his father's death. The big man cried at the grave.

But he didn't have time to live in the past. He was still a young man under thirty, and he was energetic and anxious to get on with the task of rebuilding his life.

After driving 250 miles from Waterloo to Chicago, he moved in with his sixty-one-year-old mother in the family home and obtained a job as chef at a restaurant in Chicago's Loop. Cooking was a profession that he understood and was comfortable with. Managing the Kentucky Fried Chicken outlets in Waterloo had provided valuable experience, and his work at the prison added to his skill. There were other men in prison with experience as cooks, and Gacy had watched, listened, and learned. He was especially proud of his salad bars.

Parole authorities in Iowa and Illinois were understanding and cooperative when Gacy applied for permission to move back to Chicago. Returning home seemed to offer the best opportunity for rehabilitation after his prison term. He had the support there of a loving family, and his mother provided a home for him. Most importantly he had a job. Approval was routine.

Gacy applied himself to his new job with gusto. If no one was impressed when he bragged of once being married to the daughter of the man who founded the Kentucky Fried Chicken chain, he didn't seem to notice. He continued telling the story, or other tales, about his days as a U.S. Marine, and of the thousands of dollars he won and lost at the gambling tables in Las Vegas where he said he once worked as an ambulance driver.

Jobs for cooks and chefs are plentiful, and Gacy moved around, finally landing a position at an eating spot popular with members of Chicago's professional hockey team, the Blackhawks. Although he was not an avid sports fan, any job that offered an opportunity to rub shoulders with celebrities was attractive to him.

With his gift for talking and ingratiating himself with others, it wasn't difficult for him to obtain tickets to Blackhawk games from the players. When he passed them on to cronies, he made certain that they knew he had obtained them from chums on the team.

Charlie Hill and his wife watched more than one Blackhawk game with tickets provided by their friend. Chicago was headquarters for the motel chain Hill worked for and periodically he and his wife visited Chicago for a few days on business. Hill looked forward at those times to seeking out his old friend.

Pottinger, too, visited in Chicago with Gacy, although less often than the Hills. But the onetime Iowa convict was busy making new friends and reaffirming family ties. Iowa was behind him and his immediate future was clearly linked to Chicago.

His mother was pleased at the ease with which Gacy was readjusting to civilian life. The prison experience was fading into the past where it belonged. Any worry she may have had of lingering trauma was dispelled when, some four months after his return to Chicago, her son decided that he wanted a house of his own. He had been cooped up for eighteen months in cramped spaces with thousands of other men, and a house of his own would give him some much appreciated privacy and breathing room.

It seemed that there couldn't be a better sign that he was adjusting to his new life. His mother agreed to help with the financing when he found himself a comfortable two-bedroom ranch house a few blocks outside the northwest Chicago city limits. The attractive little house was on a quiet one-way westbound street at 8213 West Summerdale Avenue in an unincorporated area of Norwood Park township. Gacy became half-owner, and his mother and sisters were named as owners of the remainder.

It was a good neighborhood to settle in. The homes were as clean and as solidly constructed as the people who lived and raised families in them. Each had its own driveway, garage, and scrupulously manicured lawn in front and back. The street was rarely used except by residents and their guests, but was convenient to busy arterial roads that carry traffic to nearby expressways, towns, and shopping centers.

The neighborhood was family-oriented. Most of the families in the neatly kept bungalows and ranch-style homes were headed by men who worked in blue-collar professions. Many were of East European stock. They were people who kept their houses in good condition inside and out. If the man of the house stretched out in front of the television set with a beer in his hand and a six-pack at his side to watch Sunday afternoon football, it was only after the grass had been mowed, the leaves raked, or the balky carburetor on his car or pickup truck readjusted.

The neighbors knew each other, and it was a good safe place to raise children. Parents didn't have to be afraid of letting their children play outside. Teenage girls looked forward to careers as secretaries, shop clerks, waitresses, housewives, and mothers. They weren't insulted if they were asked to do housework or baby-sit with the neighbor children. Their brothers tinkered with rattletrap cars, pumped gasoline, or got part-time jobs as stock boys in supermarkets. After leaving high school they followed their fathers into jobs as productionline workers, plumbers, carpenters, and mechanics.

Part of a three-block tract of homes erected in the mid-1950s, Gacy's sturdily constructed house was built with a yellow shingle front, wooden sides painted red, and a green shingled sloped roof. A garage was at the rear, with small lawns at the front and back. A previous owner had added two rooms to the rear of the house, a dining room and a playroom for a daughter. The addition was built over supporting two-by-twelve-inch joists, with plywood flooring lowered a few inches so that it was necessary to step down to enter that part of the house from the main living area. There was also a living room, a utility room, and bath.

A trap door leading to a four-foot-deep crawl space that hugged the foundation of the original house was built into the floor of a bedroom closet. Most of the houses in the subdivision were constructed similarly with a crawl space or vapor area and air vents in front and back. The back vents in Gacy's house had been closed off when the addition was constructed. Crawl spaces were more economical than basements.

The housing tract was constructed in a low-lying area, and neighborhood historians claimed that the original soil was removed from the farmland and hauled into the city for the 1933 Chicago Century of Progress. Consequently, during some seasons of the year the damaged landscape became soggy and marshlike.

The first owner of the house at 8213 West Summerdale had trouble with dampness and water seeping into the crawl space. Yet the neighboring house was constructed almost exactly the same and the crawl space was dry year-round. The Grexa family, next door, suspected that the trouble at 8213 may have been caused by an underwater stream.

By the time Gacy moved into the house, four owners had lived in it. Each, like the couple who had added the dining room and playroom, had made a few alterations to please his own tastes.

The newest owner was no different from the others in that respect. From the time he moved in until the time he left the house forever, he seemed to be constantly puttering. It appeared to his neighbors that he was forever hammering or sawing at the walls inside, or busy outside adding outbuildings, laying cement, digging holes, or fighting the dampness in the crawl space with lime. He was unfailingly able to find a project to keep him busy. When he covered the yellow shingles with an orange brick veneer and decorative outcropping to give the house a Spanish embellishment, some of his neighbors winced at his garish taste. It didn't fit in with the rest of the houses in the neighborhood.

Gacy fashioned a recreation room for himself out of the onetime playroom, installed a sliding glass door, and added a pool table, game machines, and a bar that he kept stocked with several bottles each of J&B Scotch, good blended whiskey, gin, vodka, and an occasional bottle of brandy. The icebox always held a couple of six-packs of beer and two or three cases were stacked in a corner of the utility room with still more whiskey and mix. A red "Stop" sign hung on one wall.

Despite his industriousness at home, Gacy was finding time for activities and new acquaintances that neither his family nor his neighbors could imagine.

The Greyhound Bas Terminal at Clark and Randolph Streets in Chicago's Loop is one of the busiest bus stations in the world. Every day thousands of passengers from cities, towns, and farms throughout the United States and from foreign countries arrive aboard sleek scenic cruisers. For some, the trip marks the first time away from the protective care of parents and friends.

Inevitably there are people waiting to take advantage of the vulnerability of youngsters arriving alone in the big city. Bus and train terminals are notorious as the preserves of pimps and perverts on the lookout for young girls or boys to be seduced and used for private sexual pleasure or turned into prostitutes.

On February 12, 1971, John Wayne Gacy, Jr., was charged by Chicago police with disorderly conduct on the complaint of a teenage boy. The youngster, an admitted homosexual, said he was picked up at the bus terminal by Gacy, who then took him to his home and tried to force him to commit a sexual act. The case was dismissed when the boy failed to appear in court. It had been eight months since Gacy was released from prison.

Gacy's neighbors didn't learn about his troubles with the boy. Neither did the Iowa Board of Parole. Unaware that Gacy had been accused of a sex offense in Chicago, and basing their judgment in part on reports from Illinois that he was adjusting well to his freedom, the board approved his release from parole and he was officially discharged on October 18, 1971. The discharge was signed by board chairman George L. Paul the next day. On November 22, Iowa Governor Robert D. Ray reinstated full citizenship to Gacy. Restoration of citizenship is routine and is recommended by the Board of Parole for most ex-convicts in Iowa who have successfully completed parole after first offenses.

If Gacy celebrated full restoration of his citizenship rights or his release from parole, it didn't slow his work on the house. The racket of pounding hammers and busy saws continued to emanate from the Gacy home, persevering through the day and into the night.

He moved the tub in the bathroom, shifting it to a location facing the doorway, and constructed a long vanity. Several mirrors were hung. The kitchen was completely remodeled and wood paneling was nailed conspicuously in place, with finishing nails left glaringly visible. He bought three freezers, a new icebox, automatic slicers, and a couple of dozen knives. The kitchen reflected his familiarity with cooking as a profession and was outfitted as well as those in most restaurants.

Spanish ceramics and metal sculptures of matadors and picadors were interspersed on shelves and end tables with figurines of horses and other knickknacks. Bright rainbow-hued paintings and drawings of clowns were hung on the walls. Potted plants were placed on windowsills and hung from windows. There was little evidence of planning to the decorative scheme.

In spite of Gacy's efforts, neighbors and other guests sometimes went home shaking their heads in dismay over his inept and garish decorating and uneven handiwork. He explained to friends that working on his house enabled him to show off his renovation and remodeling ideas. He worked in and around the house steadily during the years he lived there. His main problem was that he never seemed to have time to properly finish the jobs he started. And although some of his ideas were imaginative, it was obvious to several of his acquaintances who were knowledgeable in the building trades that he was not a craftsman.

He wasn't in the house long before a bricked-in patio was built between the back door and garage, and he was planting flowers around it. Some time later he constructed a new cement stoop.

Next door, Edward J. and Lillie Grexa observed the activity with interest. They had become the first residents to move into the tract of homes in 1954 and they had watched other families move in and out of neighboring bungalows. Now the house at 8213 was occupied again, this time by a bachelor. He was a man who kept busy. Only the Grexa's driveway and a few feet of green lawn separated the houses, so they were always aware of his activities as he hauled in lumber or cement and puttered with his plants or busied himself at other outdoor work. Occasionally, Ed or Lillie or their neighbor would raise a hand and wave as they went about their business, but there was no socializing or visiting back and forth—not until the new neighbor had been in his home for a couple of months.

It was Christmas Eve and the Grexas were observing the holiday with a family gathering that included Ed's mother and other relatives, when they were interrupted by a knock on the door. Their neighbor was standing outside with a large box of fruit in his arms. He greeted them with a broad smile that pushed his cheeks up, crowding the eyes into amiable slits.

"Hi. I know I should have called on you sooner, but I'm your neighbor. They tell me you have six kids here so I know you can use this fruit," he said, shoving the box toward Mrs. Grexa. "If you folks aren't doing anything tomorrow night," he said, as she took the fruit from him, "I'd like to have you come over and meet my mother and the rest of the family. They'll all be there."

He was right. With five daughters and a son, the Grexas could use the fruit. And they were pleased to accept the invitation to visit on Christmas night.

Christmas Day Mrs. Grexa baked a tray of cookies and that evening she and her husband told the children, who were busy playing with Christmas toys, that they were going to visit the new neighbor. Most of the people in the block use the back doors for visiting, and the Grexas did the same. They tapped on the door, and their genial neighbor had barely opened it so that they could walk in when his mother threw her arms around Lillie Grexa and kissed her. Ed Grexa was given more of the same.

Introductions to Gacy's two sisters and another young woman who was identified as Carole Hoff were less emotional. Two little girls were introduced as Carole's daughters.

Lillie Grexa is a confident, friendly woman with strawberry-blonde hair who bristles at being called a redhead. She loves to cook, bowl, mother, and neighbor. She is easy to talk to, alert but not nosy, gregarious but not pushy. But even she was surprised by the warmth of the greeting. Mrs. Gacy hugged her as if they were old friends.

The greeting was genuine and it wasn't long before the little group was relaxed and at ease with each other. After drinks were prepared by the host and they had chatted and listened a while to Christmas music played on his stereo, they were as comfortable as if they were indeed old friends. When they left for their home a few hours later, they had spent an enjoyable evening that was to mark the beginning of a seven-year friendship.

It was late at night on January 3, 1972. Christmas lights and pine wreaths decorated many of the windows and front porches of houses in the neighborhood. A heavy covering of dirty snow helped mask sounds along the quiet street, and residents slumbered peacefully, exhausted after the activities of the holidays. There was only one person to hear the boy's last muffled groan as the knife slashed through his young flesh and he died. That person was the man who was holding the knife.

The Grexas socialized regularly with Gacy after their Christmas meeting. Their neighbor and his mother liked to play pinochle and the Grexas dropped by at Gacy's house occasionally for conversation, a few drinks, and a hand or two of cards, or they hosted the game in their own home. Sometimes they played poker, but whatever the game was, it was always friendly for small stakes.

Often when the neighbors got together to visit or play cards Carole was also there as Gacy's partner. So Lillie Grexa wasn't surprised when some months later he informed her that he and Carole were going to marry on June 1. Although he was a nominal Catholic, he was divorced, so the ceremony was to be in the St. Paul Lutheran Church a few blocks away. He told Lillie he was disappointed that his first marriage hadn't worked out, and he was anxious to make this one a success. He said his first wife was a daughter of Colonel Harlan Sanders, founder of the Kentucky Fried Chicken chain.

Carole had just gone through a divorce, and John, the brother of two of her best friends and the boy she had once dated in high school, was there to offer comfort when she needed it. She knew he had been in prison, but was to later remember that "he swept me off my feet. I don't think I loved him, but I was still mixed up about my first marriage, and he treated me well."[1]

There seemed to be much to recommend a marriage to Gacy. He had always been an engaging, considerate companion. He was generous, industrious, and got along well with the girls. Carole, of course, already had a good relationship with her future in-laws. There was every indication that marriage into the family could provide her with comfort and security for herself and her daughters. John had even agreed when Carole suggested that her mother move in with them for a while after the wedding, even though the older woman didn't favor the marriage. There were aspects of the prospective bridegroom's personality that bothered her. His erratic temper was worrisome. He could be perfectly calm one moment and in a rage the next.

The couple nevertheless went ahead with plans for the wedding, and Gacy told his friends next door that he intended to do his own catering at the reception. It would be convenient for him to prepare the food and much of the work could be done in the restaurant he worked in downtown.

Lillie Grexa was pleased that John and Carole would be getting married. He had been a delightful and considerate neighbor since moving next door, and it was good for a man to have a woman around. Lillie said that if there was any way she could help with the reception, all he had to do was ask. She reminded him that as a homemaker and mother of six children, she also knew a few things about the preparation of good food.

"Even if I say so myself, I make a pretty good potato salad," she boasted. "Just give me an idea of how many people you're going to invite and I'll take care of the potato salad for you." She had cooked for big groups before. Sometimes at birthday parties she and her husband gave for her father, as many as seventy people were at the house for meals. The suggestion sounded good to Gacy. He would, of course, provide the ingredients.

"I figure there should be about one-hundred-twenty-

[1]*Chicago Tribune,* December 23, 1978.

five to one-hundred-fifty people here for the reception," he told his neighbor.

"We should have about fifty pounds of potatoes then," she said, "plus the other ingredients."

"No, we're going to need a lot more than that," he corrected her.

Lillie had mentally computed one or two spoonfuls of potato salad, multiplied 125 to 150 times. "John, fifty pounds is plenty," she said, her forehead wrinkling at the prospect of trays and platters heaped with mounds of leftover potato salad.

The bridegroom insisted on at least one hundred pounds of potatoes, and it was his wedding, so one hundred pounds it was. When he bought or prepared food, even at home, he did it as if he were ordering supplies for one of the restaurants he had worked at. He bought in case lots. The storeroom and closets were filled with cases of canned foods, cereal, soap, cleanser, and wrapping paper. One of his friends observed that there was always enough food and kitchen supplies in the house to sit out a war and never touch a ration book.

Lillie Grexa also volunteered to whip up two kinds of cole slaw to go with the beef, turkey, and other food her neighbor planned to prepare at work. The night before the wedding, he invited the Grexas to his house for a last-minute planning session. His mother, Carole, and a woman from the restaurant—who was going to help serve —were also there.

Gacy had decided to make sauerkraut and kielbasa, a spicy Polish sausage, at the house early the next morning before leaving for the wedding. Lillie Grexa was horrified.

"John, you can't smell up the house cooking kielbasa and sauerkraut the day of the wedding," she told him. "You're going to have the reception here in the backyard. There will be people running in and out of the house. It's June and the smell will hang over the place all day." She shook her head in disbelief. "You just can't do it. I'll cook the sausage for you at my place."

There was already an odd smell at Gacy's house, and the aroma of Polish sausage, regardless of how good it might taste, wasn't desirable for the man's wedding day.

He agreed that it might make good sense to do the cooking next door. But he wasn't sure that his neighbor knew how to make good kielbasa.

"There's nothing to it," Lillie bristled. "You use a little bit of brown sugar, some caraway seeds . . ."

"Oh, my God, no. You can't do it that way. It isn't the Polish way."

"You wait. You'll see," the woman insisted. "They'll like it."

That afternoon Lillie and Ed Grexa carried thirty pounds of sausage, a tray of spices and a box of brown sugar with them when they went home. She cooked the sauerkraut and kielbasa early the next morning. Her way. The guests ate it all.

Gacy also formed a new friendship with a young man at about the time of the wedding. Martin Zielinski was a free-lance photographer who had taken pictures for Gacy's sister and was asked to photograph the June nuptials. Gacy was pleased with his work and it wasn't long before the ex-convict and the young photographer—who knew nothing of the older man's past—became good friends.

Zielinski was barely out of high school and he was trying to get a foothold in a competitive business. Gacy gave him work, and bragged about his photography. Zielinski was susceptible to the flattery and easily accepted the older man as an entertaining and congenial companion.

After the reception, John and Carole left for a two-day Wisconsin honeymoon. Audree Grexa, the Grexa's tenage daughter, baby-sat with the girls and Carole's brother's two children.

The new bridegroom wasn't one to ignore his obligations, and to show his appreciation for Lillie's help with the reception, he and Carole decided to take the Grexas to see a performance of *Jesus Christ Superstar.* But Gacy changed his mind before the show and asked if the Grexas would care if they went instead to see two friends of his who performed as a music and comic duo at a nearby restaurant. Both Gacy and his mother knew the performers.

The Gacys and the Grexas sat through three performances. Between acts the brothers sold jewelry and visited at the table. Gacy was at his most ebullient, and gloried in the stares of other patrons when the performers joined him and his friends at their table. He talked loudly, greeted them with vigorous handshakes, and slapped their backs.

Lillie Grexa wasn't that impressed with the two effeminate men playing around in swami robes. But the outing gave her neighbor an opportunity to exhibit his show-business connections, and the evening was a gratifying diversion, even though sitting through three shows was a bit tiring. There was no denying, however, that even if he was loud and given to showing off, Gacy was a gracious host.

He proved that again one Sunday afternoon in July when the Grexas returned home from a trip to Wisconsin. It was Lillie's birthday, and she and her husband weren't home many minutes before Gacy showed up. "When you two get the car unloaded and have a couple of minutes, stop over at the house," he suggested. "I have something to show you." A few minutes later they stepped across their driveway and knocked at the back door.

John and Carole and both their mothers were waiting. He had made hors d'oeuvres and he gave Lillie a gift-wrapped bottle of whiskey. She was impressed. On the way home an hour or so later, she mentioned to her husband how nice it was of their neighbor to have the surprise party for her. Throwing surprise birthday parties for neighbors could become an expensive undertaking.

Gacy was a good neighbor, but it was a shame about the persistent musty odor in his house. The Grexas had noticed the odor for months, and it was getting worse. Carole and her mother were complaining about it. Even John's mother had said it bothered her when she visited the home.

Lillie remembered the trouble that she and her husband had with a similar stench shortly after they moved into their house. It was foul, so bad that it almost made her sick when she ate. She was certain that a mouse, or possibly a rat, had crawled under the kitchen sink and died. She had talked her husband into pulling up the sink to look for the rodent when they discovered that the odor was coming from a broken sewer tile. They notified the builder, who dug up the old tile and replaced it. The nasty smell disappeared.

The Grexas doubted that their neighbor's odor problem was caused by a broken sewer tile, because one of the previous owners of the house had installed the lines between the ground and the flooring. A broken tile would be too obvious and easy to trace.

Gacy insisted that the trouble was nothing more than "that darned moisture" and hauled in more lime. He was their friend, but the Grexas didn't lose sleep over his problem. When he installed the brick facing on the front of his house, he closed off the last two working vents from the crawl space, so the odor didn't carry as far as their house. And since he himself treated the problem so cavalierly, there was no sense in their wasting their time agonizing over it.

Gacy had other problems. They were problems that he didn't want to share with his friends and he didn't want to talk about with his wife. On June 22, 1972, he was arrested again. Police picked him up on charges of aggravated battery and reckless conduct.

The trouble started on Chicago's action-oriented Near North side. The Near North is the home of some of the city's more well-to-do citizens, as well as Chicago's playground. Some of Chicago's finest hotels and most imposing old mansions along with chic restaurants, popular singles bars, discos, boutiques, bust-out joints and stately high rises serve the beautiful and not-so-beautiful people who inhabit or roam the Near North.

A young man told police that he was standing on a street corner when Gacy swung his car toward the curb, flashed a badge and identified himself as a sheriff's deputy. The youth was ordered into the car under threat of arrest.

He said that after he got into the car he was forced to perform oral sex on the driver. After completing the act, he cowered in the passenger seat, his fright building, while the bogus policeman continued driving. In suburban Northbrook, some twenty miles from where the young man had first climbed inside, the driver stopped the car and again demanded sex. The youth shook his head and jumped out the door. The driver tried to run him down. The charges were eventually stricken, with leave to reinstate by the court. The case was never brought to trial. It would be more than six years before Gacy was again named in a police complaint.

During the intervening period, barely a year after Gacy's trouble in Northbrook, his neighbors and other Americans sat before their television sets watching in fascination and horror as news cameras focused on the activities of a sex-and-torture-murder ring uncovered in Houston.

At least twenty-seven boys and young men had died in what was described as the worst multiple murder in American history. Dean Corll, a thirty-three-year-old Houston electrician, was named as the homosexual mastermind responsible for the slayings, many of them carried out with help from a seventeen-year-old neighborhood boy, Elmer Wayne Henley.

Images of husky Houston detectives carrying the pathetic sacked remains of the victims flashed onto television screens during news shows and TV specials. Most of the remains were dug from under a toolshed. Others were disinterred from a riverbed near the southeast Texas city that was previously noted more for its oil and aerospace industries than for grisly mass murder.

Most of the bodies had been eaten away by quicklime, moisture, and mold and were so badly deteriorated that they were difficult to identify. Pathologists and police experts talked impressively during lengthy on-screen interviews about using dental charts and reconstructing faces in efforts to determine who the victims were.

Most of Corll's victims were drawn from the same area of Houston, a lower middle-class white neighborhood known as The Heights, where he had once helped run a family candymaking business near an elementary school. He developed a reputation there as a gentle young man who loved children, and was commonly known to give away candy to youngsters from the school.

Sometime after leaving the candy business, he began

sexually molesting and killing adolescent boys. Henley said that he started procuring his friends and other neighborhood youths for Corll, and was paid as much as two hundred dollars each for the victims. Many of the boys were seduced with beer and drug parties before being overpowered and tortured. Finally they were shot or strangled to death.

After almost three years of the insane activities, The Heights was nearly stripped of adolescent males. Some families lost two sons each. Yet, invariably when parents contacted police to ask for help in locating their missing boys they were told that the children were obviously runaways—and because runaways were so common there would be no official search.

The policemen were wrong. Although it began belatedly, the search got underway on August 8, 1973, when Henley telephoned police and told them he had shot Corll to death. Henley said he had delivered a teenage boy to Corll, but also brought along a fifteen-year-old girl. Corll was furious and they quarreled, but the man finally calmed down and the three teenagers busied themselves with a huffing party, using brown paper sacks to inhale the fumes from acrylic paint. One by one they passed out.

When Henley awakened hours later, his ankles were tied and Corll was snapping handcuffs on his wrists. Corll was raging and he began poking the youth in the stomach with a .22-caliber pistol, screaming that he was going to kill him because he had brought the girl. Henley begged for his life. He promised to do anything Corll told him to, and the older man finally relented. Henley was freed and told to strip the girl, while Corll began spread-eagling the other boy, who was already naked, face down on a plywood board.

Henley objected when Corll started to sexually assault the helpless boy in front of the girl, and the coconspirators began to quarrel again. The quarrel ended when Henley finally shot Dean Corll.

Less than a year later Henley was convicted of participating in the murder spree with Corll and was given six ninety-nine-year prison sentences. He was found not guilty of murder in the fatal shooting of the older homosexual torture killer after pleading self-defense.

Criticism of police work was widespread after the grisly doings of the murder ring were disclosed. Some adults, acting in alarm, established a national toll-free telephone hotline called Operation Peace of Mind so that runaways would make calls to parents to assure family members that they were alive and not among the unidentified victims. Operation Peace of Mind became a permanent hotline for runaways to relay messages to their families while keeping their own locations confidential if they wished.

While Americans were shuddering at the outrages committed in Houston, John Gacy was busy developing a reputation as a gracious and generous host. He especially enjoyed hosting theme parties, get-togethers that featured a specific time in history or a geographic location and offered an opportunity to dress in appropriate costume.

The theme parties were kicked off in 1974 with a Hawaiian luau. Lillie Grexa made leis for the guests from colored tissue paper and Gacy set up a barbecue and roasted two suckling pigs. A makeshift bar was located in the driveway just off the patio and stocked with beer and mixers. Guests who wanted stronger drink brought their own bottles. The host was usually content to sip a couple of glasses of J & B and water or drink Kool-Aid.

The Grexas moved back and forth between the two homes at his theme parties, meeting his business associates, friends, former neighbors, aunts, uncles, and cousins. Gacy had many relatives in the Chicago area and they often visited together. Although the theme parties might draw anywhere from two hundred to four hundred guests and cars were parked for blocks along Summerdale and the nearby cross streets, Gacy did not invite all his neighbors. Usually he asked only the Grexas and one or two other families.

The luau was followed with a Western theme party, and Gacy built a barbecue in the backyard on which he cooked a side of beef for his guests. He boasted that he had been the head chef at Chicago's famous Blackhawk restaurant before taking his current job and could cook anything. To others he confided that he was an honest-to-goodness, bonafide Kentucky Colonel. People who knew him well smiled and shook their heads. There didn't seem to be any harm in telling tall tales, as long as it made him feel good. But at times his stories could get hip-boot deep.

Gacy was rambling on to Lillie Grexa one time about all the jobs he had held and all the accomplishments he had to his credit when she interrupted him. "Now, John, you're only thirty-three," she reminded him, "so how the heck can you have done so many things in such a short time?"

His eyebrows arched in surprise. "Don't you believe me?" he asked, allowing his voice to betray the hurt.

"Nah. How could you do all that?" she replied, laughing.

"I'll show you. Next time I see you, I'll prove it to you."

The next time he saw the Grexas, he had a prepared list of former occupations and activities. Reading from the sheet of lined yellow notebook paper, he said he had been an ambulance driver, Marine, chef, policeman, fireman, bartender, shoe salesman, manager of a fast-food chain, and award-winning Jaycee, had served on a governor's study committee and more. Lillie reached for the list, but he pulled it away. It was his "proof." She didn't openly question his integrity again.

The year of the Western theme party was the year that Gacy went into business for himself, and started PDM Contractors, Inc. PDM stood for Painting, Decorating, and Maintenance. It was also the last full year of his marriage to Carole.

The marriage had begun going sour long before that. It wasn't that Gacy went out of his way to be unkind. But he had an erratic, volatile temper, and it seemed that he just didn't have enough time for her. He was always tired.

She once recalled that during the nearly four years of their marriage, her husband slept an average of only about two hours a night. He avoided sleep, as if his dreams swarmed with phantoms. He would get so tired that he sometimes slumped on the living-room couch, staring straight ahead, his eyes blank and his mind obviously lost in its own dark thoughts. She once sat down beside him to comfort him and he tensed, jerking away from her. Without turning to look at his wife, and speaking in a voice as papery and parched as a deathbed whisper, he asked her to move away and let him relax.

At other times his somber moodiness would turn suddenly savage. He was short-tempered, and when he was angry his powerful hands clenched into tight fists. Then his temper flared and he would scream and throw furniture. Ed Grexa works as a marble setter, and twice replaced broken marble in a coffee table after Gacy had picked the table up during one of his rages and smashed it to the floor. There was a lot of furniture broken during his outbursts, and Carole learned to watch quietly and as unobtrusively as possible while the anger swelled in her husband and he smashed their furniture into junk.

There were times when the rages stopped as abruptly as a stream of water from a shut faucet. One moment he would be raging and the next moment he would suddenly be in good spirits again, seemingly oblivious to his anger of a few seconds before and unconcerned about the broken furniture.

They had been married barely a year when he began leaving home at midnight or later and staying out until dawn. The couple's sex life became almost nonexistent. Carole remembered that during most of the marriage, her husband couldn't perform sexually. For a time she blamed herself. It was disturbing, and occasionally she let the bitterness slip out in front of other people.

There was the time that Ed Grexa saw her in the backyard a few months after the marriage, and called out jokingly:

"Hey, no little ones on the way yet, Carole?"

She turned, unsmiling, and replied: "You have to sleep with someone first."

She wasn't a complainer, but she occasionally let a hint of her troubles slip out in a remark to her sometime babysitter, Audree Grexa. Most of the time the two young women talked of other, more pleasant things, however. Audree was looking forward to her own approaching marriage and they talked of that, or of Elvis Presley. Audree was a Presley fan, and named her Norwegian elkhound "Elvis" after the superstar.

Along with the other problems that were developing in the marriage, there was the ever-present odor. The stench hung over the house summer and winter. If it wasn't the warm weather making it worse in the summer, it seemed that it was the heat in the house in the winter. But it was always there. It was increasingly bothersome and frustrating, especially considering the business that Carole's husband was in. As a remodeling contractor, it seemed that he could do something about it. But no matter how noticeable and disagreeable the odor became, he continued to dismiss it as a minor problem and said it was caused by the damp and darkness of the crawl space. When she complained too vociferously or other people began mentioning the odor to him, his solution was to haul in more quicklime.

When Carole walked outside one morning and found a huge mound of dirt piled at the far end of the backyard, she didn't suspect that it had come from the bothersome crawl space. She accepted without question her husband's explanation that he had ordered some sod and was going to fill in the backyard.

Marriage to John had its positive side. He was a good provider. No one could fault him on that. He worked long hours during the day, first at the restaurant and later at the construction job. Then he came home, had dinner and often worked far into the night. At times he puttered inside the garage or outside long after Carole and the girls had been lulled into slumber by their own soft breathing, the silence interrupted only by the occasional groan of a board in the silent house.

One day a week Carole and her husband bowled in a Sunday morning mixed league at the Monte-Cristo Bowl Alleys. Gacy was a powerful bowler with a deadly hook and was capable of regularly rolling lines in the 180s. He moved with surprising grace for a man of his bulk. He had taken naturally to the sport, something he had been unable to do with golf, which he had tried unsuccessfully during his Jaycee days in Waterloo. But he was good at bowling. He had trophies and a ribboned medal that announced he was the "World's Greatest Bowler" in his recreation room to attest to his skill.

Still, it was not the ideal marriage that Carole had hoped for. Within a year after the wedding she realized that eventually it would end in divorce. But she worried about the girls. They had already been through one broken marriage, and had quickly taken to John, calling him "Daddy" from the very beginning. The baby of the family considered him to be her natural father.

There was no denying that he got along well with her daughters and was considerate of them. He installed an oval above-ground swimming pool and built a playhouse in the backyard for them soon after the wedding. Not long after he suggested that the younger girl's bed be moved from the front bedroom. He said that he wanted to make it into a playroom for the girls and that they could sleep in the same room at the back of the house near his and Carole's bedroom.

That left the front of the house without bedrooms. The insulation was good, and Gacy was free to work in the front of the house as late as he liked without disturbing his sleeping wife or the children. On the nights that she went to bed ahead of him, which was almost every night, she seldom knew when he left and when he came home. The house was silent and not even the breathing of Patches, the family's pet Lhasa Apso that some of the neighbors referred to as a poodle, could be heard.

One day Carole found a billfold with identification belonging to a young man in her husband's late-model black Oldsmobile, which he had outfitted with a red light and radio scanner. When she asked him why the billfold was in the car, Gacy exploded in another of his rages. She learned when she found other billfolds and bits of identification belonging to young men not to ask any more where they had come from.

That was when he began openly bringing home magazines with pictures of naked males. Carole didn't quarrel with him about it, and there was an unspoken agreement that the material wouldn't be left around the house where the girls could find it. But then he never left anything out of place. He had a passion for neatness. In his house, magazines were stacked neatly, dishes were kept washed and beds were made when sleep was over.

Carole began confiding to a few intimates that her husband didn't need her any longer. He had already admitted to her that he preferred boys.

Gacy's social and professional life was progressing more favorably than his marriage. By 1975 he was becoming too old for the Jaycees. It was a young man's organization. But he missed the companionship and the ego-boosting attention and challenge of moving into a position of importance in an organization filled with vigorous imaginative men. He turned to politics.

In Chicago and in Cook County, politics is nearly synonymous with the Democratic party. There are a few offices for Republicans or Independents. One of the few Republicans to win a major political office in Cook County in recent years is Bernard Carey. He was a thirty-one-year-old lawyer in 1972, running for his first elective office, when he upended incumbent Cook County State's Attorney Edward V. Hanrahan. Carey was the only non-incumbent elected, and he was sworn into office on December 4.

Incumbent Cook County Coroner Dr. Andrew Toman, who participated in the Speck investigation, was sworn into office for the last time the same day as Carey. During his reelection campaign he had supported a referendum proposing abolition of his office and replacement by the county medical examiner system. The referendum was approved by a five-to-one margin, to become effective December 6, 1976.

It's doubtful if Gacy paid more than passing attention to either the Carey-Hanrahan contest for State's Attorney or to establishment of the medical examiner system in Cook County. But the time would come when both incidents would be significant to him.

Gacy sought out Robert F. Martwick, a prominent Loop attorney who lived in Norwood Park and was the Democratic township committeeman. The portly contractor explained that he had just moved into the community and would like to make it a better place to live. Someday he would like to run for public office, he said.

His aspirations were admirable, even though the desire to seek election to public office may have been slightly premature. Martwick suggested that before Gacy become a political candidate he become better known locally and involve himself in projects to help his neighbors in the community.

Service projects were something that Gacy had learned about when he was a Jaycee, and he knew how to involve himself in community activities. He drove away from the meeting with Martwick in high spirits, with plans to make himself known to his Norwood Park township neighbors already germinating in his mind.

He designed clown outfits for himself, and selected a catchy name, "Pogo the Clown." His generous stomach provided natural padding to fill out the front, and he topped the baggy suits with a tassled hat and added over-size shoes and white gloves. He taught himself to paint pyramid-shaped eyes and to smear on a broad smiling mouth. Only professional clowns and students of the art of clowning would recognize him as an unschooled amateur because of the sharp corners at the edges of his mouth. Knowledgeable clowns paint rounded corners so they don't frighten small children.

Zielinski took photographs of him in the clown costume, and it wasn't long before Gacy was entertaining small groups of the children and grandchildren of bowling friends and at picnics or Christmas parties sponsored by Norwood township Democrats. He talked importantly of appearing at children's hospitals, but none of his friends ever witnessed the performances.

There were other talks with Martwick. The township committeeman was impressed and pleased when the beefy contractor volunteered to use his young construction workers to keep the party headquarters clean. There would be no charge. Martwick accepted the generous offer. People didn't volunteer free services like that every day.

The Chicago lawyer had no idea that one of Gacy's first ventures cleaning up the headquarters would lead to eventual accusations (but no criminal charges) that the chubby political hopeful had tried to sexually assault a sixteen-year-old boy there.

In 1975 Tony Antonucci was a well-muscled, wiry six-footer who weighed 175 pounds and wrestled at Gordon Technical High School, a Catholic boys' school on the northwest side of the city. As the story was put together some three years later by Antonucci, Gacy made a pass at him while he and Gacy were cleaning the office. Antonucci told his boss to leave him alone, but Gacy got pushy, offering him money for sex. Antonucci said he had to pick up a folding chair and threaten Gacy with it before the man calmed down and tried to laugh off the episode as a joke.

Gacy tried again the next month. This time he came to the Antonucci apartment one night while the boy was home alone, carrying a bottle of wine and some heterosexual stag films. After they sipped from the wine and talked a while, Gacy said he wanted to show the youth a stunt with a pair of trick handcuffs he used in his clown act. He claimed there was a secret method of unlocking them and challenged his companion to figure it out.

Antonucci was agreeable and put on the cuffs. Unknown to his boss, he did not slip one of his hands all the way inside. He kept the free hand underneath him so that he appeared to be cuffed. As soon as Gacy thought that he was securely manacled he moved forward to begin undressing the boy.

Antonucci lurched suddenly forward and jerked Gacy's legs, dropping him onto his back. The young wrestler snapped the free cuff on one of Gacy's wrists, flipped him over and pressed a knee against the back of his head. Gacy squirmed helplessly face down on the floor while Antonucci took the key away from him, and a moment later both the man's wrists were pulled behind his back and cuffed. He was kept there, struggling and screaming threats, until he calmed down and Antonucci freed him.

"You're the first one to get the cuffs off—not only that, but you got that one on me," Gacy told his young employee.[2]

Gacy never tried to overpower or assault Antonucci

[2]*Chicago Tribune,* December 27, 1978.

again, although the youth continued to work for PDM Contractors, Inc. for another eight or nine months.

Martwick, of course, knew nothing about the incidents. He knew only that the husky contractor had become a dependable volunteer for the numerous jobs connected with operation of a party precinct headquarters. Gacy was unfailingly available and willing to run errands, re-hang a crooked door, wash windows, set up chairs for meetings, or fix a leaky faucet. Gacy appeared to be proving his worth to the organization and the sincerity of his desire to help better the community.

Martwick nominated him for a position on the Norwood Park Township Street Lighting District. It was the commission's responsibility to maintain street lights in the unincorporated areas. Gacy became secretary-treasurer. In 1975 and 1976 he filed ethics statements, as required by Illinois state law of appointed and elected public officials. They disclosed that a sidewalk was installed by PDM for the Norwood Park Township Road and Bridge Department at a cost of $3,500.

Gacy's appointment to the lighting commission led to an acquaintance with Sam Amirante. Young and just a few years out of Loyola University Law School, Amirante was attorney for the commission. Despite Amirante's youth, Gacy was impressed by his quick intelligence and articulate grasp of problems.

The only child of a newspaper truck driver and his wife, Amirante grew up in the adjoining town of Norridge and was president of his junior and senior classes in high school. Although he is only five-foot two-inches tall as an adult, he lettered in track and made the varsity of his high school baseball team as a second baseman and center fielder.

The competition in sports was stiffer at Loyola and he did not play varsity baseball, but the feisty student continued to shine socially and academically. He was once again elected as senior-class president. He served as administrative assistant to the vice-president in law school, and after obtaining his degree and passing the bar examination took his first job as an attorney with the Cook County Public Defender's Office. He was working there, developing and sharpening his courtroom skills, when he met Gacy.

Amirante was still an undergraduate at Loyola and haunting the courtrooms of the Criminal Courts Building on Chicago's south side when he watched F. Lee Bailey, the most famous and flamboyant criminal attorney in the country, argue a case.

The Boston lawyer and ex-Marine fighter pilot was defending millionaire horseman Silas Jayne, who was charged with conspiracy to murder in the slaying of his younger brother, George, in one of Chicago's most celebrated criminal trials. The law student sat in the courtroom of Judge Richard J. Fitzgerald for days, watching Bailey, whose brilliant courtroom work has made him a folk hero to some young lawyers. Amirante was mentally logging every detail, every maneuver, and every action of the defense.[3]

One of the most conspicuous aspects of Bailey's approach to a case, aside from his courtroom theatrics, is the obvious meticulousness of his preparation. As a practicing lawyer, Amirante too would be carefully prepared for his cases or jobs, regardless of whether, as a public defender, he was representing a penniless street-gang member charged with a mugging or solving a question of construction contracts for the Norwood Park Township Lighting Commission.

Amirante was the kind of knowledgeable and devoted worker that Gacy could relate to. Though the two men didn't become fast friends, it appeared that a feeling of mutual respect developed for the way that each handled his official obligations.

Gacy began passing out business cards prematurely, identifying himself as a precinct captain shortly after he became involved with township Democrats. Martwick overlooked the minor breach of conduct because of Gacy's record of laboring so diligently for the party and the com-

---

[3]Jayne was found guilty of conspiracy to commit murder, and not guilty of murder. Bailey described the verdict as an "acquittal," pointing out that conspiracy is a less serious offense than murder. Nevertheless, Jayne, then sixty-five, was given the maximum sentence of from six to twenty years in prison.

munity. While Gacy was building his reputation as an assiduously dedicated Democrat and minor township official, he was also cementing an even closer relationship with another acquaintance in the construction business.

Donald Czarna was a cement contractor. The men met one day while Czarna was pouring sidewalks for the town of Norridge, and Gacy interrupted him to ask if he would pour a couple of porch steps at his house. Czarna and Gacy had much in common. Both were in the construction business, and both swaggered and boasted. Czarna was a rugged man with a cowhide complexion rubbed leathery red by the Chicago sun and wind, who talked out of the corner of his mouth, filling his conversation with blustering threats and stories about people he had beaten up or laid low with a single punch. Gacy's face was darkened by a metallic-blue Richard Nixon beard that showed dark even after the closest shave, and he was also known to use bluster and threats to intimidate people he had disagreements with. The physical builds of the two contractors were as similar as Tweedledum and Tweedledee, and more than once they were mistaken for brothers.

After Czarna poured the steps the men didn't see each other again for about three months. Then Gacy contacted Czarna and asked him to do the cement work on a remodeling job he had contracted. There were a couple more jobs, and Gacy invited Czarna and his wife, Lydia, to one of his parties. They visited frequently after that and became such close friends that they took some holidays and vacations together. A few times the Czarnas loaned their cabin in Wisconsin to their friend during short breaks in his work schedule.

Although the Czarnas never saw Gacy perform in his clown costume, he was proud of his routine and liked to show off the collection of clown art and equipment he used in his act. There was a collar and stiff leash for an invisible dog, a rubber plucked chicken, and once he showed off what he said were toy handcuffs.

Gacy climbed into his clown outfit to entertain at a children's party for friends of the Czarnas, and soon moved into their social crowd, joining in more card games and other activities. Gacy and his friend worked hard, and during the slow season for construction, when the winds whipped snow and sleet through the streets and the temperatures dipped below freezing, they played hard. Las Vegas was one of their favorite play spots.

Gacy was no more compulsive about gambling than he was about drinking. Although he liked to shock his friends by telling them he had won or lost thousands at the casinos, he actually preferred spending a few leisurely hours at the black jack tables and sitting down to a fine meal with a group of companions. He was at his best and most ebullient at those times.

He and Czarna were once playing blackjack when the dealer withdrew an old deck of cards and replaced it with a new one. "I'm from Chicago and I do tricks in a clown suit for kids," Gacy told the dealer. "I go through a lot of cards and could use a few of your old decks if you don't need them." The dealer gave him a handful of cards.

"No, I mean lots of cards," Gacy said, shaking his head. "I need lots of cards."

The dealer called the pit boss, who went into a back room and returned a few minutes later. He handed the gambler from Illinois a cardboard carton full of playing cards.

Czarna was impressed. Gacy liked that. He felt good when he was able to impress his friends with his importance. He enjoyed it so much that he got carried away one time after winning a few dollars at the tables, and he invited his group, three or four couples including some bowling friends, to be his guests at an elegant restaurant in one of the casinos. Gacy was an entertaining host and talked loudly and constantly during the meal about his business successes, his luck at the tables and his plans for the future. He continued talking when the check came, seemingly unaware of its presence. The dessert had been finished, coffee and cocktails drunk, and still he kept talking, making no move for the check. Grumbling, Czarna snatched it from the table and paid for the meal.

Gacy could have afforded to pay the bill. His business was growing, and he had almost more work than he could handle building or remodeling drug stores, hamburger and hotdog shops, and ice-cream parlors. Often after doing the contracting on the ice-cream shops—he did several for the same franchise chain—he appeared at grand openings and promotions in his clown suit and gave away balloons and other favors.

There was time also to do an occasional small job in his neighborhood, and he built a recreation room in one of the houses across the street from his home. Even though he had been building things and tinkering with tools since he was a child, he wasn't a skilled craftsman. But he knew how to use others who could do professional work, and he made liberal use of subcontractors.

Czarna was one of his closest friends, but he was also observant enough to admit that, as a carpenter, Gacy was a wood butcher. It didn't take long before Czarna learned that his friend was no better qualified to handle heavy construction equipment.

Gacy was working on a repaving project in which it was necessary to remove a few inches of blacktopping along a curb to facilitate proper water flow. He asked to use Czarna's compressor, then fumbled for almost ten minutes unsuccessfully trying to get it started. Grinning at his friend's confusion as he pushed and poked at the instrument panel and steering wheel, Czarna finally shouldered him aside, turned a key and pressed the starter button. The compressor sputtered to life.

Although Gacy may not have understood how to operate some of the machinery needed on the jobs, he knew how to build his business and make money. He was a good organizer and he began to branch out, first picking up a few jobs in the neighboring state of Wisconsin and then expanding to locations even farther from his home base. At first he drove, and then he began flying to other cities to bid on jobs and bring in work for PDM.

Czarna was pleased at his friend's success, even though he himself subcontracted only an occasional job with the company. The only thing that bothered him about the way Gacy was operating PDM Contractors was his hiring of teenage boys.

"John, I just can't understand why in the hell you hire all these kids," he groused. "They don't have any experience. They don't know what they're doing. I own a construction company, and I know that if I took a fifteen- or sixteen-year-old kid out there with me and had him pouring concrete I'd have to pick up his ass and put him in the truck if he lasted the day."

Gacy was unperturbed. The boys were good workers and they followed directions well, he told his friend. He didn't mention another positive aspect of hiring the boys, although Czarna knew about it. They worked for low wages. But there were still other motives that Czarna didn't know about. There were certain benefits, which only Gacy understood, for maintaining close personal contact with a steady stream of firm-bodied adolescent boys.

4...

Disappearances

John Butkovich was working in a hardware store when he met John Gacy. An amiable, likeable boy, he was an eager worker and it didn't matter whether he was asked to stock shelves, shovel snow, or scrub floors—he stuck persistently to his chores until they were completed.

A willingness to work hard was a quality he had inherited from his father, Marko Butkovich. The older Butkovich immigrated to the United States from Yugoslavia and with his wife, Terezia, raised a family of six boys and girls, at first on the money he made as a janitor and later with additional income from several rental properties he bought and fixed up. In the late 1970s the family was living in suburban Lombard.

Johnny was good with his hands, and one of his favorite avocations was tinkering with his 1968 Dodge. But racing the souped-up vehicle was expensive. He blew out three engines and when it was time to pay for them, he was prepared to earn his own money. His parents didn't raise any spoiled or lazy children.

Most of the money Johnny made at the hardware store was spent on the car or for clothes and other expenses germane to the needs of a seventeen-year-old boy. It was difficult to make the money stretch, and he welcomed the opportunity to earn a raise and learn new skills when a remodeling contractor who occasionally bought building supplies at the store offered him a job in construction.

Johnny went to work for John Gacy. He liked the job. He was sensitive and creative, often playing a guitar he had taught himself to strum in his spare time. Decorating and remodeling provided an outlet for his creativity as well as a good paycheck for a teenager who hadn't finished high school. Like his boss, he sometimes worked long hours and there were nights when he slept over at the Gacy house. The man and the boy who shared the same first name appeared to get along well, and there was no bitterness when a bid that Gacy submitted to remodel one of the elder Butkovich's apartment houses was rejected.

Other boys near Johnny's age also took jobs with Gacy, and Carole got used to them traipsing into the house and reaching into the icebox to help themselves to a soft drink or a beer after working hard all day with her husband.

She complained once when she saw a couple of the boys passing around a marijuana cigarette in the house. She confronted her husband and told him that she didn't ever want to see anyone smoking marijuana there again. She didn't want any trouble with the police.

He was understanding and agreeable. It was the last time she ever knew marijuana to be smoked in the house, although she was aware that joints were shared a few times in the backyard or on the patio. The patio was protected from the street by the house; it was hidden from the alley by the outbuildings and shrubbery blocked most of the view from neighboring homes. It was convenient to smoke there—and to do other secret things without being spied on by outsiders.

Despite the many hours Gacy spent working around the house and in the yard or outbuildings, he constantly neglected to trim the bushes along the boundary lines of his lot. They were permitted to grow nine or ten feet high, effectively closing off any view neighbors might have of the backyard.

That didn't bother the Grexas. They were a close family, involved in activities of their own, and they had enough to do without overly concerning themselves with whatever their friend might be up to in his backyard. But they did stew a bit when his bushes were permitted to spread three or four feet across their driveway. The branches were always threatening to scratch their car, and in the winter they hogged space needed to pile snow.

When the bushes got completely out of control, Ed and Lillie Grexa would finally bellow at their neighbor, "For God's sake, John, get over and take care of those bushes or we're gonna put rock salt on them."

He would smile goodnaturedly, and later that day he or one of the boys would trim the bushes. The branches that strayed over the Grexa's drive or spread over his own lawn were cut, but he never trimmed the tops to less than six to ten feet. He liked the bushes high. After trimming they were permitted to grow again until his neighbors reminded him that they were once more in need of cutting.

Gacy valued his good relationship with the neighbors and worked earnestly to keep it friendly. Lillie once peered out her front window and observed him preparing to pour a huge concrete square in his front yard next to their driveway.

"Ed, do you see what John's doing out there?" she called to her husband, pointing at their neighbor.

Ed Grexa peered out the window. "He can't do that," he exclaimed. A decorative boulder in a front yard next door to your home is one thing. An ugly concrete block is another. Grexa walked out of the house to confront his neighbor. Gacy smiled when he saw his friend approaching.

"John, that's no good," Grexa said, pointing to the concrete form and shaking his head.

The creases in Gacy's forehead bunched in a surprised frown. "Oh?" he replied, easing the sack of cement he had just lifted uncertainly to the ground. "Okay, Ed, if you don't want it there. Look, do you want the cement? Maybe you can use it to fill holes in the driveway or something?" An hour later the forms had been dismantled and Gacy was putting the lumber and equipment away in his shed.

A more volatile threat to their friendship occurred when Gacy had a falling out with the Grexa's only son. Ron Grexa was in his early twenties when he started working for Gacy. It was a difficult period in young

Grexa's life. His marriage had just broken up, he had lost his home and his business, and he was coping with other serious problems when he moved back in with his parents and an opportunity presented itself to work for their friendly neighbor. Mrs. Grexa wasn't unhappy about the prospect of her son living at home and working next door. It would give her and her husband a chance to provide loving support while he tried to reorganize his life.

He was startled one morning when she asked him about a telephone conversation he was having with a friend. Mother and son were sitting across a table from each other when he said to his friend, "Oh, I told him he couldn't afford me."

"You mean John," his mother grinned, breaking into the conversation and bending her wrist so that her hand flopped limply, in a cruel caricature of an overt homosexual.

"Yeah. How'd you know, Mom?" Ron asked surprised.

"Oh, I just kind of suspected as much," she snickered. It was funny how children believed that the mere fact of becoming a parent somehow removed mothers and fathers from what went on in the world.

Ron conceded that he had been propositioned by his boss, but his mother didn't worry about it. He was a strong boy who knew right from wrong and could take care of himself. She had no doubts that her son was firmly heterosexual.

She was more concerned some time later when he stalked into the house, slamming the back door and announcing angrily that he was going to burn Gacy's house down.

The Grexas were sensitive about the subject of fires. Their own house had been seriously damaged by flames only a few months earlier. Unknown to them, the wood beneath their furnace had dried out. When the heat was turned on during the first chill of the fall the wood ignited. The flames spread and did so much damage that the family had to move into a motel for several weeks while repairs were made.

Lillie Grexa was upset when her son threatened to

burn their neighbor's home, even though he had some justification for being angry. His rage had nothing to do with his boss's sexual activities, but was caused by Gacy's refusal to pay him for work he had done. "John, if you don't pay me," Ron had warned, "I'm gonna burn your house down."

Gacy didn't appreciate the threat, and he called the police. Officers talked to young Grexa the same day and cooled him down, while helping to work out the dispute about the pay.

When Gacy knocked on his neighbor's door to apologize for reporting their son, the Grexas accepted his apology. He explained that just in case the threat was carried out he had wanted the report on record with the police. The Grexas didn't permit the incident to damage their friendship.

Gacy didn't show any signs of missing their son as an employee. There were other athletic young men available to work for him. One after another they showed up at his house for a while, leaving early in the mornings with him in his car or van on their way to jobs. After a time they disappeared and were replaced by other young men.

John Butkovich was one of those who vanished. He worked approximately seven months for Gacy. Then, like Ron Grexa, he quarreled with his boss about his pay. That wasn't unusual. Gacy had tangles about money with several of the young men who worked for him. He wasn't as generous with his pay as he was about hosting big parties, loaning his car, and doing favors for neighbors and township Democrats.

For one thing, he paid his young employees only for the time they were actually on the job, even though it might be necessary for them to spend half their time traveling from one work site to another.

Ed Grexa was appalled when he heard what Gacy was doing. "John, you can't do that," he said. "When we start a job in the morning, regardless of whether or not we go to four or five jobs in a day, we're paid from the time we start out until the time we're finished at night." Gacy winked at him and conspiratorily touched a finger to his lips. "Shhh," he whispered.

He knew how to get a good day's work from his young charges. He drove them hard and the sweat popped out on their lean bodies, running down suntanned backs and chests in salty rivulets as the boys struggled to carry huge armloads of boards and two-by-fours, wrestled heavy paint cans out of trucks and vans, or smacked armies of nails into fresh wood paneling. There was no sitting down to smoke cigarettes when they were on the job. Too often they were rewarded with problems about their pay. Gacy developed a wretched reputation for withholding money, especially if a boy quit or was fired.

Marko and Terezia Butkovich were surprised when their son came home one day and said he was going to look for a new job. The boy grumbled that Gacy was no good and was a liar. He wasn't going to work for PDM Contractors anymore. It wasn't because his boss didn't have work. It seemed that there were almost enough projects at his house alone to keep a couple of boys busy full time.

One of Gacy's most ambitious undertakings at the little house on Summerdale Avenue had just been completed when he attached a storage shed to the end of his garage. It didn't bother him that his neighbors might consider it an eyesore and laugh at it as "a screwed-up looking thing." If his neighbors had wandered into the adjoining garage they would probably have thought it odd that he had installed mirrors in the ceiling. It was insulated with plywood and a drywall.

When he had completed all his alterations, the garage was the only one on the block that didn't have the door at the end of the driveway where the interior was visible from the street. It was necessary to make an awkward sharp right turn to drive through the door. With the addition of the attached shed, the garage was also the only one on the block that covered the entire back section of the lot.

Gacy spent hours working in the garage and so needed the extra space that the shed provided. The garage and shed were his private areas. If the house was considered to be his wife's domain, the shed and garage were his. Soon after the shed was constructed, he outfitted it with a durable concrete floor like the one that Czarna had poured for the garage. Dirt had already been turned over and the surface prepared when Czarna arrived to pour the concrete.

"This would be a helluva place to put bodies," Czarna joshed as he spread the cement. Gacy didn't laugh.

Butkovich didn't mention his former boss again until several days later when he began to complain that Gacy hadn't mailed him a check for his last two weeks' work. Marko Butkovich told his son to advise the stocky contractor that if he didn't pay, authorities would be tipped off that he wasn't deducting taxes from earnings as he was required to do by law. Johnny and two of his buddies, Robert Otera and Joseph Meronicki, went to Gacy's house to collect.

There was a fierce argument. When Johnny mentioned the tax deductions Gacy began screaming and warning him not to make threats. The boys gave up and left, and soon afterward Johnny dropped his pals off and drove away in his Dodge. It was August 1, 1975.

He didn't come home that night. The Butkovichs are old country in some ways, and they raised their children to respect them and their feelings. The parents provided a good home, and in return the children were home on time for meals, helped with the chores around the house, and made a habit of keeping their elders informed of their whereabouts when they were away. It wasn't like Johnny to stay out all night or to go somewhere without letting his parents know his plans.

He had decided to move into one of the apartments his parents owned, and it was said that Gacy had even begun to help him redecorate before their falling out. The boy spent two thousand dollars on carpeting alone. But even though he was planning to move, while he was still living at home he wouldn't stay out all night without first telephoning his parents.

The next day his 1968 Dodge was found parked about a block away with the key in the ignition. His jacket and wallet with forty dollars in it were on the seat. The elder Butkovichs were certain that something was seriously wrong. They contacted the police and reported their son missing.

Seventeen-year-old boys and girls in the greater metropolitan Chicago area leave home every day without telling their parents when or where they are going. Most of them return home when they run out of money, get hungry, or when friends who are sheltering them tire of the freeloading and kick them out.

The report on the Butkovich boy didn't sound much different from those of other teenagers who had gotten itchy feet and left home. It sounded like he was a runaway, police told the worried parents. And if so there was nothing they could legally do to make him come home, even if they found him. According to Illinois law, boys and girls are no longer classed legally as juveniles when they reach seventeen. At seventeen they are considered to be minors, old enough to leave home if they wish.

Marko Butkovich got upset. The more excited he gets, the heavier his accent becomes. The conversation with police was going nowhere. It was obvious that the police weren't going to look for the boy, even though the parents were certain that he had gotten into trouble. Considering their son to be a runaway didn't make sense to either parent. If he had run away, the worried father argued, he would surely have taken his wallet and jacket with him. But there was no reason for him to run away. He had a loving relationship with his family, friends, money in the bank, and a car of his own. It was a good life for a teenager and there was nothing to run from.

Butkovich telephoned Gacy. The husky contractor said he was sorry to hear that the boy was missing and asked if there was anything he could do to help. There were other contacts with police by Marko Butkovich, urging them to look for his son and to talk to the contractor who had quarrelled with the boy over a paycheck. Police told him that they tried to talk to Gacy and he refused to answer their questions.

About a month after their son disappeared, the Butkovichs received a collect call from Puerto Rico and a woman told them that Johnny was living there. Then she hung up. The Butkovichs told police about the anonymous tip, but later worried that it may have hindered the investigation by opening up false leads.

Every week for more than two years Butkovich telephoned police, often asking if they had talked again to Gacy. Eventually police quit answering his calls. Investigators were later to complain that Butkovich didn't give Gacy's name to them until two weeks after the boy had disappeared.

Terezia Butkovich was heavyhearted and puzzled that police could accept the disappearance of her son so lightly. Her husband was more frustrated and angry than puzzled. His son was missing and the police wouldn't look for him.

He telephoned Gacy several more times but there was never any news about the missing boy. Gacy always said he hadn't heard from him and apologized for not being able to help. Johnny Butkovich wasn't seen in the neighborhood, and to his friends he seemed to have suddenly vanished from the face of the earth.

Police moved on to other more pressing investigations, and Gacy continued with the business of running PDM Contractors. He knew how to bring work into the company and he knew how to satisfy his customers. Most of the people he worked for were pleased with his efforts to do a good job.

One businessman whose shop was remodeled by Gacy met him after a general contractor selected PDM to subcontract much of the work. Gacy impressed the businessman with his diligence and speed. He worked on the job with a crew that ranged in size from two to ten other men of varying ages. Some of the more skilled workers were over forty years old, but there were others who were younger and handled the menial labor.

The shopkeeper was more impressed with the efficiency and speed with which the jobs were handled than by the age of the construction crew. Gacy got the right people for the job and he held time down to a minimum.

Regardless of how busy Gacy became, he always had time to do little jobs in the neighborhood and to take care of the projects that kept coming up around the house. It was still Gacy who showed up with a plow after heavy snows and, unbidden and unpaid, cleaned neighboring walks. It was also Gacy who gave away valuable buckets of paint left over from remodeling jobs. And it was Gacy who showed up at the Grexa's back door with an armload of expensive leftovers after hosting another of his parties. He had added Christmas parties for his employees to the popular summer soirees and smaller dinners that he and Carole were becoming locally famous for. He habitually ordered and prepared too much food.

Lillie Grexa shook her head one evening when she answered a knock at the back door and was confronted by her neighbor, balancing a huge tray in his arms stacked high with sliced beef, corned beef, and turkey.

"Can you use it?" he asked, grinning and pushing the tray toward her.

"You're darned right we can use it," she replied, looking down on at least thirty dollars worth of meat. "How much do you want for it?"

"No, I don't want any money," he said. "I over-ordered again. I always want to have more than enough food on hand for the parties."

While John and Carole were building their reputation as party hosts, their marriage was deteriorating beyond salvage. He became brusque and domineering, locking the telephone so that his wife could not make outgoing calls. He locked his office and restricted her and her daughters to the kitchen and bedroom area.

The long anticipated divorce action was finally filed. She accused him of seeing other women. He accused her of not preparing his meals. Carole and the girls continued to live in the house with him until the divorce became final on March 2, 1976. Despite all their differences, she never felt that either of them had been abusive to the other, and the breakup was more amicable than might have been expected. When she left the house he moved her furniture and personal belongings as well as buying new carpeting for her apartment. In return, she allowed him to keep the icebox and stove.

Carole's mother, who works in a beauty parlor, hadn't been pleased with her son-in-law from the beginning of the marriage. She became disenchanted with him as rumors of his sexual involvement with young men inevitably surfaced. She once overheard a quarrel he had with one of the boys. There was a shoving match over money that Gacy allegedly owed him. During the exchange the angry youngster screamed that Gacy had tried to rape him.

Carole and John continued to see each other after the divorce and in some ways their relationship was better than it had been during the marriage. It was more relaxed. Carole was concerned about her former husband's welfare and helplessly agonized with him when he talked to her for long hours about his bisexuality. She had never known a homosexual before, and she had no idea what she could do to help the troubled man she had once been married to.

To others, he maintained the front of self-confident efficiency that he had striven so hard to create for himself: John Gacy, generous neighbor, successful businessman and sound citizen.

He began inviting politically important people to his parties, and if they didn't attend it wasn't because he didn't make the effort. Chicago Mayor Richard J. Daley was invited to a theme party and disappointed the exuberant host by not attending. Gacy bragged, however, that some aldermen attended.

Jim Van Vorous, a business associate of Gacy's, co-hosted three of the theme parties. Carole also helped out as hostess at one of the gatherings after their divorce. The 1976 party was logically planned with a Bicentennial theme and hosted on the Fourth of July. Both Gacy and Van Vorous dressed as Colonial gentlemen in outfits complete with knee-length pants, long white sox, and white periwigs to greet their guests. Gacy said he was George Washington, the father of the country.

The Bicentennial fete was followed in 1977 with a Southern Jubilee, when Gacy dressed as a Confederate general, and in 1978 with an Italian festival, when he wore a peasant's costume. Southern fried chicken was served at the jubilee and spaghetti and meatballs at the Italian party.

The median age of Gacy's party guests grew progressively younger each year. It seemed to Lillie Grexa that young men in their late teens and early twenties were all over the place when she and her husband mixed with the group at the Italian event.

At the parties he co-hosted, Van Vorous pitched in to help Gacy with the cooking, and they split the cost of the beer, mixers, and a four- or five-piece band. When Gacy's mother was visiting from her home in Arkansas with her youngest daughter, she stood in her walker and, ignoring the discomfort of arthritis, later aggravated by a broken hip, sang for the guests. The guests also sang and danced. The more fun everyone had, the happier it made their host. Gacy loved being surrounded by friends and he loved to entertain.

The Grexas were intrigued by their somewhat eccentric neighbor and his entertaining. His activities were amusing to watch. You never knew what he was going to do next. Sometimes his shenanigans could be funny, even when they weren't meant to be.

Lillie loves to tell the story about the time that a neighbor from a house down the street asked to borrow Gacy's power saw to cut down a tree. "Yeah," Gacy said. "You can borrow it, but I better go along and show you how to use it." A short time later Gacy, who had told his friends that he was worried about a heart ailment, was twenty feet above the ground sawing off limbs. Afterward, the neighbor received a bill in the mail charging him three hundred dollars for the tree cutting.

Lillie puzzled about her neighbor's weak heart. It was true that he was overweight and had an oxygen tank and mask in his house. But he had cut down three or four trees in his backyard by himself, he thought nothing of operating the business end of a wheelbarrow loaded with cement or dirt six or eight hours a day, and he seemed to be always climbing on ladders. He once tumbled off a ladder after making a misstep and broke a leg. He was back at work a few days later wearing a cast.

Lillie's capricious neighbor seemed to be committed to a regimen of work, punctuated by work, hardly an ideal life-style for someone with a weak heart. "John, you better watch out for your heart," she sometimes cautioned. He would smile, reassure her that "It's okay, I'm fine," and return to whatever he was doing.

The divorce didn't appear to have damaged Gacy's zest for living. It was just the opposite. He applied himself to his business with renewed vigor, socializing with his neighbors, and occasionally slipped off for an abbreviated vacation of two or three days, once making the trip to Las Vegas with Carole. The neighbors always knew when he was home. On those days the house hummed with activity as muscular young men in ten-year-old cars pulled in and out of the driveway and trooped into the house or busied themselves working on some project with Gacy in the yard or garage.

The nights were busy, too. One night when Gacy came wheeling home in his Oldsmobile at about 2:30 A.M. with a gang of boys, they made so much noise that Ed Grexa walked next door to point out the late hour and ask everyone to quiet down.

At other times, long after most of the hard-working people who were his neighbors had clicked off their television sets and gone to bed, Gacy was still up puttering in the backyard or busy in the garage. Sometimes Ed Grexa would tap on the garage door, point to his watch, and ask, "John, don't you know what time it is?"

Gacy usually looked startled, and replied, "No, I didn't know." Then he would apologize and say he was sorry that he had disturbed anyone. If anyone had been watching a few minutes later they would have seen him pull the garage door shut, lock it, and go in the house or drive away in his car. The Grexas wondered about his late hours. It seemed that he was so busy, there just wasn't enough time in the day to get everything done that he had to do.

Not long before Gacy's Western theme party, Grexa spotted him digging a hole in the backyard and walked over to see what was going on. His burly neighbor was almost chest deep in the pit. "What are you doing, John," he kidded, "digging a grave?"

Gacy jammed his shovel into the dirt and looked up. "That's an awful thing to say," he replied, his face contorting into a mirthless smile. A couple of days later he had constructed a permanent barbecue over the pit. It was completed in time to use at the party.

The parties were growing in size as PDM Contractors prospered and he widened his circle of business associates and acquaintances and hired more employees. He had no trouble finding help. There was a limitless reservoir of boys with lean, well-muscled bodies in the city and northwestern suburbs to hire, boys like Gregory Godzik.

Greg was a handsome seventeen-year-old youth with clear gray eyes and stylishly long blond hair that his parents were badgering him to cut. His good looks were enhanced by an effervescent personality that made it easy for him to attract girl friends at Taft High School, where his academic record unfortunately trailed his social accomplishments.

Although he had some academic problems and a reputation for occasionally cutting classes, he was well liked by the school faculty as well as by his classmates. If he wasn't with a girl friend he was likely to be lounging with a couple of buddies or riding somewhere in a car.

Like most boys his age from the northwest side of Chicago, he was anxious to earn his own spending money. When Gacy asked him to go to work for PDM Contractors, Greg eagerly accepted. The job provided all the excuse he needed to invest in an old car, which he tinkered with until it would run. Then he announced that he had transportation to get to and from work.

Although he carried only about 110 pounds on a slight five-foot nine-inch frame, he was sinewy and tough and the cleaning work and other tasks he was given to do for PDM didn't bother him. He loved it, and once confided to his buddy, Tim Best, that it was the best job he had ever had. His parents were pleased when he told them that he had an afterschool job. It would keep him off street corners and out of mischief.

Greg appreciated the good things that happened to him, and he had a cheerful and confident outlook on life. Judy Patterson, a fellow student at Taft, wasn't at all surprised when he told her, as 1976 was nearing to a close, that it had been the best year of his life.

Having an optimistic nature, of course, didn't mean that the lighthearted high school senior didn't have an occasional problem. Near the first of December he mixed it up with another boy who was trying to date Judy, and came out of the fight with a small cut above his right eye.

But by December 11 he was sitting down in the family recreation room drowning cookies in a glass of milk, watching television, and talking excitedly to his mother, Mrs. Eugenia Godzik, of the date he had that night with the pretty sophomore he had fought over.

A lunchroom attendant with the Chicago public schools, Mrs. Godzik was on her way to church with her husband, John, and she swelled with pride in her handsome son. He was wearing a new shirt he had just brought, and it was the first time he had dressed up specially for a date.

Greg dropped Judy off at her home after their date, at about 12:30 A.M., reminded her that he would telephone later, and drove away in his battered car.

He didn't come home that night, and he didn't telephone his girl friend. It wasn't like him to stay out all night. It was something he never did. He didn't like to be away from home. The few times he was out of town with relatives or with his hockey team, he got homesick and wanted to come home. Anytime he was gone from the house for an unexpectedly long time he telephoned to inform his parents where he was.

The Godziks called Judy and she told them what time he had taken her home and of his promise to telephone. She hadn't heard from him. Although they had quarreled earlier in the week, they had patched up their differences and got along well together on their date. The girl said she was sure that he would have told her if he planned to run away. His buddies were no more successful than his date in trying to shed light on his whereabouts. They hadn't seen him or heard from him.

His parents contacted the police and talked with Police Area Five youth officers. They were told that their son was probably a runaway. It was a supposition that they couldn't accept. Despite their son's sometime lack of attention to academics, and the fact that several of his friends had dropped out of school, he expected to graduate in a few months. He was dating a girl that he cared a lot about. And there was no trouble at home that was more serious than an occasional suggestion that he trim his hair, or gentle grumbling about his habit of using the family recreation room as his bedroom. There was certainly no trouble serious enough to cause him to run away without even talking over his problems with his parents or his friends.

Furthermore, he had a job that he liked and he had just acquired his first car. Police found the car the Sunday afternoon after his date. The 1966 maroon Pontiac was abandoned, unlocked, behind a pet store in Niles, another of the so-called O'Hare Corridor communities that bunched around Chicago's northwest boundary.

The boy's parents couldn't believe that he would have willingly walked away and left his unlocked car in Niles after having lavished so much loving care on it. He was so proud of it that even when it was parked at his home he always doublechecked to make sure that it was locked if he had to leave it for a few hours.

Mrs. Godzik remembered once meeting a boy who said he had run away from home, and had been taken in by her son's employer. Greg also had three or four days' pay coming, money he would surely need if he was leaving home. It seemed possible that he could have driven to his boss's house to pick up the money after dropping off his date. Mrs. Godzik telephoned John Gacy.

Gacy had a rule that his young employees should telephone before coming to his house, unless their arrival was expected. He told Mrs. Godzik that her son called a few days after his unexplained disappearance and left a message on the telephone tape machine saying that he would be in to work at noon the next day. He never showed up.

The worried mother asked Gacy to play the tape for her. He said he couldn't—it had already been erased. The next time Mrs. Godzik talked to Chicago police she told them about the conversation with the contractor and suggested that they talk to him about her missing son.

Gacy's name had, of course, come up in the investigation into Butkovich's disappearance. But Butkovich lived in Police Area Six on the north side, whereas Godzik was from Police Area Five on the northwest side. There was apparently no communication between the officers from the two districts and no one recognized the name that was the common link which could have tied the two missing persons reports together. Nor did policemen from either district bother to check Gacy for a prior arrest record, although he was one of the last people known to have seen Butkovich and, according to his own statement, was one of the last to have talked with Greg.

Harold Thomas, commander of the Chicago Youth Division, later defended the seemingly slipshod police work. "There was no reason to check his record," Thomas said of Gacy. "We don't run a check of everyone we talk to in our investigation unless there is some reason. You must realize that you don't treat every missing case as a possible homicide."[1]

A couple of tantalizing reports of people who reputedly saw Greg after his disappearance reached the Godziks, but none of them was confirmed. A security guard at Taft said he talked to the boy in the school lunchroom on Monday, December 13, two days after he was last seen by his parents. The guard said that Greg left after he was asked if he was supposed to be in class.

The Godziks also visited the editorial offices of their neighborhood weekly newspaper, *The Lerner Times*, and talked reporter Carolyn Lenz into writing a story about their son. Reporters don't often write stories about missing teenagers unless there is strong evidence to indicate that violence or an abduction has been involved. Like police, they are aware that tens of thousands of boys and girls leave home every year.

But Greg didn't fit the mold of the typical teenager who runs away because of trouble at home, school, or with a sweetheart. His parents had come to her for help, and the reporter, a slender young woman with rust-colored short hair, didn't turn them down.

On February 9, 1977, the story of the disappearance of Greg Godzik appeared in *The Lerner Times* under the reporter's byline. Among other people, she had talked to his former employer, misspelled in the article as "John Gasey."

Gacy told the reporter that, contrary to what the

[1]*Chicago Tribune,* January 7, 1979.

boy's parents believed, Greg had been talking about quitting school and running away. He said he last saw the youth on a Friday afternoon, the last day Greg attended school, and that he had left hurriedly, apparently angry. He didn't say why the boy was upset.

The contractor confided that Greg had not come to work regularly and that he was rebellious. Charitably, he added, however, "I don't think he's a bad kid." The reporter thanked him for his assistance. He had been very nice, very cooperative.

The reporter later recalled that Gacy handled the conversation smoothly and appeared to be anxious to help. "I had no reason to think he wasn't telling the truth," she said. "He wasn't at all evasive."

The newspaper story didn't help. Greg still didn't show up. His parents talked to a Navy recruiter, and with his help checked all the branches of the military service to determine if their son had enlisted. They knew he had previously taken and passed a Navy aptitude test. But Greg wasn't in the service.

By the time Carolyn Lenz wrote a follow-up story about Greg nearly a year after his disappearance as part of a series on teenage runaways, his parents had hired private investigator Anthony Pellicano to search for their son. Although Pellicano was said to have located some four thousand missing persons, he could not find Greg.

On January 20, 1977, less than two months after Godzik vanished, John Szyc was reported missing. The nineteen-year-old youth had known Godzik and Butkovich. He had also been an acquaintance of John Gacy, although he hadn't worked for PDM Contractors.

Szyc graduated from Main West High School in Niles in 1975, the year that Butkovich dropped out of sight. Soon after completing school he found a job in Chicago, moved to an apartment on the north side where he had friends, and bought a 1971 Plymouth Satellite.

A car can be an important extension of a teenage boy's personality. Buying a first car is a sign of the transition from childhood to manhood, a move out of the nest, and a readiness to begin accepting adult responsibilities. It also helps to get a date. Young Szyc was understandably proud of his car, and when he dropped out of sight the car vanished with him.

Although he was living by himself, he had kept in close touch with his father, Richard, a truck driver, and his mother, Rose Marie. When they didn't hear from him for some time and they learned that he hadn't been seen at his apartment or by his friends, they notified police. Police recorded the information and filed it.

Like Butkovich and Godzik, who had earlier disappeared so mysteriously, Szyc had no history of running away and had nothing to run from. He had independence, privacy, his own apartment and a car. He had no reason to run. Yet, despite an agonized search among his friends and hangouts, the Szycs could find no trace of their son.

It was nearly nine months before an incident occurred that reminded police of the missing boy and provided a solid clue linking him to the same man thought to have been one of the last people to see or talk with Butkovich and Godzik.

Police picked up Mike Rossi after a service station attendant accused him of filling the tank of a 1971 Plymouth Satellite with gas and then driving away without paying. The eighteen-year-old motorist told police that the man he was living with could explain everything. Once again authorities were drawn to the house at 8213 West Summerdale Avenue.

Gacy's loquacious salesmanship paid off and he not only took care of the problem about the tank of gasoline, but also convinced the policemen that he had purchased the car from Szyc and sold it to Rossi. Neighbors had seen Rossi around the house for weeks, and other employees said they were as close as "father and son."

The contractor said that Szyc sold the car to him in February because he needed the money to leave town. Oddly, although investigators obviously did not bother to check, there was no resemblance between the signature that Szyc signed on the title when he purchased the car, and his name as it was written on the title transfer eighteen days after his parents reported him missing.

A few days after investigators talked with Gacy, police sent a letter to Szyc's parents advising them that although they had been unable to locate the boy, they had learned that he had sold his car and told the buyer he needed the money to leave town.

The police made no effort to explain why, if Szyc needed money, he had left behind two paychecks, all of his personal possessions, and had purchased new license plates for the car on January 20, the day he vanished.

5

Lavender City

It was June 13, 1976, the nineteenth birthday of his brother Robert, and Billy Carroll, Jr., slept until mid-morning before rolling out of bed and pulling on a pair of blue jeans and a tight-fitting orange T-shirt.

Officially it wasn't yet summer, but a few blocks away trees and shrubs along the lakeshore were splashed with green and vibrantly alive. People were lounging or strolling in cutoffs and bikinis or languidly lobbing tennis balls back and forth.

In the Carroll apartment it was stuffy and hot and the rooms were stifling. There was no breeze in Uptown and the air was moist and putrid, hanging heavily over the moldering streets where garbage and dog droppings sprang up as profusely as spring flowers might bloom in tidier, less soiled neighborhoods.

Shadows cast by the streetlights were stealthily shifting in the early evening gloom by the time Billy slid into a seat in an old green car and rode away with three friends. He had promised his parents that he would be back in an hour. He never saw the apartment or his family again.

The last time Frank W. Landingin, Jr. saw his cab-driver father, they quarreled. It was shortly after an acquaintance posted a one-thousand-dollar bond on November 3, 1978 to get the young man out of jail, where he had been held on a charge of assault and battery for beating up his girl friend. His girl friend, like most of his peers, called him Dale. It was a name he chose for himself, bastardizing it from "Del," the nickname his father had given him because he was born in Delaware.

When father and son met outside a restaurant on an Uptown street corner, they quarreled over Dale's failure to hold a job, his abuse of drugs, and his unsavory friends. The angry words they shouted at each other were the last words they ever exchanged.

Billy Carroll and Dale Landingin had much in common, even though they apparently did not know each other. They were about the same age. Billy was sixteen when he disappeared, and Dale was nineteen when he vanished two years later. Both were precocious children of the streets. And both were apparently sexually straight but used their good looks, youth, and charm to take advantage of men who cruised Chicago streets looking for boys. Billy specialized in procuring other boys for adult homosexuals for a commission. Dale accepted cash and gifts for promises of sex and then slipped away before the payoffs.

Both youths were living in Uptown when they disappeared. Much of Uptown would be described by social scientists and urban planners as blighted. The worst sections are for the defeated or for the newly arrived who go on welfare or work at day labor agencies, and settle into cheap hotels or festering apartments owned by absentee landlords.

The lucky and the industrious are eventually able to move to better neighborhoods like Rogers Park, Wicker Park and Lakeview or to pleasant middle-class homes in the northwest suburbs of Norridge, Des Plaines, Harwood Heights, and Park Ridge.

Most, however, are trapped in Uptown, where they live miserably in a physical environment that is intrinsically hostile to them. There are areas of Uptown where mothers hang beds from ceilings with ropes to keep their babies from being chewed on by rats, fathers worry about getting shoes for their kids to wear to school, and the winos parade as unsteadily as a shell-shocked army.

The people are poor Appalachian whites, blacks from southern dirt farms or backwoods bayous, American Indians who have left the security and poverty of reservations and a polyglot assortment of foreign immigrants from countries as diverse as India, Vietnam, Mexico, Jordan, Poland, and Yugoslavia.

The Appalachians account for one of the largest ethnic groups. Between 1940 and 1960 more than 350,000 people from Appalachia migrated to Chicago. Thousands more followed in the nearly two decades since then. And most of the wave of new urban poor settled in the cheap, crumbling apartment buildings of Uptown, squeezing themselves in next to the rainbow host of poor already there.

The adjustment is difficult. Most of the newcomers have no training to help them make the transition from what was basically a rural agricultural society with strong familial, church, and neighborhood ties, to a new urban existence of factory work, fearsome unfriendly streets, and a social life tied more closely to dingy corner saloons than to church.

In the city, bars with jukeboxes blaring country tunes by Conway Twitty, Willie Nelson, or Loretta Lynn have become the center of cultural activity for the newcomers and a refuge where they can go to escape northern prejudice against "hillbillies" who talk funny, ride in old cars, and listen to shit-kickin' music. They have become crisis-oriented, living from job losses to apartment evictions to victimization by burglars, muggers, and sneak thieves. Their world has turned upside down.

If adapting to urban life is difficult for adults, it can be totally devastating for teenagers. Told to attend schools where integration is more important than education and it may be necessary to fight their way to and from classes, where their southern accent is about as easily understood as Ethiopian and they are mocked for their redneck image, the boys and girls become truants and dropouts. The streets are waiting for them.

There are areas in Chicago where boy prostitutes favorably compete with, if not completely overshadow, females. Uptown is one of them. Dressed casually in blue jeans and T-shirts, the sallow-faced young men slouch insolently in front of bars and restaurants waiting for dates wearing business suits who drive in from the suburbs in big cars. For a few dollars the boys climb into the passenger seats and ride to secluded side streets, the murky shadows under elevateds, or a few blocks east to parking lots in the park along the Lake Michigan beach. A few minutes later, after completing a single surreptitious act, the boys are dropped off again to await their next date.

In New Town, a few blocks south, the atmosphere is less defeating, the boys are younger, and the action is even more open. Prostitutes of both sexes work the gaudy, bustling neighborhood near the lake. New Town never sleeps, and the girls who parade along Broadway in hotpants or miniskirts, filmy nipple-punctuated blouses, and boots are available morning and night. They are as close as a street-corner meeting, a telephone call—or a wrong number.

More than one New Town couple has awakened at 6 or 6:30 A.M. and, after sleepily groping their way to a door buzzer, been greeted by a voice over the intercom announcing: "This is Karen. Did you send for me?" In New Town it is easier to get a hooker to make a house call than a doctor.

Residential New Town is a neighborhood of young singles, many of them gay males and females who moved to the city seeking jobs and the society of people who accept them for, or regardless of, their sexual preferences. The gay life-style comes closer to total acceptance in New Town than in any other part of the city, than probably anywhere in the Midwest. Public behavior is tolerated in New Town that would be totally unacceptable in other areas. There are gay weight watchers, over-forty clubs for gays, political and gay rights organizations, groups for gay alcoholics and Catholic, Protestant, and Jewish churches and temples for gays. One summer a "gay patrol" was organized from among gays trained in karate and kung-fu who volunteered to douse the enthusiasm of young toughs who had developed the disturbing habit of prowling the streets of New Town on weekends and evenings looking for homosexuals to pummel.

New Town has been called a gay ghetto, but in reality it is a free and easy mélange of gays and straights. A few blocks east of Broadway, New Town's main promenade, Lake Shore Drive accommodates high rises occupied by doctors, lawyers, bankers, wealthy real-estate investors, and retired professional men and their wives.

On Broadway, Belmont, or Diversey, a few blocks west of the high rises, wives and daughters of the more conservative residents of the area have been mistaken for prostitutes and propositioned while shopping for groceries or clothes. When the vice activities began interfering with commerce, a neighborhood association complained to police and a crackdown was initiated. In less than one week shortly before Christmas, in a vice sweep incongruously dubbed "Operation Angel," police picked up some thirty males and females accused of prostitution and more than six hundred men identified as prospective clients.

New Town tourists learned then that not every sexy blonde that they approached on the street is female. Many are drag queens and transsexuals who climb into cars, accept twenty dollars for a rapid act of oral sex and leave without their client ever suspecting that he has just had a homosexual experience.

New Town is Chicago Bohemia. The Hull House Association's Jane Addams Center on Broadway offers photography, dance and art classes, and activities for senior citizens. There are practicing witch's covens, Latino Santeros, theater groups, singles bars for gay and straight clientele, head shops, an art fair, boutiques, Japanese, Korean, Thai, and vegetarian restaurants, resale shops, antique stores and botanicas where customers can buy ingredients for magic potions or statues of saints and Yoruba gods and goddesses.

There are meetings of sadomasochism societies, wife swappers, adult bookstores, a boutique for transvestites that carries size-eleven pumps, and the Pleasure Chest— a sex supermarket that features sales on whips, flails, manacles, rubber suits, and giant plastic dildos.

For cruising adult homosexuals, even the exotic offerings of the Pleasure Chest pale beside the lure of the young men and boys who frequent the discos and street corners, lounge in all-night restaurants and coffee shops, or who promenade at curbside wearing skintight trousers or tiny cutoffs and blouses that have been knotted and pulled up at the waist to expose a wink of belly button.

Some of the youths are ethereal and pallid with long bleached hair, earrings, and shrill voices. Others are butch with short hair, earrings, and shrill voices. Others are butch with short hair, work boots, leather jackets or tight black tank tops and jeans that show off their slender-hipped ruggedness and draw the eye to the genital bulge at the crotch. The colored bandannas or kerchiefs draped from the back pockets identify the type of sexual specialty the owners find most enjoyable. There is instant recognition for those who know the color code.

Annually in June, a phalanx of grim-faced motorcycle policemen are drafted to lead the annual gay rights parade of shiny convertibles, floats, musicians, drag queens and chanting gay male and female marchers along the major streets to the park for a picnic along the lakefront. The parade is the climax of gay pride week.

Billy Carroll, so far as any of those who knew him were able to ascertain, was heterosexual. But he knew the streets of Uptown and New Town and familiarized himself with their homosexual haunts and hangouts.

If there was anyone in his family who looked like a survivor, it was Billy. He had a fast, agile mind, and according to a truant officer and others who knew him, fingers that matched his brain in their swift stickiness. He was a child of the city and he learned early that a person, no matter how young, could survive if he was capable of approaching the streets on their own terms.

The lessons he learned best were not those that he learned in school. He attended school fitfully and once was ordered into special classes for truants. The lessons he most readily absorbed were those he learned on the streets.

His brother and his parents, William Carroll, Sr., and Violet, are candid about Billy's talent for getting in trouble. He was an active, mischievous boy. At three years of age he fell from a moving car after pushing the back door open with his foot while the family was driving to North Florida to see his grandparents. Robert yelled that his little brother had fallen out, and when his father turned to look, Billy was rolling end over end down a grade. He was patched up in a hospital with a few stitches in his head.

A few years later there was another visit to a Chicago hospital and more stitches in his head when he fell from a tree. He returned home from the doctor as recklessly adventuresome as before.

He was only nine years old when he snatched a purse and wound up in the juvenile home. His father recalled that his son was more fortunate another time and found himself three hundred or four hundred dollars richer after he reached out the window of a slow moving elevated train and grabbed a purse from a woman standing on the platform.

By the time he was eleven, Billy was in the bicycle business. A local Fagin had organized several of the young boys in the neighborhood, and when the man was finally caught by the police they used three patrol wagons and a squad car to move the bicycles and other loot he had accumulated in the fencing operation. Billy had been one of his most industrious and successful associates.

He had wisely left the wasteland of empty lots, broken bottles, and exhausted lives in Uptown and headed for the suburbs where he found English racers, shiny new Schwinns, and expensive ten-speeds from Holland, Germany, and Belgium. He traded one of the bicycles for a black and silver-haired puppy which he brought home and named King. Most of the bicycles he sold.

Somehow Billy learned to make strip keys, which could be used to open almost any padlock. Eventually he acquired a collection of about twenty-five padlocks, which he tinkered with, experimenting and familiarizing himself with the action of the tumblers.

He was about fourteen or fifteen when he was caught with a .38-caliber Smith and Wesson automatic pistol. Friends told his father that he had been shooting it at people to scare them. He liked to watch them run.

When Billy wasn't roughhousing with King or on the street, he was exercising to build himself up physically. As a teenager he helped keep his body firm and evenly muscled by lifting weights, boxing, and wrestling. At sixteen he was a scrappy five-foot, nine-inches tall and as game as a fighting cock. Even his teeth were good and were marred by only two small fillings.

He had his own boxing shorts and gloves and squared off in the Clarendon Park District's boxing program in matches against other youths in his weight class. Watching the 1972 Olympics on television interested him in wrestling.

The Parkway Cinema near the three-way intersection of Clark, Broadway, and Diversey probably shows as many kung-fu movies or action films starring Clint Eastwood, Charles Bronson, and Burt Reynolds as any other theater in Chicago. Billy and his friends sat through entire afternoons watching Bruce Lee and other heroes, sometimes seeing double features twice. His interest in the Oriental fighting styles stimulated by the movies, he bought books on kung-fu and karate and took a few lessons, earning an orange belt.

At other times he ice-skated or jogged around Graceland Cemetery a few blocks south of his Uptown home. He didn't smoke tobacco, but occasionally sipped from a bottle of wine—and, according to friends, shared a joint if someone was passing one around. But he cared too much about his body to move deeply into alcohol, tobacco, or drugs. He talked vaguely about keeping in good shape so that he could someday strike out on a cross-country bicycle trip.

He liked money and one of the places to find it was at the corner of Diversey, Broadway, and Clark. The corner is constantly crowded with urban commuters waiting for Chicago Transit Authority buses. A blind man who holds a tin cup and dangles a blaring transistor radio from his belt has taken over one spot on the corner, and a newspaper kiosk has another. Shops and stores offer snacks of pizza, ice cream, Cantonese rice and noodles, gyros, cocktails, Big Macs and Yankee Doodle Dandies.

To Billy and his friends, the intersection had other charms not confined to the shops, restaurants, and cinema. They knew they could make money if they hung around long enough. He met street hustlers, a boy named Jaimie, another named Jerry, and others who were less cautious than himself about climbing into cars with strangers when the price was right. Made conspicuous by their short haircuts, neckties and white shirts, the strangers cruised the streets with the driver's window rolled down until eye contact was made with the right person.

The motorists were almost invariably middle-aged or older and lived in suburbia with wives and children or with parents, posing as sexually straight during the day and cruising the city streets at night once a week or so looking for young boys. Avowed homosexuals with nothing to hide had their own friends and frequented their own bars.

Stories were passed around about boys who returned from rides with their eyes blackened and noses bleeding or doubled over in pain from less obvious injuries. The boys had to be cautious. Jerry once climbed into a car with a solid, tough-looking man who was so rough and threatening that the boy jumped out of the car and ran. The youthful hustlers learned quickly from friends or by sad experience that a certain breed of man enjoyed inflicting fear or pain.

Billy knew what went on in the cars, and he sometimes parleyed at curbside with motorists or permitted someone to buy him a taco at a restaurant. But he never got in their cars. He arranged for other boys to go for rides, and when they returned he was waiting for a share of the money they brought with them. Billy Carroll's parents said that their son was too smart to voluntarily ride away in the car of a stranger, and he was too scrappy to be forced.

When Billy was a regular on the corner there were stories about a big, rugged chunk of a man who cruised in a new black Oldsmobile with a spotlight. Young men like Jaimie, who trades on his thick-lipped likeness to Mick Jagger and is a regular at homosexual hangouts, believed they narrowly escaped serious injury or death after encounters with him. He told of a frightening confrontation with the big man in the sleek Oldsmobile in an article by Gene Mustain and Gilbert Jimenez in the *Chicago Sun-Times*. [1]

[1] *Chicago Sun-Times,* December 31, 1978.

The encounter began at Bughouse Square, about a half mile north of Chicago's Loop, when Jaimie was introduced to the man by another male prostitute known on the street as Speed Freak Billy. Bughouse Square acquired its unique name years ago when the block-long park on the near north was a haven for soapbox oratory. Day and night, self-appointed experts climbed on top of wooden crates, overturned buckets, and park benches, or merely stood tall and lectured to anyone who cared to listen on subjects as diverse as Marxism and the evils of big business, to the universal draft, prohibition, or flying saucers.

By the 1960s the park had changed. The speakers were gone and had been replaced by winos with faces and bodies as vacant and exhausted as worked-out coal mines, and by young boys—runaways, truants, or just kids whose parents didn't care where they went and whether or not they came back. It became known as a chicken park where young boys patrolled the sidewalks near the curbs with no underwear on and socks wadded up inside their pants to make their genitals bulge. When a car slowed and a motorist looked interested they might rub the front of their pants suggestively or "throw the basket out," pushing their crotch enticingly forward. They patrol year around in all types of weather until they earn the price of a supper, an ounce of grass or carton of cigarettes, and another night in a hotel room.

Jaimie said he was driven to a house on Summerdale Avenue in Norwood township. The big-bellied man who drove him was John Gacy.

The first meeting was uneventful, even though there was something discomforting about the house. It was almost too still and the young hustler was bothered by "bad vibrations like spirits." He was uneasy being alone with his host. But once they had shared a couple of drinks and talked, Gacy drove him back to Bughouse Square, after giving him thirty dollars and a handful of pills. "See, I'm okay, you can trust me," Gacy reassured him. "You'll be seeing me again."

It was a couple of weeks before Jaimie saw Gacy at Bughouse Square again. A full, gibbous moon had fumbled its way out of the clouds, dimly illuminating the dark shadows of the park in a brackish yellow glow, when Gacy smilingly approached the second time. Gacy's smile groped for the corners of his mouth and his eyes squeezed into pleased slits as the young man climbed into the car and accepted an offer of thirty dollars for mutual oral sex. When they pulled away in the big car Jaimie was embarking on a different sort of evening than he had spent with his companion earlier.

As the story was reconstructed, there were no pleasant interludes of friendly conversation or drinks. Jaimie's husky host led him into the bedroom, where both of them stripped. Gacy told Jaimie to get busy doing what he was being paid to do, but before the youth could comply his head was jolted back with a sudden slap. Suddenly Jaimie was being beaten. He tried to scream but the noise was smothered by powerful hands that closed around his throat.

Jaimie had been a prostitute since he was twelve, and he realized that he was with one of those people who were sexually stimulated by hurting others. The trick was to defend himself but not to fight so hard that it made his attacker even more violent and more dangerous. Tears were welling in his eyes and he was trying to wriggle free when Gacy did something that terrified him even more. From somewhere, Gacy produced a pair of handcuffs. Jaimie picked up a vase and shattered it over the man's head. He grabbed at the handcuffs and hurled them against a window, then gripped Gacy's wrist and bit down until he tasted blood.

As his attacker clutched his wrist and jerked away, Jaimie screeched that a friend had taken down the Oldsmobile's license number. That was how the boys protected themselves, he lied.

Moments later Jaimie was lifted off his feet and heaved onto the bed. The man threw his own heavy body onto that of the youth, smashing him into the mattress. Jaimie couldn't move. He was smothering. The man on top of him was groaning.

Abruptly the man rolled off the boy, got to his feet, and snapped on the bedroom lights. He was panting heavily and smiling. It was time for them to get dressed so that Jaimie could be driven back to the park, he said. Before leaving the house. Gacy gave the frightened boy fifty dollars, the thirty-dollar promised fee and a twenty-dollar tip, and added another handful of pills.

Jaimie was silent on the ride back. After he left the man who had beaten him, he took a month off from the streets. It had been a terrifying experience. Much later Speed Freak Billy casually mentioned to Jaimie that he was a specialist. His clients were sadists, masochists, and bondage freaks.

Jaimie had more than he wanted of sadists, and he told his friends about the man from Norwood Park. He warned them to stay away from the man if he came around again.

He came back. Various boys talked of seeing him around the square, in leather bars on the near north and in New Town clubs like Cheeks, Broadway Limited, and Blinkers. All the clubs were known for their gay clientele. At other times he was spotted cruising in his Oldsmobile farther north on Broadway, his eyes gleaming hungrily at curly-haired boys carrying shoulder bags, youths in cutoffs and sneakers walking hand-in-hand past pizza and gyros restaurants, leafing idly through stacks of rock albums or leaning against the brick-and-glass fronts of gay bars and discos. Streetwise hustlers avoided him. The word was out.

There was also talk of the same man in a black Oldsmobile cruising the meaner, grimier streets of Uptown looking for young boys. It was said that although he could be generous with his dollars, he was also dangerous. It was best to stay away from him because he was as rough and mean as an oilfield bully.

There was speculation that he might have been involved in the disappearance of a nine-year-old boy who was a known prostitute and pimp for other children. Nine years old is not too young for boy prostitutes. There are men who find pleasure in sex with even younger children. In street parlance men who seek sex with boys are called chicken hawks. By eighteen or nineteen a boy hooker can be burned out and so old for the street that the price for his services has dropped precipitously.

An hour or so with a nine-, ten-, eleven- or twelve-year-old can bring one hundred dollars to a don, the man who acts as go-between for the extremely young and their clients. Men who desire sex with preteens are reluctant even to circle known pickup spots at parks or street corners where youth or vice-squad officers may be watching to make embarrassing arrests or to record license numbers. It is safer to make the arrangements with a don to pick up the boy at a certain location and take him from there to a hotel or to an apartment.

By the time boys become fourteen or fifteen years old, even those new to the business, they are usually working on their own because they no longer need a go-between. But by that age their value as sexual partners has already begun to drop. Their bodies are becoming too muscular and hairy, and their voices too deep.

When the nine-year-old vanished from his old hangouts, other boys provided Area Six Youth Division officers with a description of the man in the black Oldsmobile. Driving the car with the red spotlight on the side, he wasn't difficult to find. With fellow officers from Area Five, the police tailed him through the grimy streets of Uptown and through the lively streets of New Town. Eventually he led them to the bungalow on Summerdale Avenue. During a two-week stakeout, several youths seen going in and out of the house were questioned. None of them had anything incriminating to say about the man who lived inside.

Like earlier policemen who had been led to the house on Summerdale, none of the youth officers bothered to check the computers to determine if there was an arrest record on John Wayne Gacy.

While Gacy was becoming familiar to boy prostitutes and youth officers, he was also making new friends in straight bars and neighborhood clubs. He was drawn to clubs like the Good Luck Lounge, a working-class saloon with a predominantly young Polish clientele on North Elston Avenue in the neighborhood where he had attended Schurz High School.

Occasionally he showed up at the tavern with Carole, both before and after their marriage, or with a young female cousin. A couple of times he walked in wearing his

Pogo the Clown outfit, explaining that he had been entertaining at a children's hospital or private party and had stopped for a drink before going home to change clothes.

The young men who drank bottles of Old Style and Bud or shot pool with the sleeves of their T-shirts rolled up to show off the tattoos on their forearms might have been suspicious of the newcomer at first. The Good Luck Lounge wasn't the kind of bar where a man can set his drink down and squeeze the leg of the fellow next to him or announce that he would like to meet cute young boys.

The young men were there, but they were not the type who carry shoulder bags or bleach their hair blond. If they wear leather in the bar it's because they have just parked their motorcycles outside. And when they drink and dance to the conversation-crushing rock music that crashes from the jukebox or to the live bands that play on weekends, it's with girl friends who wear blue jeans, have shoulder-length blond hair and ask for beer or whiskey straight up.

The heavyset man with the small black moustache behaved himself. The women he brought with him from time to time were vivacious and pretty. And he was in the construction business, an occupation that many of the robust tavern patrons knew about firsthand.

As the noisy young crowd got used to the large friendly fellow who came in to sip Scotch and follow the action, they began inviting him to play pool on a table placed conveniently near the front door or to pit his skills against a local favorite on one of the two pinball machines at the far end of the bar. It didn't matter that he was about ten years older than everyone else.

Like many others at the Good Luck Lounge, Daniel Rosasco found Gacy to be entertaining and good company. Rosasco, who worked for two years as the club bouncer, visited dozens of times at Gacy's home. Gacy was a good host, despite the strangely musty odor that continuously hung over the house.

Rosasco worked days as a mechanic, but the jobs could be spotty and he was quick to accept when his contractor friend asked him to help out with some remodeling. A few others from the tavern had worked part-time for the contractor and the money was welcome. Few of the people who gathered at the lounge had too much money, and jobs were often difficult to find.

Rosasco was impressed with the zeal that Gacy applied to the work. The man was always pushing to get each job done as quickly as possible so that he could get on with the next. A couple of times when Rosasco arrived at Gacy's house early in the morning, the burly contractor was at his desk, rubbing at his eyes and sleepily doing paperwork. Gacy would explain that he had been up all night.

After Gacy had been a regular at the tavern for a few months, stories inevitably began to circulate, amid jokes and chuckles, that the big fellow liked boys better than girls. They were stories that people like Gacy's sturdy bouncer friend found difficult to believe. The few times when Rosasco was riding with him and they saw someone who was overtly homosexual, Gacy would snort and tell him to "take a look at the weirdo." If someone was telling dirty stories and the butt of the joke happened to be an unfortunate homosexual, Gacy always laughed the loudest.

The two men got their biggest laugh the day Gacy was driving them back from a job and he noticed two black men in a car behind him passing what appeared to be a marijuana cigarette. He loved to play policeman, and he told his passenger that he was going to make the men think he was a cop. He slowed until the two cars were abreast, then turned his spotlight on them. Gacy and Rosasco roared with laughter when one of the black men swallowed the dope.

Gacy liked the good times he had at the lounge, and was upset when he learned that it was going to be sold. When the new owners took over he stopped coming in as often as he had previously, and confided to some of the regulars that he was thinking of buying his own bar. Soon after that, he stopped in a tavern on the northwest side that was for sale. He talked to the owner and impulsively announced that he had decided to buy and would leave a down payment after picking up his checkbook. About a half hour later he returned and wrote a check for the deposit.

The tavern owner couldn't believe that the loquacious customer was serious about doing business so impulsively and he put the check on the counter behind the bar and forgot about it. He didn't hear again from the prospective buyer, but a couple of weeks later remembered the check and took it to his bank. Payment had been stopped.

Gacy was busy with other matters. People at the Good Luck Lounge were talking about their friend, Robert Sipusich. They were telling each other that the out-of-work construction man called Snags by his buddies had been lured to the big guy's house with a promise of drugs and sexually assaulted.

It wasn't a story that Snags was proud of. It was a disturbing, nasty tale that he talked of frankly and honestly, however. Snags had seen Gacy around the Good Luck Lounge for some time before the older man suggested one night that they could have a drink at his home and that he would give his young friend a few hits of speed.

Speed is a common street name for amphetamines, the tablets and capsules that housewives and kids take to lose weight, for a quick rush of euphoria, or for extra borrowed energy to help carry them through a rough day or night. The tablets and pills have myriad nicknames like white crosses, black beauties, and hearts. And they can be deadly if too many are taken at once or if they are used with alcohol.

Snags' work was slow and it had been a while since he had a job. When Gacy suggested that he had some speed for him, Snags was agreeable.

Initially the older man impressed him as a considerate host. Minutes after they walked into the house on Summerdale, Snags was relaxing in a comfortable chair with a whiskey and Seven-Up. A few minutes later Gacy slipped a pre-rolled marijuana cigarette into his hands. As Snags sipped at the whiskey and toked on the joint, Gacy talked about other drugs. The young man was impressed with his host's knowledge of the subject. He had been somewhat suspicious of all the bragging about owning so large a supply of drugs. Gacy talked like he operated his own pharmacy.

Snags realized the boasting was based on facts when his host began pulling brown bottles full of capsules and pills from a shelf and lining them up on the bar. There were hundreds of Preludins, and new unopened bottles of Darvon, Valium, and Placidyl. Snags began listening with more respect as Gacy talked of being some kind of law-enforcement officer. It sounded reasonable. He wouldn't be the first policeman who kept confiscated drugs.

When Gacy asked him if he had ever used poppers, Snags replied that he had. Poppers are thin glass capsules filled with amyl nitrite. Amyl nitrite stimulates and speeds up the heart. When the top is snapped off and the fumes are sniffed there is a quick rush of sexual excitement and exhilaration.

If Snags was expecting his friend to produce a popper, he was wrong. Gacy pulled a rag from behind the bar, inviting him to try it.

Snags pressed the rag loosely over his mouth and nose. The odor was heavy and unpleasant, and the fumes smashed through his consciousness like a giant fist. He was immediately dizzy and his stomach convulsed, causing him to vomit on the floor. Gacy shoved a towel into his hand and told him to clean up the mess. The young construction worker leaned over and wiped at the vomit with the towel. His head was spinning as he straightened up, and he was helpless to prevent the rag from being pressed to his face. He blacked out.

Sometime later, when Snags regained partial consciousness, a naked body was pressed against his. It seemed to the twenty-three-year-old that somehow he had gotten into bed with a woman. Slowly he realized that he wasn't with a woman, but that the hairy contractor from the lounge was sprawled on top of him.

Snags yelled and weakly pushed at the gross, corpulent body, as fright and nausea rose in his throat. Gacy lifted himself up and slid to his feet beside the bed. He walked out of the room as Snags struggled to chase the dreamy terror and confusion floating through the dark hollows of his mind, and to regain control of his uncooperative body. He was still straining to get to his feet when Gacy returned and again pressed the cloth to his face. Snags lost consciousness once more.

The next time he awoke, light was beginning to blush faintly at the bedroom window and Gacy was looming over him, embracing him. Snags bellowed in alarm, pushed the heavy body away, and stumbled from the bed.

Nonchalantly easing himself to his feet and acting as if the trembling young man had panicked over nothing, Gacy told him to relax. Picking up his clothes and beginning to dress, Gacy explained that he was bisexual. He was troubled by his problem, he said, and had recently met a woman who was going to help him.

Snags didn't care about Gacy's sex life or his problem with bisexuality. He was pulling on his clothes as quickly as he could. He said that all he wanted from Gacy was help getting back to his car parked at the Good Luck Lounge.

That would be no problem, Gacy said. He would drop Snags off on his way to Sunday morning Mass.

After Snags' unsettling experience it became more difficult for Gacy to meet and make friends with young men at the tavern. But if the people at the Good Luck Lounge were beginning to learn of Gacy's homosexuality, most of his other close friends and business associates would have bet money that he was as masculine as anyone.

Czarna was beginning to believe that his friend might be spending too much time chasing women. Sometimes when Czarna was pouring concrete, Gacy would show up at the job site neatly dressed in slacks, sweater, and necktie, but with red eyes and a drawn, pale face that was pasty gray from lack of sleep. Czarna would shake his head.

"Man, you really look sucked out."

"Yeah," Gacy would reply. "I'm tired. I was out until about five this morning."

"What the hell do you do out there?" Czarna would ask, speaking from the side of his mouth in an affected drawl.

"I couldn't sleep."

"I don't know about you, John," Czarna would rasp. When a man had gotten used to living with a female around, it was no good to suddenly find himself alone again. "You need a woman."

Gacy's mouth would sliver into an exhausted smile and he would turn and begin yelling at one of his young workmen, accusing him of not doing the job right or of not moving fast enough. Gacy was rough on the youngsters who worked for him. He was more respectful to older tradesmen and to the subcontractors he dealt with. But his bragging also created occasional problems with them.

It bothered Czarna when Gacy walked onto job sites with customers and pointed to the workers and equipment pouring concrete and bragged that they were his men and it was his machinery. Czarna had been in business some twenty years, Gacy for five or six. The two friends exchanged a few sharp words over Gacy's habit of assuming on-the-spot ownership.

Gacy did the same with carpenters and other subcontractors. They generally accepted it as merely another of his crazy quirks. It was mildly bothersome, but even Czarna eventually put up with it because some of the jobs he did with Gacy were worth as much as fifty thousand to sixty thousand dollars.

Gacy liked Czarna's work and arranged for him to pour a new driveway at the house on Summerdale. The old concrete was broken up and the earth underneath prepared for resurfacing late one night. When the forms were placed and only the pouring remained to be done, Czarna promised that he would be back the next morning to complete the job.

The next morning when he arrived at the house with his mixer, the forms had been changed. Gacy explained that he decided during the night that he wanted the driveway to cover more area so that cars and trucks could swing wider. He had even planted flowers and set up a bicentennial sign overnight. It was Gacy's driveway. Czarna poured the surface.

Although the two men didn't do more than a half dozen jobs together, they were seeing more and more of each other socially and their friendship was growing. Gacy was considerate and friendly to Czarna's wife, remembering anniversaries and birthdays with gifts and cards. She also developed a fondness for the blustery, busy contractor.

The men hadn't known each other long when Gacy advised Czarna that there was something he had to tell him. "You know," he said, "I've been arrested."

"So you've been arrested. I've been arrested, too," Czarna replied, unimpressed. "Everybody gets caught with traffic tickets."

"No, not that," Gacy said. "I did some time."

Czarna became more interested. "For what?" he wanted to know.

"Prostitution. It was for prostitution. And there was theft in it too. Yeah," Gacy said, shaking his head as if his mind was boggled with his own daring. "I ran prostitution."

Czarna told him that if he had done his prison time and was released, the debt was paid. There was no reason for Gacy's past to affect their friendship.

Gacy agreed. He said that he had serious problems in Iowa, and divorced his first wife there after catching her in bed with another man. It was a terrible blow to his sense of self-esteem. The trouble was compounded when he had to pay her $250,000 and turn over four fried-chicken franchises to her as part of the divorce settlement.

At first Czarna had been sympathetic, but the story was preposterous. At the time, Gacy was about thirty years old, and by his own admission a few months before, had spent eighteen months of those thirty years in prison. Czarna had built a healthy business for himself and earned good money but it was improbable that Gacy could have accumulated enough to make the kind of settlement on his former wife that he claimed.

The braggadocio got under Czarna's skin at times. If he mentioned that he had successfully bid in a $100,000 job, Gacy would boast that he had bid in a $150,000 job. Gacy always had to be the biggest and best, even if it involved going to jail and negotiating a divorce settlement with his wife.

During the years that they knew each other there were other strains on their friendship. Regardless of his sometimes generosity, Gacy could be slow paying business debts. He made his money work for him as long as possible, withholding payments when he could until the last minute. That system worked reasonably well with the young men and boys he employed. It was less workable when he tried it on Czarna.

As Czarna later recalled the incident, Gacy had owed him a couple of thousand dollars on a job for several days, when the concrete contractor telephoned at about seven thirty one morning and said it was time to pay off the debt.

"You'll have to wait and take the right channels. I'm not ready to pay it yet," Gacy said.

Czarna has an explosive temper, and he saw red. "Pal, the only channel you got to take is to write me a check, or you'll wish to hell you had when I get done with you," he bellowed into the phone.

"You can't talk to me that way," Gacy yelled back, slamming down the receiver.

It was the wrong thing to do. Czarna shoved his stockinged feet into a pair of shoes and, with the laces still flopping, grabbed a light jacket and exploded out the door. Gacy's home was six or eight blocks away, still within sight of the imposing domes of St. Joseph Ukrainian Catholic church, a neighborhood landmark on bustling Cumberland Avenue. Czarna's pickup truck skidded to a stop in front of Gacy's house a few minutes later and the angry contractor bounced out of the cab and began pounding his fist against the front door.

Rossi answered the door, his smooth chest bare and his eyes blinking in the glare of the early morning sun. Czarna barely had time to roar that he wanted to talk to Gacy before the owner of the house loomed in the doorway beside his young friend.

Gacy's hair was still uncombed and sprouted from his head in odd angled clumps. He was also shirtless and his hairy belly sagged obscenely over the beltline of his trousers. His face was purple with anger.

"John, I want that money now," Czarna demanded, straining the words through clenched teeth.

"Get out of here or I'll throw your ass out," Gacy shouted back, pushing the youth aside and closing his fists as he stepped forward. Gacy knew that Czarna was left-handed. He was watching that hand when Czarna's right fist buried itself in his belly.

Gacy slid down along the door frame to a sitting position, without making a sound. His eyes were wide in shock and pain. "Call the police," he gasped to Rossi when he finally got his breath. Rossi hesitated, glancing uncomfortably at the fuming cement contractor, who stared coldly back as if he were daring him to move toward the telephone.

The police were never called. By the time Gacy pulled himself to his feet, his anger had abated and he apologized for withholding the money. Czarna left with a check in his hand. Their friendship resumed almost as if nothing had happened, except that Gacy treated his friend with new respect and a certain amount of caution. It wasn't long before Gacy was again calling his friend "Schultzie," the pet name he had coined for him.

Later, when Gacy helped construct a new bathroom in Czarna's summer cabin in Wisconsin and badly botched the job, he didn't argue about his mistakes. He returned and did the job properly.

The fight cleared the air and the men got along fairly well together, despite their blustering ways and volatile tempers. Gacy was a man that Czarna could relate to. Gacy could handle his whiskey, he did healthy outdoor work (even if it wasn't always done well) and he enjoyed the company of other rugged men. The concrete contractor never suspected that his macho pal was homosexual.

Homosexuals were people that Czarna wouldn't tolerate. He once threatened to walk off a job when he saw magazines with pictures of nude men in a house where he was working. He finished the job after the magazines were stowed in drawers and the owners agreed to stay out of his way.

He relishes telling a story about the time when he was a young man and a homosexual made a pass at him. Czarna kicked him in the face, loosening several teeth. "I can't stand he-shes," he explains.

But he had no such suspicions about his friend Gacy, despite the perpetual presence of young boys in and around the little house on Summerdale. That's why he was surprised at the violence of his own reaction when the young man who was engaged to his daughter told him that he had been invited to move in with Gacy.

Steve Katelanos was a tall, good-looking boy with a broad smile and dark eyes who was having trouble at home. He was growing up and away from the ways of his old-country parents, and there were bitter quarrels over early curfews, the amount of money extracted from his paychecks for room and board, and other problems created by the difference in generations and cultures. It was decided that Steve would move in with his future in-laws.

Czarna's first son, the oldest of four children, including two middle daughters and a boy who was the baby of the family, had moved out of the house not long before. The oldest daughter was also married, so there was plenty of room. But Czarna also had house rules. Although they were not as confining as those of Steve's parents, Czarna applied them to his future son-in-law just as he had with his own children. Among the stipulations were understandings that Steve would pay twenty-five dollars per week for room and board, and that he would be home no later than 1 A.M. It was the same curfew Czarna had set for his son, who was two years older than Steve.

Steve objected, and Gacy told Czarna that he was being too strict with the boy.

"Keep your nose out of my business," Czarna snarled. "This is my house and I run it the way I want to run it."

Gacy backed off, but he and Steve continued to see a lot of each other at Czarna's home and developed a warm, easy relationship. Steve's girl friend was working nights, and he developed the habit of driving to Gacy's home every few days to drink beer and shoot pool or just talk with the host and some of the other youths who habitually hung around.

Czarna didn't like the idea of Steve idling at Gacy's house, and he said so.

"All we're doing, Pop, is drinking some beer," Steve told him.

"You want to drink beer, come home and drink it," Czarna replied.

Steve's finacée defended his visits to the house on Summerdale, and reminded her father that Gacy was one of his closest friends. It was difficult for her to understand why her father was so opposed to Steve's spending a few hours at the house.

"He don't belong with John. John's too old," Czarna said. "Let him go out with friends his own age."

Regardless of the quarrels it was causing, when things got too quiet at the house, with his girl friend at work and no one to talk to but his future in-laws, Steve would get restless and drive to Gacy's house. Gacy never made a pass at the young man and never acted overtly homosexual in front of him.

One day Steve told Czarna that he was going to move in with Gacy. Rossi was already staying at the house, but there was plenty of room for another guest. Although it went unspoken, Steve was aware that at Gacy's there would be no bothersome curfew.

"Pal, you move in with John and you can forget about marrying my daughter," Czarna boomed. The threat was a knee-jerk response, made without considering the implications. But it was a threat that he was prepared to back up if necessary.

It wasn't necessary. Steve elected to stay where he was, and when he married his pretty dark-haired girl friend a few months later, Gacy and his mother attended the wedding. Marion Gacy stood in her walker and sang for the guests.

The elderly woman sat in on the card games and other get-togethers with her son and his friends when she visited him. Being with him then was almost as comforting as the old days. There was some of the same serene close-ness between mother and son as there had been when he was a little boy who played on the floor with his train set, or sat on the neighbor's porch on quiet summer nights singing songs or listening in wide-eyed fascination to sto-ries of ghosts and ghastly murders.

She was pleased with her son's friendship with the Czarnas. It appeared to Czarna that at times she almost looked upon him as an older brother of her son.

"Don," she once said, "you got to watch John."

"Why? He's a big boy."

"I mean watch out to help him," she said. "He's kind of sick."

"Mom, he's as healthy as you or me," Czarna replied. He was suspicious of his friend's reputed heart ailment. Gacy complained about attacks, but he said many things that weren't altogether true. So it was difficult to tell if he actually had a weak heart or if his stories of attacks were merely another plea for attention.

If Gacy sometimes talked about things that weren't true, there were other times when he didn't talk about things that were true. Like the disappearance of Billy Carroll.

When Billy didn't come home the day after his brother's birthday, his parents began to worry. Although they didn't immediately notify police, his brother began moving among Billy's friends in Uptown asking about him. No one had seen the missing boy.

The family speculated for a time that Billy might have lied about his age and joined the Army, Navy, or the Marines, or hitchhiked to North Florida to see his father's kinfolks. But as time went on and they didn't hear from him, those ideas were discarded. He was just missing, like other boys from Uptown and nearby north-side neighborhoods had been missing in recent months.

Seventeen-year-old Michael Bonnin had dropped out of sight only ten days before Billy was last seen. A few weeks before that, fifteen-year-old Randall Reffett and his friend Samuel Dodd Stapleton were first missed by their family and friends.

Rick Johnston wasn't from Uptown, but the seventeen-year-old boy was last seen there when his mother dropped him off on August 6, in front of the Aragon Ballroom where he was going to attend a rock concert with friends.

Michael lived in Lakeview a few blocks south of Uptown and within walking distance of Wrigley Field, the home of the National League Chicago Cubs. Randall and Sam were from farther north nearer to the edge of Uptown, but still within reasonable distance of Wrigley Field. Sam was known among his friends for the bracelet he wore permanently welded to his wrist.

Gacy *(left)* dressed as George Washington, presiding over a July 4, 1976 bicentennial party at his home. The man on the right was one of Gacy's business associates. *(Courtesy Chicago Tribune)*

To John Gacy,
Best Wishes
Rosalynn Carter

First Lady Rosalynn Carter autographed this photo for Gacy, taken at a private reception honoring her when she visited Chicago in 1978. The man at the right is believed to be Mrs. Carter's advance agent. Gacy is wearing a security clearance button, issued by the Secret Service.

Gacy modeling clown suit for publicity shots taken at his home in December 1976. (Professional clowns say that the corners painted at the edges of the mouth should be *rounded*—in order not to frighten children—rather than sharp, as Gacy painted them.) (*Courtesy Chicago Tribune*)

Cook County Sheriff's Police remove the remains of at least four victims from the crawl space beneath Gacy's home. *(Wide World Photos)*

Cook County Medical Examiner, Dr. Robert J. Stein, identifying skeletons of bodies found under Gacy's home. *(Wide World Photos)*

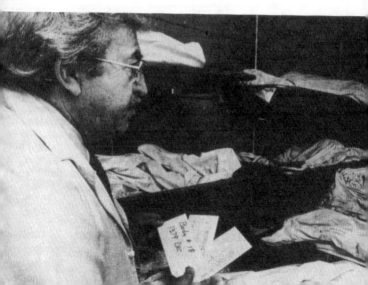

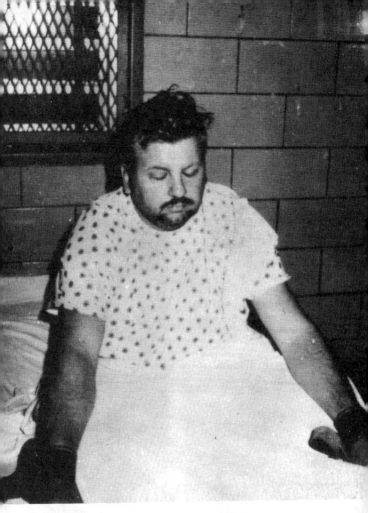

I.D. photo of Gacy taken at the Cook County Jail Hospital. A guard at the hospital resigned after jail officials threatened to suspend him for the removal of this photo from jail files. *(Courtesy Chicago Tribune)*

Billy Carroll, Jr., got into a car one evening with several friends, told his parents he'd be back in about an hour, and was never seen again. *(Wide World Photos)*

John Butkovich was another youth employed by Gacy's construction company. He disappeared the day after a heated argument with Gacy concerning his paycheck.

Russell Nelson walked outside of a bar with a friend while vacationing in Chicago. Distracted by a group of people, the friend turned away for a moment. When he turned back around, Nelson had disappeared.

Martin Zielinski was a young free-lance photographer whom Gacy befriended and hired on several occasions to take photographs. *(Courtesy Chicago Tribune)*

Gregory Godzik disappeared after taking his date home for the evening, just a few months before his high school graduation. *(Courtesy Chicago Tribune)*

Frank Wayne "Dale" Landingin, Jr. Nine days after his disappearance, Landingin's body was pulled from a marina on the Des Plaines River.

Wreckers tear down roof of Gacy's home, April 11, 1979. *(Photo by Chicago Sun-Times)*

Diagram of Gacy's property in Des Plaines, a suburb of Chicago. *(Wide World Photos)*

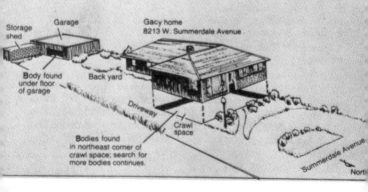

The toll of bodies climbs

Storage shed

Garage

Gacy home
8213 W. Summerdale Avenue

Body found under floor of garage

Back yard

Driveway

Crawl space

Bodies found in northeast corner of crawl space; search for more bodies continues.

Summerdale Avenue

North

Michael was last seen alive by his family when he told them he was going to catch a Chicago & North Western train to Waukegan and meet his stepfather's brother, Konrad G. Stein. Michael, who liked woodworking and carpentry, had been refinishing an old jukebox for his uncle and was planning to complete the job that weekend.

Earlier he had spent about three weeks sanding and finishing a boat for one of Stein's friends, and was proud of the opportunity it provided for him to practice his skills. Even though his grades were good, he had dropped out of Luther North High School a few months earlier so that he could go to work at the tasks he enjoyed. But he had later begun talking about returning to school in Waukegan and probably living with his uncle in nearby Gurnee.

Stein waited at the train station for the good-looking, muscular young nephew he called "Mikey," who had promised to visit with him on the Friday after Memorial Day, but the boy never arrived. Immediately, Stein began searching for him.

Michael liked to fish and Stein had given him permission to use his cottage at Briggsville, Wisconsin, where the family had spent the previous weekend together. The cottage was one of the first places Stein looked, but there was no trace of the boy. Michael could not be found anywhere else that his uncle looked.

Stein contacted his brother, Donald, and Michael's mother, Shirley, and told them of the unsuccessful search. They notified police that their only son, the baby of a family that included two older sisters, was missing.

Family members were annoyed when police indicated that they believed Michael to be a runaway. As the months progressed and there was still no word of him, they began to think that he might indeed have run away, but puzzled about his reasons. He had been an easygoing, considerate son who trusted other people, and he had not been having trouble at home.

Randall Reffett had also acquired a reputation as an easygoing boy before the May afternoon when he failed to return home from Senn High School. At Senn, he hadn't been especially successful scholastically. But he got along well with most of the other students, even though shortly after enrolling there he had gotten into a fracas and was sent to Weiss Memorial Hospital for treatment of a stab wound.

He had been more successful scholastically when he attended the Joseph Stockton Elementary School. Teachers there considered the quiet, brown-haired boy to be an excellent student who never got into trouble and had an outstanding attendance record.

Randall's mother, Myrtle, did not immediately notify school officials at Senn that her son had vanished, and truant officers began searching the Uptown area for the mother and son after he missed several days of classes, but couldn't find either of them.

Rick Johnston never returned from the rock concert to his home in suburban Bensenville. By daylight the next day, his mother began frantically calling his friends, and before noon she notified the Chicago Police Department and the Bensenville police. They weren't impressed, although the Bensenville police finally agreed to send an officer to her house to talk with her. But if the police didn't initially take the disappearance seriously, the family did. Mrs. Johnston, her other son, Greg, her daughter, Kari, and her divorced husband, began an exhaustive search that would not end for two years—tragically.

Responding to the suggestions of Bensenville police and of newspaper reporters, that Rick might have joined the Moonies religious sect which was actively seeking converts in the neighborhood around the ballroom, family members even journeyed to Washington, D. C., where the Reverend Sun Myung Moon's Unification Church had scheduled a massive rally. He wasn't there.

A simple mix-up by Bensenville police added to the family's anguish when the date of Rick's disappearance was improperly logged in the original missing person report as June 8, 1976 instead of August 8, 1976, when he actually dropped from sight. Consequently, journalists and others were led to believe, and to erroneously report, that Mrs. Johnston had waited two months to notify authorities that her son was missing.

No one, police included, thought to put together the amazing string of disappearances of young boys from the north side of Chicago and adjoining suburbs. No one wondered at a possible connection between the disappearances of Randall Reffett, Samuel Dodd Stapleton, Michael Bonnin, Richard Johnston, and Billy Carroll, in the space of less than three months.

Most of the boys, of course, were not promptly reported missing. Billy's parents didn't make an immediate report to police, although neither his brother nor his friends had turned up any trace of him.

A girl he had been friendly with since they were both small children often wondered about him and said that she sometimes had disturbing dreams of Billy, of lights and of concrete. And when William Carroll, Sr., walked past the vacant lots, abandoned derelict cars and crumbling graffiti-covered graystones of Uptown, pulling his frayed gray overcoat closer about him to keep out the wind sweeping off the lake, he often found himself peering into the faces of young men he met or turning to stare at them after they passed. There was the merest chance that one of them might be the missing son he called "Sugar Pie—because he was such a sweet baby." William Carroll, Sr., is disabled and living on social security and a veteran's pension, so he had time for his walks. But the walks never turned up a trace of his missing son.

Much later people also wondered what had happened to Dale Landingin. People like Mary-Jo Romero, the twenty-seven-year-old waitress he had charmed and moved in with after meeting her at a rock concert in the Aragon Ballroom—the same Aragon Ballroom where Rick Johnston had planned to attend a rock concert five months earlier. Before that Dale had lived in a succession of hotel rooms and apartments. And he had worked in a succession of jobs,—busboy, shoe salesman, and waiter—before finally going on public aid.

Mary-Jo insisted that Dale had wanted to work, but was frustrated by employers who for various reasons continued to fire him. His real ambition, however, was to become a singer. He had a good voice. His girl friend played guitar and he talked to her often about getting everything together some day and starting their own group.

He also talked of getting married and having children with her. But they didn't get along as well as she might have hoped. He erupted into terrible fits of violence, at times becoming so agitated that his dark, longish hair swirled wildly around his head while he screamed and shook with anger. Like John Gacy, Dale would pick up household items when he was angry and slam them against the walls or the floor. He also beat his girl friend.

He was dealing in marijuana, PCP, and LSD, and it was when he was sampling too much of his own wares that he became mean and violent, Mary-Jo said.

Eventually he would calm down and apologize, but the damage to the waitress's bruised feelings and body didn't vanish as quickly as his temper. The tantrums were occurring two or three times a week when he finally drove her out of her own apartment and she had to move in with her mother. That's when she filed charges against him.

It wasn't the first time he had been in trouble with the police. His problems started some six years earlier, about the time his parents divorced shortly after moving to Chicago from New York City. His father recalled that Dale took the divorce hard. He first quit Lake View High School, and was picked up for stealing cars and selling marijuana.

Dale never indicated that he had a sexual interest in other men, but his girl friend was aware that he had dealings with homosexuals and frequented their hangouts. It wasn't an interest in sex that led him to the association with gays, Mary-Jo realized. Dressed casually but neat, he used his appealing 120-pound, five-foot, five-inch frame and arrogantly handsome face to attract guys who would spend money on him or give him money and presents. He was little but macho, and they flocked around him.

"He made them think he was going to have sex with them. But he didn't have any intention of doing it. When they got wise, they'd stop seeing him," Mary-Jo remembered. He used gay men the way some really pretty girls use men. He said he enjoyed using them."[2]

[2]*Chicago Sun-Times,* December 28, 1978.

Nine days after Frank Wayne Landingin, Jr., dropped from sight, a naked body, water-soaked and bloated, was pulled from a marina on the Des Plaines River in the small community of Channahon, south of Joliet. The bearded young man had been strangled to death. His bikini undershorts had been stuffed into his mouth and jammed with vicious force down his throat. Police began the job of identifying the corpse.

6

Buried Dreams and a President's Wife

The last thing Jon Prestidge's friend said to him when the Michigan youth stepped out of the apartment to begin a night of barhopping was:

"Be careful. You're not in Kalamazoo anymore. There are plenty of crazy people in the world and a lot of them are here in Chicago."[1]

Jon had heard warnings like that before, as recently as the previous day. On March 14, 1977, he had telephoned his mother, Mrs. Nancy Cassada, of Gobles, near Kalamazoo, and told her he planned to stay in Chicago a couple more days. He said he was going nightclubbing.

Mrs. Cassada cautioned her son to be careful. She worried about him going out alone. He usually carried forty or fifty dollars with him and wore turquoise rings

---

[1]*Kalamazoo Gazette*, January 13, 1979.

and other jewelry and she was afraid he might be mugged. Even his older brother Michael worried about Jon and warned him to beware of strangers. The brothers were close and Michael knew that Jon could be naive and dangerously trusting of other people.

The gangly twenty-year-old blond youth was a free spirit, who was sure that he could take care of himself. He had graduated from Kalamazoo Central High School after transferring there from Gobles in his senior year and going to live with his father, Lewis Prestidge, a musician. Although he was bright and learned quickly, he preferred farm work and the outdoors to studies. He dropped out of Kalamazoo Community College after attending only a short while and began working intermittently at various motels in the area. He had a cheerful, outgoing personality and got along well with the other employees. But he was adventuresome and believed in taking advantage of the footloose years between school and full adult responsibilites. So he traveled, and his friends learned that he might leave a job at any time to hitchhike to some faraway state.

He always told his family where he was going when he left on trips, and kept in touch at least weekly with telephone calls. For a while his calls were from Philadelphia, where he stayed several months working for a contractor.

He was enjoying life, seeing the country and making new friends. But by early 1977 he had begun to think seriously about a career, and when he telephoned home from Chicago he told his mother he planned to check into a nursing school that had a program for men. He thought he might like to specialize in anesthesiology, and had arranged for an interview on March 16.

Medicine appealed to him. As a member of the profession, he would be exposed to the excitement of working in hospitals, as well as having the satisfaction of knowing he was helping other people.

He liked being with others, and New Town, with its twenty-four-hour bluster of activity, offered new experiences and new friends. The apartment he was staying in with a friend of his grandfather was a mere few blocks from Broadway discos and young people's bars like Crystal's Blinkers, Broadway Ltd., The Phoenix, and the Fat Black Pussy Cat.

Jon may or may not have known that Blinkers and the Broadway Ltd. were frequented primarily by gay crowds, and the others by mixed male and female couples. But part of the fun of club hopping was exploring new places. Chicago and Illinois liquor laws permitted nineteen- and twenty-year-olds to drink beer and wine and most of the clubs along Broadway catered to clientele of those ages or a few years older.

No one will ever know if Jon remembered the warnings of his mother and his brother, or his host's admonition not to trust everyone, as he walked the half dozen blocks to the neon-lighted action on Broadway. No one will know because he was never heard from or seen alive by his friends again. He never returned to the apartment and he never showed up for the interview at school. He just vanished.

Nine days later, on March 24, his family reported to police in Chicago and Kalamazoo that he was missing.

Mrs. Cassada knew something was horribly wrong when a week passed after Jon's last telephone call and she hadn't heard from him again. She had expected to hear about the school interview, or about his arrangements to drive a new car from Chicago to Colorado the following week to go skiing.

"He had a lot of things planned—that's how I knew something had happened," Mrs. Cassada said. "He'd never run away or anything, he had no reason to. He did as he pleased anyway."[2]

Chicago police recorded the information provided by Jon's mother. He was not a juvenile and there was no evidence of foul play. He was listed as voluntarily missing, as were an increasing number of other youths last seen in New Town or Uptown.

The information about Jon was filed with reports on 19,455 other men, women, and children listed by Chicago police in 1977 as missing from the city. Of those, about

[2]*Kalamazoo Gazette,* January 11, 1979.

14,000 were minors, including approximately 6,700 children under seventeen officially classed as juveniles.

The necessary reports and investigations created mountains of paperwork. An average single report fills six sheets of paper, and detailed investigations fill many times that number. Youth officers have pointed out that no human can struggle through that much paperwork and pinpoint similarities between cases. Hours can be consumed going through the reports to determine which cases demand priority attention.

In the same year 175,557 boys and girls under eighteen were reported missing nationwide, according to the Federal Bureau of Investigation uniform crime reports. Most of them come back when they have had enough of the streets and the strain of living hand-to-mouth—if their families want them. Not all familes do. Some children called "throwaways" by professionals, have been pushed out of their homes for economic or other reasons and have nowhere to return to. Many of those who don't return are forced or seduced into prostitution or pornography. Some are murdered.

Regardless of their age, all missing persons reported to Chicago police are the responsibility of the Youth Division, headed by Commander Harold Thomas. Part of a metropolitan police department with some thirteen thousand men and women, the Youth Division has fewer than six hundred officers and a handful of clerical employees available to handle missing reports averaging more than fifty daily. Additionally, they have all the other duties traditionally assigned to officers who work with missing persons and minors. Several of the nation's larger cities have even fewer officers assigned to trace thousands of missing children.

Except in unusual cases where known violence or an abduction has occurred, the missing juveniles get most of the attention, especially those children thirteen years old and younger. Thomas refers to those youngsters as "tender-age children." One of the reasons that tender-age children are given priority is their vulnerability to sexual exploitation and street violence. Searches begin as soon as the child is reported missing. Police in squad cars and on foot comb the neighborhood, interviewing residents and looking in alleys, basements, abandoned buildings, garages, and anywhere else a child is likely to be hiding, in trouble, or dead. Perhaps second only to the fear that a child is dead is the fear that he or she may be abused sexually.

Amazingly, the problem can become even stickier when older children are involved. Such bewildering laws and regulations have been passed to protect the civil rights of juveniles that it is becoming increasingly difficult to protect them. One of the problems preventing police from making the most effective possible use of computers to locate missing persons is fear of violating rules of confidentiality.

Youth officers are prevented by the confidentiality rule from circulating lists of missing children under seventeen across the country to brother police departments, according to the commander.

"You cannot expose the child according to our law. And I understand this," Thomas says. "They assume that this child is going through a problem period, a troubled time. And if we have the services for this child we can turn him around before he is an adult. We don't want to label him or stigmatize him by putting his picture in the paper."

Nevertheless, a Federal Bureau of Investigation computer network lists more than 21,000 disappearances, most of them juveniles and young adults, and the information is available to local police departments. Indications of foul play are considered serious enough in only about 5,200 cases to justify automatic notice to local law-enforcement agencies. There is also a state computer as well as the local Chicago police department computer, but by the beginning of 1979 none had been programed to pinpoint common denominators in seemingly dissimilar cases.

Parents can publicize information, including pictures of their missing children. Policemen cannot. Police departments do, of course, exchange information about missing children, but according to Thomas, most of the data is passed by personal contact or by telephone. Other youth officers have been quoted as saying that sharing of information between departments in Chicago and the suburbs is practically nonexistent. The problems that exist between overlapping police jurisdictions are especially troublesome in missing-persons cases.

A good-looking, even-featured man with a smooth acorn-colored complexion, Thomas leans forward in his chair at the Police Administration Building on South State Street and looks people confidently in the eye, talking in firm, sincere tones when he discusses the job of protecting minors in a city of more than three million people.[3]

"Somewhere along the line I think we've said that children have the same rights as adults and that's the way it will be," Thomas says, shaking his head. "But children are *not* adults, and they need help."

John Prestidge was neither a runaway nor a juvenile. Nor was Russell Nelson. But like Jon, Russell made the innocent mistake of visiting Chicago's New Town at the wrong time.

Both young men were about the same age. They were each from Midwestern towns much smaller than Chicago. And they had been in the city less than a week when they disappeared.

One thing they didn't share was scholarship. Russell graduated as an honors student from his high school in Cloquet, Minnesota, a small town located between Duluth at the southwest end of Lake Superior, and the Fond du Lac Indian Reservation. Most of the town's 8,700 inhabitants trace their livelihood to one of the three large lumber mills that produce wood and paper and are the foundation for the area economy.

Russell's father, Robert, is a crane operator for the Continental Oil Company in a nearby community. One of Russell's older brothers found a job as a baker and the other a job as a laborer on a Burlington Northern Railroad construction gang, but Russell planned to be an architect.

[3]The 1970 U. S. Census listed a Chicago population of 3,369,357. A later estimate by the Census Bureau in 1975 reported the population had dropped to 3,099,391.

He was bespectacled and bookish. He admired the work of architect Mies van der Rohe. He liked the music of singer Donna Summer, and teamed with a girl friend to win several disco contests. A slight five-foot, eight-inches tall and 130 pounds, he shied away from his high school hockey, football, and ski teams and elected instead to apply himself to reading, art, photography, and drama. In his junior year he acted in *Oliver,* and the next year he was in the cast of *South Pacific.* He managed to sandwich activities as a Boy Scout and work as a stock boy in a Cloquet store between his studies without hurting his grades. In his senior year he won both a community scholarship and a VFW scholarship.

In September 1974 he enrolled at the University of Minnesota in Minneapolis as a major in pre-architecture. A few weeks after beginning classes he met Thomas Maurer, a sixty-year-old clergyman with the United Church of Christ and a lecturer in sexuality at the university's medical school. Russell moved into Maurer's condominium in the Towers, a posh apartment complex.

According to reporter James Warren in an article in the *Chicago Sun-Times,* Maurer acknowledged that he is homosexual, but insisted that he never had sexual relations with his young roommate. He said that their ties were closer to a father-son bond. It was a relationship approved of by Russell's parents. "I think Russ became the son Tom never had," Mrs. Norma Nelson was quoted as saying.[4] Maurer went so far as to change his will, making Russell the sole beneficiary.

But Russell had sprung from people and a community where youngsters are taught to make their own way. He interrupted his classes after two successful years and told his friends that he planned to make as much money as possible and return to school in the fall. Still living with Maurer, he began working eighty hours a week as a custodian at the medical school and as a waiter at the First Street Station, a popular restaurant. His mother said he had also once worked sixteen hours a day, six days a week, as a draftsman, and established trust funds for nieces and

[4]*Chicago Sun-Times,* January 16, 1979.

nephews. He told her several times that if he died young he wanted to donate his eyes to science.

His work at the restaurant was so impressive that he was promoted to combination waiter-host in the evenings. His fellow employees overlooked occasional subdued boasting about living the good life in the Towers. He also liked to give the impression that he was street-wise and knew his way around, a not too unusual bit of posturing for a college boy.

The young man avoided alcohol, tobacco, and coffee. "Yet it is clear, despite the parents' protests to the contrary, that Nelson did socialize in the city's gay community," Warren reported. "To gay friends he affected the name 'Parker' Nelson . . ."[5]

Despite his crushing work schedule, he was young and full of energy and after completing his night shift at the restaurant he sometimes stopped in at The Gay 90s, a onetime strip joint converted into a gay bar. It was apparently there that he met Robert Young, a twenty-eight-year-old from Belle Fourche, South Dakota, who reportedly worked at a variety of jobs, including carpentry. Russell called his new friend The Cowboy.

In October 1977 Russell quit both his jobs and drove nearly six hundred miles to Belle Fourche with his new friend. They stayed with Young's parents for a few days before returning to Minneapolis. Russell then told his parents that he and his companion were going to travel to Chicago, Canada, New England, and Florida. The youth took $2,600 in cash and traveler's checks with him when they left in Young's van on their way to their first stop— Chicago. The Cowboy knew a contractor in Chicago and had other friends there.

One of the first people they met in Chicago was Jim Burnett, a waiter at a north-side restaurant and a friend of Young's. Russell and The Cowboy were apparently sleeping in the van and Burnett agreed to permit them to take showers at his apartment. They stayed overnight on Tuesday, October 18.

Burnett was impressed with the aspiring young archi-

⁵*Ibid.*

tect from Minnesota and considered him to be intelligent and sensitive, but naive. Russell was excited about investigating the architecture program at the Illinois Institute of Technology, and the prospect of looking over Chicago buildings which Mies van der Rohe had worked on.

He and his friend made the visit to IIT on October 19. The moon was full as the two men, who had been in Chicago fewer than seventy-two hours, headed for Crystal's Blinkers in New Town that night. There is something about the full moon that science has never quite been able to cope with. Countless phenomena associated with it have occult overtones. They range from the old beliefs linking it with werewolves to scientifically documented studies which have shown that postoperative surgical patients bleed more profusely and birth rates rise when the moon is full. Almost any policeman who has been on the job long knows that people act more irrationally than usual during the full moon, and murder and suicide rates often go up. Sexual desires are also believed to be heightened.

The full moon that hung over the city that night was apparently the last ever seen by Russell Nelson. Young later told police that after some time in the bar he and his friend left and were standing outside when he was distracted by some other people. When he turned back Russell was gone. The Minnesota youth didn't return to the van or to the apartment, and Burnett said that thousands of dollars and valuable personal possessions were left behind.

Young filed a missing-persons report with the police and contacted the Nelson family, asking for money to finance a search.

The Nelsons refused to give him the money, but Russell's older brothers met him in Chicago when they arrived there to search on their own. The effort was fruitless. The brothers rejected an offer by Young to get them jobs with a local contractor while they were in the city.

Young didn't mention the contractor by name, but John Gacy was in Roseville, Minnesota, remodeling the Setzer Pharmacy in June 1977—only four months before

Russell Nelson's fateful trip to Chicago. Roseville is a suburb of St. Paul, the twin city of Minneapolis.

Gacy's work was increasingly taking him outside the Chicago area to other communities in Illinois and to dozens of states. The Grexas were socializing with him less frequently, and other friends saw less of him. Occasionally they would see him and he would say that he was flying to New York the next day, to Minnesota a few days after that, and then to Texas or New Jersey or Florida. He once told the Grexas that he was expecting to receive an award for flying one hundred thousand miles. Several times he returned to Springfield, where he had lived from 1964 to 1966, to do remodeling jobs.

Although he was branching out to other states, Gacy still managed to find much of his work in his home area. One of the stores he remodeled was the Ksiazek Pharmacy on Chicago's southwest side. Owner Ed Ksiazek later observed that although pharmacists try to guard against thefts, it would be possible for someone to help themselves to handfuls of drugs without the owner noticing when construction or remodeling is underway. There is no law requiring all prescription drugs to be locked up out of sight.

Czarna once agreed to pour the foundation and concrete floor for a pharmacy for Gacy, and Gacy escorted him through the back door to introduce him to the owner. They were surrounded by thousands of pills and capsules as they waited for the pharmacist, and it would have been simple for either of them to have helped themselves to handfuls of drugs without anyone knowing they were missing.

Gacy subcontracted twenty-five or thirty drugstore remodeling jobs with Ted Gladson, a respected contractor from a far Chicago suburb. Operator of the P & E Systems in Lisle, Gladson specialized in drugstore and supermarket jobs and referred several young men to Gacy for jobs, when he himself didn't have work for them.

Gacy had plenty to keep them busy. Amazingly, after so many years of fixing up his own home, he still had jobs for them to do at 8213 West Summerdale.

His photographer friend, Martin Zielinski, was at the

house one day when Gacy had a teenager crawling through the space under the house to repair a minor plumbing leak. Gacy put both Rossi and Cram to work digging out sections of the crawl space at other times. He told them where to dig, explaining that he was having drainage problems and wanted to install tile.

It was awkward, nasty work. The crawl space was narrow, cramped, and musty. A sour odor mixed with the sweat of the teenagers as they hacked at the dank earth with trenching tools provided by their boss. It was not an ideal working space for a man with Gacy's humpty-dumpty build, or with his reputed heart ailment.

Yet, Zielinski had once joined him on a job that required them to work in a crawl space similar to the one under Gacy's house and the young photographer was amazed at his boss's performance. Despite Gacy's corpulence, he worked in the cramped tunnel for eight hours on his knees. He grunted and sweated but he showed surprising physical endurance for a man of his size.

The day the boy repaired the plumbing leak, Zielinski crawled after him just to see what the underside of his friend's house looked like. The tunnel was lighted by a single bulb that shriveled and bent the shadows as they played over the smooth dirt. Zielinski wasn't aware of any particular odor, although there were dark puddles of standing water.

Zielinski's relationship with the man he called "Johnny" was often turbulent during the half dozen years they knew each other. In addition to the photographic work he did for Gacy, Zielinski also occasionally helped out on construction jobs.

The money came in handy because Zielinski was working toward a degree in business administration at the University of Illinois, Chicago Circle campus. But even though the money was welcome, it didn't always come easy. There were constant differences about the pay or working arrangements. Working for Gacy eventually became more trouble than it was worth and the young photographer began avoiding him. But not before he had gotten an inkling of his friend's unorthodox sexual attitudes.

Gacy once asked him to go to a porno movie, and Zielinski agreed. He was surprised when he got to the theater and discovered that the film had an all-male cast. He was also bored, and showed it. Perhaps, he reasoned later, that was why Gacy never made a pass at him.

Another time Gacy asked him to shoot revealing pictures of homosexuals, and Zielinski refused, saying that it was illegal. Gacy told him that if he was smart he wouldn't get caught, Zielinski recalled, and that he should consider it because there was good money to be made and homosexuals love to be photographed.

The chunky contractor talked about other shady dealings he was supposedly involved in, but wasn't specific, although he claimed that he had been questioned by the FBI and local police. Gacy told some of the younger boys that he was a hit man for the Mafia, and offered to take care of anyone who was giving them trouble.

Zielinski said that he was threatened during one of their quarrels after demanding payment for photo work. Gacy reputedly sent word that he had friends who would put Zielinski in a hospital if the photographer didn't back down. "I do a lot of horrible things, but I do a lot of good things too," Gacy once told him.[6]

Apparently, one of the bad things that Gacy did got him into trouble in the late summer of 1978 when he was beaten and kicked in the groin. He was taken to Loretto Hospital by Cicero police at about 1:15 A.M., and admitted with injuries to his groin, chest, and face. He told police he was mugged, but his doctor said Gacy claimed he was beaten after getting into a quarrel in a tavern. When regulars at the Good Luck Lounge heard about it they chuckled and told each other between beers how the big fellow had made the mistake of propositioning a karate instructor. Gacy's friends in Norwood Park township heard still a different story, that he was beaten by Rossi and another teenager during a quarrel. Whatever version of the incident might be true, if any, Gacy remained in the hospital four or five days.

[6]*Time* magazine, January 8, 1979.

Earlier he spent a longer period of time in a northside hospital after making a nude dash across his back lawn to put out a fire in the playhouse he had built for Carole's daughters. It was a snappy, cold November day when officers in a passing suburban police car noticed smoke coming from the outbuildings and alerted the Norwood Park (township) Fire Protection District.

Gacy was taking a shower when the policeman pounded at his door. Without waiting to dress, he sprinted across the lawn, covered only by a towel clutched around his hairy belly, and began battling the flames. The fire was extinguished before firemen arrived, but Gacy was hospitalized for treatment of smoke inhalation and bronchitis.

During one of his hospital stays he gave his business card to a nurse and asked her to refer young men to him for construction jobs. She never sent him any prospects, but he had no trouble finding willing young workers elsewhere. He contacted some of the boys who worked for him by posting a notice on a bulletin board at a supermarket at Harlem and Lawrence Avenues near his home. One boy who took his girl friend along when he asked for a job was rejected. Gacy told him he was too skinny.

Robert Gilroy was the son of a Chicago police sergeant who worked at the city's central auto pound, and lived near the supermarket where the notice was posted. On September 15, 1977, the youth left home to join about fifty other young people who belonged to an equestrian club and were going to be bussed several miles for a day of horseback riding. A student at the University of Illinois, Chicago Circle campus, which Zielinski attended, he was an outdoorsman who often went camping with his parents, Mr. and Mrs. Robert E. Gilroy, and their policeman friends. The active eighteen-year-old never showed up for the bus ride. After waiting for a while, friends contacted his parents and told them he was missing.

Robert's father and some other policemen began looking for the youth, who had been talking of possibly earning some money to help pay for a transfer to school in the East where he could study animal husbandry. An official at the Blue Ribbon Riding Center in Northbrook said he hadn't attended his lessons for weeks.

He had been scheduled to check into the Potomac Horse Center in Gaithersburg, Maryland, for a special class on September 29—exactly two weeks after his disappearance. Sergeant Gilroy telephoned the center on September 27 and confirmed that his son had not checked in. The boy's riding gear was still at home in Chicago. Gilroy filed an official missing-persons report. It had been almost two weeks since he had seen his son.

The official probe of Robert's disappearance eventually filled a forty-four-page report, including twenty follow-up investigations by police and additional information gathered by his father. The elder Gilroy's search turned up a report by the doorman of a luxury high-rise apartment building on North Lake Shore Drive that the boy may have accompanied a resident of the building inside on November 6, nearly three weeks after he presumably left home to meet his equestrian friends. No workable leads materialized from that report. Other reports indicated that the youth spent some time around the three-way intersection of Clark, Diversey, and Broadway in New Town. Nothing turned up in the investigations specifically linking him to Gacy. And nothing in the investigations led his father or other policemen to the boy.

Barely two months before Robert was last seen by his family, eighteen-year-old Matthew Bowman of Crystal Lake, some thirty miles northwest of Chicago, disappeared.

On September 25, nineteen-year-old John Mowery was seen alive by his family for the last time. John's disappearance was especially alarming to his family because his only sister, Judith, had been savagely murdered five years earlier. John, then fourteen, had discovered the body.

The twenty-one-year-old woman had been released early from her job as a clerk typist with the Cook County Assessor's office the previous afternoon because it was an election day, and returned to her apartment about a block from her grandmother's home. She had moved into the modest three-room walk-up only two months earlier so that she could keep pets.

She was in the habit of visiting her grandmother nightly and when she didn't show up for two nights in a row and couldn't be reached by telephone, John was sent to her apartment to look for her.

He found his sister sprawled fully clothed on the living-room floor, stabbed nine times in the chest and back with a knife that was long enough to have punctured her lungs. Three frightened eight-week-old puppies were huddled against her body. The killer was never caught and the case remains open in the files of the Chicago Police Department.

The family of Johnny Mowery, which included one older brother and one younger, closed around each other in support and he survived the trauma of finding his only sister murdered. By early 1977 he was discharged after serving eighteen months in the Marines and was taking his first steps toward a possible career in accounting.

He had returned to his family home only briefly after completing his military service, before moving into an apartment with a friend that his family knew only as "Mike." One night not long after that, he told relatives that he was going out for the evening. He didn't say where he was going. He wasn't in the habit of doing that. They never saw or heard from him again.

Early the next year on February 16, Mary Jo Paulus said good-bye to her boyfriend for the last time. William Wayne Kindred had telephoned and gone to see her every day or night since the previous July when he had given her and her girl friend a ride as they were hitchhiking on the north side.

They were talking about getting married as soon as the muscular nineteen-year-old youth could find a good job. In the meantime, he supported himself by doing odd jobs. Friends said the youth they knew as "Shotgun" also knew how to make money on the street and was a familiar figure at hangouts in New Town frequented by street people.

He didn't telephone his girl friend on February 17, and he didn't stop to see her at her home. When she looked for him at his apartment, he was gone but had left his clothes and other belongings behind.

Mary Jo reported to police that he was missing. For many nights, after getting off work as an office clerk, she drove and walked around New Town and other areas of the city looking for him.

While Mary Jo Paulus was continuing her fruitless search for her boyfriend, Sergeant Gilroy was passing around pictures of his missing son. Questions were being asked about John Mowery in areas of the north side he was known to frequent. Jon Prestidge's friends had given up combing Chicago bars and hanging "Information Wanted" posters in New Town with his picture on them. In Michigan, however, his mother and stepfather, Alan Cassada, had in desperation consulted a psychic. The psychic told them that Jon was dead but couldn't pinpoint his location or the manner of his death. The Cassadas began sending Jon's dental records to different communities in Michigan where the unidentified bodies of young men were found.

Gacy, meanwhile, was busily continuing to build his reputation as a good neighbor, good Democrat, and community worker.

He posed for photographs in 1978 while shaking hands with Mrs. Rosalynn Carter, wife of the President. The First Lady later autographed one of the pictures taken by a White House photographer; "To John Gacy. Best Wishes. Rosalynn Carter."

The occasion was Chicago's Polish Constitution Day Parade on May 6, marking the 187th anniversary of democratic government in Poland. It was the third consecutive year that Gacy had been director of the parade, which in 1978 consisted of fifty-four floats, twenty bands and some ten thousand marchers.

Ed Dziewulski, a spokesman for the Polish National Alliance, said Gacy was recommended for the job by Colonel Jack Reilly, Chicago's special-events director under Mayor Richard J. Daley. Reilly was credited with promoting the contractor for the task because of the excellent job Gacy had done on one of the Democratic Day parades in Springfield during the Illinois State Fair.

Gacy wore a lapel pin bearing the letter "S" while he

and about fifty other people shared the parade-reviewing stand in Chicago with Mrs. Carter. The pin indicated he had been cleared by the Secret Service, which guards Presidents and their families. The Secret Service was provided with the names, addresses, birth dates, and social security numbers of Gacy and three assistants, among those of others expecting to share the reviewing stand or attend a reception for Mrs. Carter in the Daley Center during her near four-hour stay to participate in the festivities and to work at improving relations of her husband's administration with Chicago Democrats.

Prior to the parade, the Secret Service sent the "S" pins to the Polish National Alliance for distribution to the people whose names were on the list. A Secret Service check of the backgrounds of the people recommended for clearance should have turned up information about Gacy's sodomy conviction in Iowa. Before issuing clearance, the agency is known to consult with the FBI, the National Crime Index, regional Secret Service agents, and local police. Gacy's sodomy conviction record followed him when he was paroled and became available to Chicago police when he left Iowa. However, the Secret Service did not learn of his felony conviction.

About the same time his picture was taken with Mrs. Carter, Gacy also posed for a photograph while shaking hands with Chicago Mayor Michael Bilandic at a groundbreaking ceremony for a senior citizens' facility near Resurrection High, not far from Norwood Park. Both photos, with pictures of Gacy dressed as Pogo the Clown, were prominently displayed in the office in his home.

Martwick's advice to become involved in community and Democratic party activities was being followed to the letter. Gacy was becoming a familiar figure in local Democratic party circles, and in 1978 his name appeared in six ads, four of them full page, in the Norwood Park Township Democratic organization's dinner-dance program. The ads identified him as being among "community leaders," listed PDM Contractors, Inc., showed him posing with other members of the street-lighting district, and extended best wishes to Martwick from Pogo the Clown.

Gacy introduced himself as a Democratic precinct

captain when he approached Loop attorney James E. Noland with a young man who had been given a traffic ticket. Gacy explained that he often did favors for constituents, and during a subsequent two-year period he referred about forty people who had picked up tickets for speeding and other offenses to the attorney. Gacy usually paid the legal fees himself.

Several times young men referred to Noland by Gacy appeared for one or more court hearings and then failed to show up at others. Gacy himself was arrested for speeding on a Chicago area expressway at 4 A.M. on January 5, 1978, and Noland helped him to obtain an acquittal.

If Gacy's neighbors heard about his speeding arrest, they probably weren't surprised. If he had any obvious fault that bothered Lillie Grexa, it was his habit of tearing out of his driveway with the Oldsmobile's tires squealing and its motor roaring as if the devil were after him. Many of the families on the block were young and she worried about their children.

After Carole moved out, Gacy's neighbors noticed that a heavy-set woman occasionally came to his house. He said she was his bookkeeper. But the appearance of a younger, slimmer woman was more surprising. The woman, who appeared to be in her late twenties, moved in with him.

Some time after that when Lillie say Gacy he grinned and asked: "Guess what?" He answered his own question before she could reply. "I'm getting married again."

The Grexas had been busy with other things and hadn't met their neighbor's new girl friend yet, but Lillie told him that it was "nice" that he was going to settle down again with a wife. Gacy was pleased. He said he had already given his fiancé an engagement ring.

When Lillie again saw her neighbor a few weeks later, he casually mentioned that he was going to take Carole to some party or business function.

"I thought you were engaged?" Lillie asked, puzzled.

"Oh, I kicked her out," Gacy said. "She was such a slob. She didn't even clean up after herself." The Grexas never saw the woman again. He told his friends, the Czarnas, that she had given his ring back before she left.

A similar motive for severing a relationship was cited when Zielinski once asked what had happened to a young man who had been living in Gacy's house, and suddenly wasn't seen there anymore. Gacy said he had evicted the boy because he was dirty and was drinking all the liquor in the house.

Gacy continued to see his former wife Carole for months after they broke up. The last time they were together was on Memorial Day, 1978, when they journeyed to Paddock Lake to visit some of his sister's in-laws. On his way to drive Carole home, they stopped at his house so he could show her how he had remodeled the kitchen. It looked good. But one thing about the kitchen bothered her.

"John, it's sure a nice kitchen," she said, "but that odor that used to be in the front room seems like it's coming right from the sink now."

"I know," Gacy said, "I have to check on the sewer pipes. I must have put them in wrong."[7]

'*Chicago Sun-Times*, January 8, 1979.

7

The Rack

Jeffrey Rignall shivered as he stepped away from the apartment building into the post-midnight chill. He liked Chicago. It was nice to be home, and the stay in Florida during the winter had provided an opportunity to return to the city with an unseasonable tan that gave his slender face a healthy beachboy look under his curly mop of sandy hair.

But New Town wasn't Florida. It was late night on March 21 and it was cold. The crisp, dark sky was punctuated with the merest flecks of clouds and a brisk breeze off the lake whispered through the streets, scattering discarded papers onto lawns and ruffling his hair like a capricious hand. Even though the temperature had inched a couple of degrees above freezing, Rignall's sinewy frame shook in the frigid air.

He first noticed the sleek, black late-model Oldsmobile with spotlights on the side after it had slid quietly in front of him, blocking his path. Rignall began to step around the car when a heavyset man with genial features and a Santa Claus smile leaned out the rolled-down window and complimented him on his tan.

New Town is a friendly neighborhood where people often talk to strangers. The hum of activity and the music and laughter drifting from discos and taverns can provide a false sense of security and trust, and many meetings are by chance. Rignall replied goodnaturedly that he had picked up the tan in Florida.

When the stranger invited him to share a joint and

take a ride, the twenty-seven-year-old bachelor didn't give it a second thought before popping inside the car. He was thankful to get out of the cold, and looked forward to loosening up with some marijuana. The decision was instantaneous—and fateful.

Rignall began to relax as he pulled the soothing smoke into his lungs and leaned back into the comfort of his seat. The cigarette was passed a couple of times. He was contented and off guard when the big man suddenly whirled and shoved a rag over his face. Rignall tensed, flailing his arms and legs in alarm and drawing in his breath. Then he passed out. The rag was soaked with chloroform.

There were moments of fuzzy semiconsciousness during which he remembered opening his eyes and being dully aware of brief chimeric visions of street signs and a familiar expressway exit before the rag was once more pressed against his face and he lapsed again into total darkness.

Sometime later he experienced a dreamlike feeling of being carried in powerful arms into a house, through another doorway and down into a lowered room. As the veiled darkness began to clear from his mind and his eyes focused on the confusing miasma of shapes swimming in front of him, he realized he was lying on a couch, fully dressed. The rag was pressed to his face again. The next time he regained consciousness he was naked. His wrists and neck were locked in a pillorylike rack. The man who had chloroformed him was standing in front of him, also naked, his huge, hairy belly bulging obscenely. Several whips, chains, and dildos were lined up on the floor.

Rignall was groggy, but his eyes widened in alarm as the stranger told him in cool, even tones exactly how each of the implements was going to be used. The words rolled off his tongue like an incantation. Then the torture began.

Rignall was in the power of a sadist who used one instrument after another, waiting before each new assault until he saw the young man's face bleach gray in fear and pain, then smiling and applying the chloroform again. As soon as Rignall regained consciousness, the torture resumed.

Between the sessions of physical abuse and unconsciousness, the big man bragged that he was a policeman. He once said that he would just as soon shoot his pain-wracked victim as look at him. The abuses being performed on Rignall were so horrible and excruciatingly painful that there were times when he didn't care if he died. But at other times he pleaded for his life and babbled to his tormenter in mindbending terror that he was from Florida and would return there if he was freed.

Once as he was being tortured during a period of groggy semiconsciousness, Rignall was aware of a light being turned on in the kitchen area. He vaguely wondered who was there, allowing the idea to crouch on the edge of his consciousness until the pain and the chloroform caused the blackness to close around him again. He didn't expect to live through the night. Finally, after the darkness had enveloped him for the last time, he forced his eyes open and realized that he was sprawled under a statue in Lincoln Park near the lake. He was fully clothed but dishevelled, and his body was trembling from the shock of the ordeal he had just undergone, as well as from the chill of the early morning air. He had his billfold and his money, but, oddly, his driver's license was missing. It was just after five o'clock, and although it was still dark, birds were already beginning to stir and fill the crisp air with their cries.

Rignall stumbled a few blocks to his girl friend's apartment and collapsed on the bed. Several hours later he reported to police that he had been kidnapped, tortured, and raped. Policemen took him to a hospital for treatment. He was there six days. The chloroform had permanently damaged his liver, he had facial burns from the chemical, and was bleeding from the rectum.

Police told him that they were pessimistic about finding his attacker, because of the scarcity of information. Rignall had no name for the man, no license number, and no address.

He wasn't willing to permit the matter to drop, however. He had been kidnapped and his body outraged and permanently damaged by the unnatural trauma of the assault. It took courage to report the rape in the first place. It is estimated that as few as one heterosexual rape in ten is reported, and only one homosexual rape in one hundred, primarily because of embarrassment. Rape can also be one of the most difficult offenses to prove. But Rignall was hurt, and he was angry. He decided to do his own detective work.

He remembered the vague images he had become aware of while being driven along the Kennedy Expressway, of the road signs that teased his consciousness with foggy visions of Bryn Mawr and Cumberland Avenues. Other images were even more clear, those of the hulking sadist who had abused him, and of the black Oldsmobile with the spotlights.

Rignall rented a car and drove to the expressway exit he remembered from the night of his abduction and rape. He spent four to fifteen hours a day for about two weeks searching streets in the area for the car or sitting by the exit, sometimes accompanied by friends, waiting for it to drive by. His patience finally paid off when the black Oldsmobile turned off the expressway one day and passed him. He jotted down the license number and followed the Oldsmobile. The car turned into a driveway at 8213 West Summerdale Avenue in unincorporated Norwood Park township, a few blocks from the expressway.

The amateur sleuth's next steps were to check the license number and real-estate records. Rignall was familiar with real-estate records because he had managed real-estate properties and did other work in the field for a law firm.

The records turned up the name of John Wayne Gacy, Jr. Rignall took his information to Chicago police.

Police subsequently informed him that Gacy had a criminal record from Iowa, where he was convicted for sodomy. It would take about three weeks, they said, to obtain a photograph of Gacy. When the photograph was available, Rignall picked it out from among a thick book of pictures they showed to him. He swore out a warrant for Gacy's arrest, but police took their time acting on it.

It appeared that Gacy was developing a pattern of getting off easy after young men had accused him of kidnapping, physical abuse, and rape.

In December 1977, approximately four months before the assault on Rignall, an agitated nineteen-year-old told police that Gacy had kidnapped him from the north side at gunpoint and forced him to engage in unnatural sexual acts.

In a news article by John Gorman in the *Chicago Tribune,* the boy was quoted as saying that police treated him as they would someone who was high on drugs when he complained about Gacy.[1] He believed they were influenced against him because he had been arrested three months earlier for possession of marijuana when police found three joints in his pockets.

Police reported that Gacy was taken into custody and admitted to the sexual encounter, including the brutality, but insisted that both he and the teenager were willing participants. He claimed the boy tried to blackmail him and was angry because the attempt failed.

Officers later pointed out that they were faced with two people telling conflicting stories, and there were no other witnesses. Authorities refused to file charges because of lack of evidence. Off the record, investigators noted that current permissive attitudes toward sexual conduct have also made it difficult to prosecute sex offenses.

Gacy's associates never saw him with a gun. But he talked about guns a few times. He told Czarna that he had sealed a handgun he claimed belonged to his former mother-in-law in the concrete stoop at the back entrance to his house. He didn't explain why.

And Art Peterson said that Gacy once made a veiled threat about a gun in an attempt to frighten him. Peterson was a strong and supple twenty-five-year-old when he knocked at Gacy's door late in 1977 and asked for a job. The contractor invited him in for a beer.

Recalling the incident, Peterson said that one of the first things Gacy did after handing him a beer was to announce that he was a bisexual. Then Gacy suggested that since the young job seeker hadn't immediately punched him, that he (Peterson) might also be interested in men.

[1]*Chicago Tribune,* January 7, 1979.

They debated bisexuality over their beers for about fifteen minutes before Gacy tried to molest him. When Peterson pulled away, Gacy became angry and said he had a gun collection. It would be an easy feat to kill someone, roll the body in a carpet, and dispose of it in a trash dumpster, Gacy warned. The contractor added that he had in fact already killed people. Peterson didn't believe him.

Gacy eventually calmed down, and Peterson worked for him for a few days. During that time Gacy offered him three hundred to four hundred dollars to engage in sexual relations, and also offered him nine or ten dollars an hour to be his traveling companion on business trips, Peterson said. He wasn't interested in the extra-curricular activities and quit his job after a few days because he was dissatisfied with the pay. Before he quit, however, Peterson asked where all the bottles of pills and capsules came from. Gacy replied that he got them from pharmacists.

Both Peterson and Dominique Joscziniski, who worked for Gacy for about two years, said many of the employees were propositioned and that they regularly joked about their boss's sexual peccadillos. Josczinski said that Gacy had made sexual advances to him, but he rejected them. Gacy didn't try again.

On June 30, 1978, the nude body of a young man washed ashore in the Illinois River near the Dresden Locks in Grundy County. The name "Tim Lee," tattooed on his upper left arm, was the only identifying mark on the body.

Jeff Rignall, meanwhile, was becoming impatient waiting for police to act on the warrant for Gacy's arrest. In early July the plucky young man drove to the house in Norwood Park and knocked on the door. An elderly woman answered the door and said she was John Gacy's mother, and that her son was away but would be back soon. She inquired if Rignall was planning to come to her son's Italian theme party. It was going to be a big one with hundreds of guests.

Rignall said he wasn't interested in the party, but would return later. He walked to his car and parked it nearby, to wait for Gacy's arrival so that he could telephone Chicago police and ask them to serve the warrant. The police arrived before Gacy showed up, but when they got there they realized they could not make the arrest. The house was outside the city limits, and thus outside their jurisdiction.

While the men were standing outside their cars talking, Rignall was approached by a soft-spoken man about his own age who had driven up in a late-model red Chevrolet with a white vinyl top. The newcomer, who was neatly dressed in clean working clothes, asked Rignall not to mention the rape complaint to Gacy's mother. The problem could be handled without bringing the woman into it and needlessly upsetting her. The stranger didn't mention his name, and identified himself only as a friend of Gacy's.

Rignall saw the man once again a couple of months later when he showed up at a scheduled court hearing. The mystery man said that he worked for Gacy and his boss needed a continuance because he was out of town. He left without his name being entered in the court records. Rignall and Fred Richman, Rignall's attorney, followed to obtain his license number, but he drove away in a van owned by DM Contractors, Inc. Rignall was intrigued by the possibility that the man might be the individual who had been in Gacy's home the night of the assault, and talked to police about his suspicions.

Gacy had always been considerate of his family. He kept in close telephone contact with his mother and visited at least twice a year. He never forgot birthdays or Christmas and was generous with his sisters and their children. When his older sister's home needed repairs, he gave her money to help with the expenses. And when his younger sister's deep freeze broke down, he purchased her a new one. He was always available with help when family members needed it.

During the Thanksgiving holidays in 1978 he traveled to Arkansas to visit with his mother and his sister's family. It was a relaxing break in his busy schedule and he went Christmas shopping with his sister to buy presents for his nieces and nephew, his mother, and other family members.

The family of James Mazzara also spent Thanksgiving together. Like Gacy, James was a considerate and loving son who remembered birthdays and holidays and called his parents at least once a week. But he slept only occasionally at the family home in suburban Elmwood Park—preferring to exert his independence and stay with friends.

Carrying 110 to 120 pounds on a five-foot, two-inch frame, he was small for a twenty-year-old, but he had been taking care of himself by working at a variety of part-time and unskilled jobs since dropping out of Elmwood Park High School a couple of years before. The youth, who was called "Mojo" by his buddies, was good-looking, healthy, and genial, and it appeared that there was still plenty of time to get serious about carving out a career. So it was a happy occasion when he sat down to Thanksgiving dinner with his family. When he left that evening it was with the understanding that he would be home again for Christmas, if not long before. His older sister, Annette, didn't begin worrying about him until well into December after James hadn't telephoned or visited his parents' home. She asked a few of his friends if they had seen him recently, and when some of them replied in the affirmative, she was somewhat relieved and settled down to wait for Christmas or earlier to hear from her errant, dark-haired brother.

Meanwhile, Rignall's persistence was beginning to pay some dividends in his drive to elicit satisfaction from Gacy for the March 22 abduction and rape. Police had finally arrested the contractor on a misdemeanor charge of battery of July 15. They refused to file a more serious felony charge, despite the urging of Rignall and his attorney Fred Richman. It was explained to the perturbed young man that if he had been chloroformed as he claimed, it would be difficult for him to positively identify his assailant even though he had talked with the man outside the car and for several minutes while smoking the marijuana.

Rignall had also moved, through Richman, to recover some of the expenses he was piling up for medical attention. He was continuing expensive treatments for the liver damage, he had lost forty pounds, and his vitality was sapped as a result of the ordeal. He was admittedly saddled with serious emotional disturbances and was facing financial ruin. There were nights when he would awaken at 3 or 4 A.M. and sit staring blankly at the wall of his bedroom. When he went to the hospital for the shots that were making road maps of his arms and legs, he fidgeted, his nerves humming like hot wires, as he struggled to understand why he had been singled out to be the victim of a madman.

Richman notified Gacy that he planned to file a civil suit on behalf of his client to collect for the medical bills. Gacy at first suggested that they meet to talk things over in a west suburban restaurant, but later agreed to come to Richman's office. The attorney had arranged for Rignall to wait in the outer office. As Gacy walked in, Rignall got his first good look at him since March 22. Rignall was certain he recognized the man he believed to have attacked him. But Gacy gave no indication that he recognized his reputed victim.

At the meeting, Gacy assumed an air of muddled innocence as he listened to a reading of the proposed suit. When he left he indicated that he wasn't worried about the possibility of the suit being filed, but in a subsequent telephone conversation advised Richman that the matter had been referred to attorney LeRoy Stevens. Stevens was the registered agent for PDM Contractors, Inc.

When Stevens talked with Richman, he reportedly remarked that he didn't believe Gacy was capable of carrying out the acts described in the proposed suit. Nevertheless, about ten days later Gacy offered a settlement of $2,800 through Stevens if Rignall would promise not to file the suit. At that time, Rignall had already run up $7,000 in medical bills and he had no medical insurance. He was worried that without police cooperation he would have difficulty proving that Gacy was the person who had attacked him. After negotiations, he agreed to accept $3,-000. He also obtained a promise that Gacy would drop a counter-complaint charging him with battery. The battery charge against Gacy, of course, still stood.

Gacy continued to maintain his usual facade of self-confidence, but privately he may have been beginning to feel the pressures of the problems building around him.

Even his reputation as a man who could always hold his drinks was beginning to slip. It was late fall when Zielinski ran into him at the Harlem-Irving Park Plaza Shopping Center a few blocks from Gacy's home. Gacy was drunk, Zielinski said. When Zielinski asked his friend how business was, Gacy replied that it was good. Zielinski should have continued working for him, Gacy said, because he was paying his employees big money.

Lillie Grexa had a short conversation with her neighbor at about the same. time. He told her that his house was becoming too small for him and he was thinking of building on another floor and adding three rooms.

That was foolish, she said. If he felt that way he should sell the house and buy a bigger one.

Perhaps she was right, he agreed, nodding his head in assent. It might be better to sell the house and move on.

8

The Apocalypse

Robert Piest didn't want to be late for his mother's birthday party, so she was anxious to be on time to pick him up at the pharmacy when he got off work.

Elizabeth Piest was forty-six years old on Monday, December 11, 1978, and she and her husband, Harold, had two other children. Kenneth, twenty-four, was a medical student at the University of Illinois, Chicago Circle campus, and a daughter, Kerry, twenty-one, was an office worker.

But Robert was the baby of the family. Mrs. Piest was not being overly protective when she picked him up at school and drove him to work, nor when she promised to give him a ride home so he wouldn't have to wait at bus stops and walk the dark streets of the northwest Chicago suburbs. He was an intelligent, active, and adverturesome boy, but he was, after all, only fifteen.

He was the kind of son that any parent could be proud of. Descriptions like "clean cut" and "All American Boy" were coined for youngsters like Robert. He earned good grades at Maine West High School in Niles, and even though he was an underclassman, he was already a letterman in gymnastics. He had always made his parents proud of him in every way.

At about the time the new school term started, he was working a part-time after-school job at the Nisson Pharmacy in nearby Des Plaines and saving his money to buy a car. Elizabeth Piest was proud of him, as she was of all her children, and looked forward to returning home with him so that the family could cut her birthday cake.

She arrived at the store with ten minutes to spare before her son was to finish work at 9 P.M. A couple of minutes before he was to leave for the night, he asked Kim Beyers, a fellow employee, to watch the cash register a few minutes because "that contractor guy wants to talk to me." Then he turned to his mother.

"Mom, wait a minute," he said. "I've got to talk to a contractor about a summer job that will pay me five dollars an hour." He was earning $2.85 at the pharmacy, and the new job would mean that he could buy a car sooner. Mrs. Piest agreed to wait inside the store for a few minutes, and her son pulled on his light-blue hooded ski jacket and walked out the door.

When his mother realized that it was almost 9:30 P.M. and he hadn't returned, she went outside to look for him. He wasn't in the parking lot or anywhere else in sight. Alarmed, she asked inside the store if anyone there knew what might have happened to him. No one could tell her much more than she already knew. Her son had apparently gone outside to talk to the contractor about a job. Her anxiety growing every minute, Elizabeth Piest drove home to tell her husband about Robert's mystifying disappearance. He wasn't the kind of boy who would deliberately walk out on his mother without saying a word about where he was going, and she knew he had been looking forward to the cake cutting. At 11:30 P.M., after they had waited three hours for their son to come home, the Piests reported to the Des Plaines Police Department that Robert was missing. Officer George Konieczny filled out the reports, making careful note of the suspicious circumstances of the boy's disappearance—and including the name of the contractor, John Gacy. Information about the missing boy was entered on state and national computers at 1:54 A.M., December 12.

Tuesday morning Lieutenant Joseph Kozenczak walked into his office in the Investigations Division of the Des Plaines Police Department and began checking over the previous night's reports. Konieczny's report about the missing Piest boy was among them. Minutes later, Kozenczak was talking to Mrs. Piest, who had come to the station at 9 A.M.

The five-foot, eight-inch, 140-pound Boy Scout didn't fit the description of a typical runaway. Kozenczak had three children of his own, one of them a fifteen-year-old son who was a fellow student of the missing Maine West sophomore. The hard-nosed, analytical-minded police lieutenant was aware that the similarity between his own son and the missing boy may have influenced him to focus on the Piest case. But he also realized that Robert was a "straight kid" who had never been in trouble or given his parents problems.

After spending most of his career in patrol work, Kozenczak had been named chief of detectives less than a year earlier when Lee Alfano moved up to head the department as chief of police. As the new division head, Kozenczak instructed his detectives to carefully scrutinize all missing-persons reports and to pursue especially closely those that did not resemble routine runaways. Robert was not a casual runaway. He was obviously a well-behaved, industrious boy with no problems in school or with his family.

Kozenczak took personal charge of the case. He was a no-nonsense investigator who understood and accepted the value of dogged attention to detail in police work. He immediately launched an in-depth investigation and search for the missing boy. Detectives began questioning everyone at the pharmacy in Des Plaines who had known the missing youth—clerks, customers, and the owner. A clerk said that Robert had left to speak with the contractor, who was parked outside in the lot in a pickup truck, and was described as a gray-haired, middle-aged man. The owner of the pharmacy disclosed that Gacy, who owned a pickup truck among various other vehicles, had done some remodeling work at the store. Furthermore, he was in the store on two different occasions Monday night and apparently talked to Robert and offered him a job. That afternoon, Detective Ron Adams of the Juvenile Bureau telephoned and asked Gacy if he knew anything about the missing boy. Gacy said he did not.

By 9 P.M., however, Kozenczak was in Norwood

Park township, accompanied by three other investigators, and was knocking at the door of 8213 West Summerdale Avenue. When Gacy answered the door, Kozenczak asked him to come to the police station for questioning. Gacy replied that he had to wait at home for an important telephone call from his mother in Arkansas, regarding an uncle who had just died. A boy was missing, Kozenczak pointed out, and stressed that it was imperative that Gacy talk in detail to investigators as soon as possible. He asked Gacy either to telephone his mother immediately or to leave the telephone call until later and go to the station to give a statement. Gacy didn't like being pressured, especially so soon after losing a beloved uncle. He accused Kozenczak of having "no respect for the dead."

The hefty contractor was obviously upset but he finally agreed to take care of his business and report to the station in a couple of hours. He stumbled into the police department sometime after three o'clock the next morning with his shoes and clothing caked with mud. The detectives who were to take his statement had left hours before and he was told that he could return home, but to report back to the station later that morning.

By 9:15 A.M., Gacy was in the Investigative Division offices being questioned extensively about possible connections to the missing boy. He emphatically denied that he knew anything about Robert's disappearance, and was eventually permitted to leave. Soon after that, routine background checks Kozenczak had ordered on various people believed to have known or come into recent contact with the boy paid off. He was notified that Gacy had a criminal record and had served eighteen months of a ten-year term in an Iowa prison on a sodomy conviction. The charge involved a teenage boy. Kozenczak went to Circuit Judge Marvin J. Peters for a search warrant, citing Gacy's criminal background, the boy's exemplary reputation, and other factors to show probable cause.

Lillie Grexa was coming home from a shopping trip and although it was only four o'clock in the afternoon, the heavy December sky was already gray and sodden, hinting of new snow in the early winter that was about to settle over the Midwest. But she was used to gray skies and cold winters. She was more interested in the assemblage of cars in her neighbor's crescent drive. So was her husband.

"What's up next door?" he asked, as his wife walked inside and began unloading packages.

"Oh, maybe John's having an early Christmas party."

"If that's what it is, it's a funny way to have a party," Grexa replied. "His own car isn't even there."

Lillie was opening packages and beginning to put things away. "They might be waiting for him," she suggested. She was sure that whatever her friendly but eccentric neighbor was up to he could take care of himself. Shopping had tied up most of her afternoon and she had work to do. She hadn't even thought about starting supper yet. She was puttering in the kitchen when the back door slammed and her red-haired fourteen-year-old daughter walked in carrying an armload of schoolbooks.

"Mom, it looks like they're searching Mr. Gacy's house," she said. "There's a light on in every room and it looks like people are going through things." Lillie Grexa called to her husband and repeated the story. "Maybe you'd better go next door, Eddie, and see what's what," she suggested. They were used to their neighbor knocking on their door and asking them to keep an eye on his house for a few days while he was away on one of his frequent business trips. He returned the favor when he could by watching their house for trouble while they were away on vacation or visiting.

Grexa, however, said he didn't think he should get involved in whatever was going on. His wife repeated her urging to check things out next door. He shook his head "no." But a few minutes later, when a couple of men walked outside the house next door and began taking photographs, he changed his mind and told his wife that he was going to John's to talk to them.

"What's going on?" he asked, after cutting across the lawn and confronting the men with the camera and waving his arm toward the house. "You know, I'm about ready to call the police."

One of the men reached in his pocket, took out his billfold and flipped it open to show a badge clipped inside.

"Don't worry," he said, "we are the police." Grexa was impressed but unintimidated. He asked what they were looking for, and the policeman replied that he couldn't talk about the search. "Well," said Grexa, turning to leave, "if you're searching for something, you know there's an attic and a crawl space in there."

Lillie telephoned Gacy's bookkeeper and said there was trouble next door. She asked how she could locate her neighbor. The bookkeeper said that Gacy was planning to attend a wake that night and promised to try to get in touch with him. Shortly after, the bookkeeper called back and said Gacy hadn't shown up at the wake and couldn't be found.

Meanwhile the search of the house was bearing fruit. When the Des Plaines detectives and an evidence technician from the Cook County Sheriff's Department eventually left, they took with them:

> A section of rug with stains on it.
> Clothing, including a pair of yellow undershorts.
> Color photos of drug stores.
> An address book.
> More than a dozen books, including *Bike Boy, Pederasty, Sex Between Men and Boys, Twenty-One Abnormal Sex Cases, Tight Teenagers, The American Bi-Centennial Gay Guide,* and *The Rights of Gay People.*
> Seven erotic films.
> A hypodermic needle and syringe.
> A quantity of crushed green plantlike material and rolling papers.
> Bottles of pills, including capsules thought to be Valium, and another containing amyl nitrite.
> A scale.
> A switchblade knife.
> A pistol, and a bag containing possible gun caps or rivets.
> A pair of handcuffs and keys.
> A length of nylon rope.
> A thirty-nine-inch-long two-by-four board with two holes in each end.

A temporary driver's license issued to Michael B. Baker.

A Maine High School class ring with the initials J.A.S.

A driver's license issued to James G. O'Toole.

A receipt from the Nisson Pharmacy for a roll of film being developed.

At that time, police also confiscated Gacy's 1979 Oldsmobile Delta 88, the second new car he purchased in 1978; a 1978 Chevrolet pickup truck with the words "PDM Contractors" inscribed on it and the attached snowplow; and a late model van, also identified as the property of "PDM Contractors."

Bits of hair were found in the trunk of the car, which was taken to the police garage. The door of the car and those of other vehicles in the garage were opened and a trained dog that had been given articles of Robert's clothing to smell was released inside the building. He scampered past the other vehicles and jumped inside Gacy's Oldsmobile. The hair, which was the same color as the missing boy's, was sent to the police crime laboratory for further examination.

Investigators were especially curious about the film receipt they had found in a kitchen trash basket. They suspected that it did not belong to Gacy and felt it might be an important factor in leading them to the missing boy. By 9 P.M., the Piest family had confirmed that the receipt was for film that belonged to Kim Beyers.

The sixteen-year-old girl subsequently explained that she was with Robert a few days before his disappearance and he had given her his jacket to wear because she was cold. She said she left the film receipt in the jacket pocket and recited the last two digits of the serial number for police. By that time, Kozenczak had few doubts that Robert had been in the house on Summerdale Avenue. The tenacious detective ordered twenty-four-hour surveillance on the contractor, hoping that Gacy would lead them to the boy. Police surveillance teams made no attempt to hide their presence, as other officers spread out to talk to the suspect's friends and associates. Several officers began working double shifts. The Investigations Division, which combines the Detective and Juvenile Bureaus, operated with a total of fourteen policemen.

Czarna was one of the first of Gacy's associates to become aware that his friend was in trouble when Gacy drove to his house in a rented car to complain that police were persecuting him and trying to tie him to a drug offense. Police even parked a few yards away and watched as Gacy sold Christmas trees near an area shopping center, an enterprise he had undertaken for two or three years. The Czarnas believed him when he said he was innocent, and they sympathetically agreed that the around-the-clock surveillance would be nerve-wracking. They were his friends and they listened as he talked of his troubles and joked sarcastically about his police "bodyguard." He was worried that police would get another search warrant and "break in" his house again, and feared that they might be inside even then or had already been inside and left. Czarna couldn't understand Gacy's distress about a search. There should be nothing to worry about if there was nothing to hide, he reasoned.

Nevertheless, Gacy continued to fuss and worry until Czarna finally agreed to drive to the house and check inside just to put his friend's mind at ease. Gacy handed him the keys to the rental car and prepared to wait for his friend's return. A police car slid from its parking place and followed the cement contractor as he drove the half dozen blocks to Summerdale, pulled the vehicle into the rear driveway, and parked. The police car stopped in front. The house hadn't been searched again.

The next day, Gacy knocked at the Grexas' back door. He had some specifications to drop off for a job involving marble installation that Ed Grexa's boss had bid on. Lillie answered the door. Her neighbor was hollow-eyed and drooping.

"I should have been here earlier with these, but I've been kind of busy," he apologized, as he handed the plans to her.

"Yeah, what's going on?" the woman agreed, nodding her head in knowledgeable assent.

"Well . . . I got company wherever I go. I even had to hire bodyguards," he joked.

When Lillie asked him why he was being followed, he replied that the police were trying to tie him to a murder. It took a moment for the remark to sink in. Then she remembered hearing that one of the boys who worked on her neighbor's construction jobs for a while had disappeared. "Is it that kid that used to work for you?"

"Oh, no. Not him," Gacy said. "He's in another state." Gacy indicated that the trouble was drug-oriented, but emphatically denied that he had anything to do with drugs and said the whole incident was a misunderstanding. He knew how strongly she was opposed to drug abuse. Then he apologized because he had to leave, but before turning to go, he told her, "If anyone comes and asks any questions, just refer them to my lawyer." He gave her his attorney's name and office numbers, and told her not to worry because the trouble would all be over soon.

The search for the missing boy was taking other avenues as well as the surveillance of Gacy. Dogs and a Coast Guard helicopter were called out to comb portions of the forest preserve and along the banks of the Des Plaines river in the northwest suburban area. Robert's family and friends circulated flyers with pictures of him throughout Des Plaines. Some were left near the cash register at the Nisson Pharmacy. He was described as having medium-length brown hair and wearing a tan T-shirt, tan levi pants, and the blue jacket. Several people responded with information that they hoped would be helpful, and policemen were assigned to check out the data for workable leads.

Gacy, meanwhile, took the offensive against the people he claimed were tormenting him, by filing a $750,000 civil-rights suit in U.S. District Court in Chicago against the city of Des Plaines. He asked for an injunction to halt all investigations and sought damages for mental anguish, loss of reputation in the community, deprivation of liberty, and loss of personal property. Specifically naming Chief Alfano and other officers, he claimed that he was being harassed by Des Plaines police and accused the Illinois Bureau of Investigation of participating in the abuse. He and his attorneys were apparently unaware that the state agency had been defunct since 1977, when its functions were assumed by the Division of Criminal Investigations in the State Department of Law Enforcement. The name of Sam Amirante, Gacy's acquaintance from the Norwood Park Township Lighting Commission, appeared on the suit with that of Stevens. It was also Amirante whose name Gacy had given to Lillie Grexa.

The contractor complained that his right to privacy had been violated and he had been exposed to illegal searches and seizures during the investigation. His vehicles were improperly seized and held and he, himself, was detained on December 13 from 1:30 to 9:45 P.M. Police were additionally accused of harassing his friends, employees, and associates by detaining and questioning them.

Gacy's attitude toward the policemen who were trailing him blew hot and cold. He alternately shot photographs of them, led them on long rambling car chases in apparent efforts to lose them, and invited them into his house. In the early evening of the day the suit was filed, Gacy approached two officers parked in a police car near his driveway and invited them into his home. Officer Robert Schultz, an eight-year veteran of the department, recognized the heavy cloying odor pervading the house the moment he stepped through the kitchen door. Temperatures outside were near zero and the furnace was on, emphasizing the stench of putrefied human flesh. It settled over the rooms like an odiferous blanket. It was an odor that Schultz had smelled dozens of times before at the Cook County Morgue and on other occasions when he was near the cadavers of people who had been dead for some time. The odor of human tissue that has putrefied clings to a room or enclosed space like gangrene.

Czarna was beginning to feel some of the pressure of the intense investigation focusing on his friend. He was interrogated for the first time on the same day that Schultz was invited into Gacy's home. Detectives told him they were investigating the disappearance of the Piest boy and wanted to know if Gacy was a homosexual, if he was known to be violent, and how he treated his employees. The affair was becoming more and more frustrating and difficult for Gacy's friends, and Czarna's irritation was beginning to surface. A police car had been parked outside his own house several times, yet his friend kept assuring him that the investigation was a terrible mistake and that everything would soon be cleared up. Police questioned more than one hundred people during the first four or five days of the investigation.

The pressure on Gacy was also mounting. When Des Plaines detective David Hachmeister relieved other officers and picked up his shift of surveillance one minute after midnight on December 21, he had been with the department's youth division only three days after serving six months in the department's tactical unit "Delta." Hachmeister took over his shift with a partner outside Amirante's law offices in Park Ridge, across the Des Plaines River, a few miles southeast of the town of the same name. Temperatures were again near zero, and Amirante walked out to the car and invited the policemen inside. He motioned them to chairs and poured hot coffee, explaining that Gacy was asleep on a couch in an inner office.

By 8 A.M., the plainclothesmen were back in their car when Gacy lurched from the office, apparently highly disturbed and agitated. He climbed into his car and roared out of the driveway, with the officers behind him. The car ripped through speed zones and continued erratically along busy streets until the policemen finally pulled him to the curb and warned him to drive more carefully.

Gacy nodded his head and drove away again, slower and more carefully, heading southeast to a Park Ridge service station near the Niles town line. As the policemen watched from about six feet away, he stepped out of his car and took a plastic bag of what appeared to be marijuana from his pocket and stuffed it into the pocket of one of the station attendants. The officers did not make an arrest at the time despite the virtual invitation because they were still hopeful that Gacy would somehow lead them to Piest. Gacy walked inside the station to talk to the owner, but left a few moments later and drove the few blocks to his house.

He stayed only long enough to take his little gray dog across the street and leave him with neighbors, Sam and Jennie De Laurentis. They were curious and asked him why he was being followed by police cars. Everyone in the neighborhood was aware that he was involved in something serious.

"They're trying to pin a murder rap on me," he said.[1] Then he joined the couple laughing at the seeming preposterousness of the idea. When he stopped chuckling, he said he would nevertheless appreciate it if they would keep Patches with them until he could get the matter straightened out. It was odd, he said, but the dog was nervous and didn't appear to like being left alone in the house anymore. That night Sam De Laurentis opened the door to talk to a neighbor and Patches scampered outside. He never came back.

It was a few minutes after 10 A.M., and Czarna was in the washroom when Gacy pounded at the door. Lydia Czarna let him in and was appalled by his haggard appearance. His eyes were sunken deep under his brows and shone wildly from his tired sallow face, which was darkened by at least a day's growth of whiskers. He looked worse than she had ever seen him and he was moaning, "I've been a bad boy." Perplexed, she motioned him to a seat at the kitchen table. He had barely sat down when he asked for a drink of Scotch. That was surprising because lately he had been turning down drinks, explaining that he was trying to lose weight. She had never seen him drink so early on a workday.

Czarna had walked into the kitchen and was staring at his friend. "John," he finally asked, making no attempt to hide the exasperation in his voice, "what's your problem?"

Gacy reached for the glass on the table and lifted it to moist lips, his trembling hand causing the ice to clink as he swallowed deeply. He set the glass back down on the table and turned to Czarna. "The end is near," he intoned, his voice cracking.

"What the hell are you talking about, 'The end is near'?" Czarna exploded.

"The end is near," Gacy repeated.

Czarna couldn't figure it out. It sounded like his

[1]*Chicago Sun-Times,* December 29, 1978.

friend was expecting to die. "What are you gonna do, kill yourself?"

"No," said Gacy. "They're trying to pin a murder rap on me." He sipped the Scotch again, got up, and began walking toward the door. Czarna asked where he was going and Gacy replied that he had a job to do.

"I thought you had something you wanted to tell me," Czarna spluttered. Gacy walked outside without answering but immediately turned and walked back in. The words were forced out in a hoarse croak as he approached his friend. "I killed thirty people," he said, "give or take a few."

Czarna was stunned, but managed to ask who the victims were. "Bad people," Gacy said. "They were blackmailing me. They were baaaad people." Leaning his head on Czarna's shoulder, he began to cry.

By 10:55 A.M., Gacy had left his bewildered friends and driven again to the service station, where he stayed a few minutes before heading to the home of David Cram. Rossi was also at Cram's house. Both youths had lived with Gacy for a time. As he entered the house, the policemen overheard him tell Rossi, "I'm glad you could make it. Come inside. This is the last time you'll ever see me."

Rossi left the house alone at about 11:30 A.M. About fifteen minutes later, Cram left with his friend and former boss. Before getting in the car, Gacy approached Schultz, who was tailing him by that time, and announced that Cram was going to chauffeur him "if it's okay with you." Schultz was puzzled that Gacy would ask him but indicated that he had no objections.

Gacy added that he and the youth were going to a restaurant in northwest Chicago for lunch, and the policemen followed them there. Gacy slid from his seat and began walking to the restaurant, but as he reached the door, he apparently changed his mind and returned to the car. Cram walked to the police car and leaned toward the window to talk to Schultz. The boy appeared to be frightened. "We're going to Maryhill Cemetery," he said. "John wants to say good-bye to the grave of his father."

Schultz noncommittally nodded his head. "Don't you guys know?" Cram asked. "When John was with his attorney all last night, he admitted to him that he had killed at least thirty people. He's practically suicidal. I hope you stay close to us."

The man and the boy never reached the cemetery. Unknown to them, Schultz was notified by radio moments after talking to Cram that other officers had been ordered to arrest Gacy for possession of marijuana, a charge stemming from the incident at the service station. Less than five minutes after Cram drove away from the restaurant, officers from the Des Plaines Police Department, Cook County Sheriff's Department, and the Illinois State Department of Law Enforcement, Division of Criminal Investigations, stopped the car and took Gacy into custody. A companion charge of possession of a controlled substance (Valium) was later added to the marijuana offense. During arraignment in Circuit Court, bail was set at a total of one thousand dollars on the two counts. Until his arrest on the drug charges, Gacy had still been free on nominal bail awaiting action on the misdemeanor charge filed earlier in the Rignall case.

In a Chicago restaurant early Thursday evening, December 21, Florece Branson consulted the cards again. Czarna had asked his wife to have a reading on his behalf. He was worried that he would be drawn deeper into the legal problems of his friend, and he wanted to know the true nature of Gacy's troubles. Although the Czarnas were not directly involved, the reader advised, there was serious trouble affecting a person close to them. The problem involved drugs and the disappearance of someone. The advisor warned that their friend was shady, dishonest, and had an obsession that had entangled him in the predicament. His distress would grow still greater.

At about 7 P.M., the Grexas noticed police cars again collecting in front of the house next door. Another search warrant had been obtained and Des Plaines's and Sheriff's police returned to the house with Gacy. This time, Ed Grexa didn't bother to go next door to ask what was going on, and the family spent most of the evening at the back of their house where they had their family room and television.

Investigators had already looked through all the rooms in the house, including the attic, and they told Gacy that it might be necessary to rip up the flooring in their search for the missing high school student. Obviously alarmed, Gacy blurted out that he had killed a man in self-defense. But it wouldn't be necessary to rip up the floorboards of the house to find him. Gacy said he had buried the body under his garage and offered to show detectives the location of the makeshift grave. Flanked by Assistant State's Attorney Lawrence Finder, a half dozen policemen and his own counsel, Gacy led the group to the garage, where he pinpointed the burial site with an "X" drawn on the concrete floor with spray paint.

Instead of immediately breaking up the concrete, the investigative team returned to the house for a look at the crawl space. A few minutes later, everyone understood why Gacy hadn't been anxious for them to poke around under the flooring.

Back in Des Plaines, Gacy was complaining of chest pains, and fire department paramedics were called. His blood pressure was checked and was slightly high. He was taken on a stretcher to a local hospital, examined more closely, and returned to the police station the same evening.

Investigators worked into the night. At 10 P.M., Cook County Medical Examiner, Dr. Robert J. Stein, answered his telephone in north suburban Highland Park. He is traditionally an early riser who plans to be at his office near the Cook County Hospital by 5:30 or 6 A.M. on weekdays, and a few minutes later he would have been in bed. The telephone call changed that.

"There's a body or something in the crawl space of a ranch house near Norridge," a sheriff's policeman told him.[2] Stein telephoned an aide and instructed him to bring disposable coveralls and meet him at the house in Norwood Park township. Almost a dozen law enforcement officers were waiting when he arrived. Sheriff Richard J. Elrod had designated Deputy Chief Richard Quagliano and Lieutenant Frank Braun, head of the Major Investiga-

[2]*Chicago Tribune,* December 30, 1978.

tions Unit, and others, to work with the town policemen because Gacy's house was in an unincorporated area and the investigation was reaching into various jurisdictions within northwest Cook County.

Officers repeated the information that remains of at least one human body had been found in a crawl space, and led Stein inside the house. He was met by an odor familiar to anyone who has worked with dead bodies. It was a death house. As soon as he had slipped on the coveralls, Stein dropped through the trap door into the dankness below. An evidence technician pointed to material that appeared to be human hair. At the other end of the tunnel, another technician called out that there was a bone for Stein to look at. The yellow beam of a flashlight illuminated skeletal human remains of at least one human being. Bones that had been part of two human arms were uncovered. Other suspicious mounds were crowded elsewhere in the dark space.

Stein crawled out of the tunnel and sat down at a table for a conference with other law enforcement officials. The medical examiner is in legal charge at the scene of any death he is investigating. It was quickly determined that efforts to recover the remains would be postponed until the following day. At that time, Stein said, the bones would be disinterred as carefully as if the site were an archaeological dig to insure that all possible evidence was preserved. He ordered the house sealed overnight and guards posted.

While Stein and other investigators were preparing to continue their probe of the nauseating horrors of the thirty-by-forty-foot crawl space, the man police believed to be responsible for the atrocity was still talking at the Des Plaines police station. He had engaged Amirante as the second attorney to represent him, and the thirty-year-old lawyer was present during questioning. Sheriff's department officers were standing by along with Des Plaines police. Assistant State's Attorney, Terry Sullivan, chief of the Northwest Suburban Division and County Sheriff's Investigator, Greg Bedoe, who was assigned to the State's Attorney's staff, were also helping with the interrogation.

The tightness had been closing in on Gacy more intensely every day and he appeared to be relieved that the chase had come to an end. Investigators confronted him with evidence they had been collecting, read him his rights, and he made a rambling verbal confession. By early Friday morning, he had confessed that he had murdered at least thirty people. He told of using his experience as a clown, offering to show his victims "a trick" to lure them into permitting themselves to be handcuffed, and after they were helpless, sexually abusing them and forcing them to perform unnatural acts. He killed them by moving behind them and throttling them with a rope or a board that he held at both ends and pulled back against their throats.

The bodies were interred in the crawl space or elsewhere on his property until a combination of poor health, that prevented him from doing more digging, and a lack of space in the makeshift burial ground forced him to seek a new method of disposal. Consequently, he dumped the last five victims into the Des Plaines River. Piest was one of those, and Gacy confessed that the body was still in the attic when Kozenczak was downstairs on December 12. Gacy admitted keeping the bodies in the house for several hours but would not say if he sexually molested them after death, one investigator told newsmen.

He said he was so unnerved by the appearance of the detectives that after they left, he crammed the body into the trunk of his car and drove to the Kankakee Bridge on the Des Plaines River south of Joliet. He dropped his grisly cargo into the water and tossed the boy's clothing after him. The bridge is about fifty miles from Gacy's home.

The story was given some credibility when a tow-truck operator from the town of LaGrange reported pulling Gacy's Oldsmobile from a two-foot snowbank on the Tri-State Tollway at about 2 A.M. on December 13. Bob Kirkpatrick, who held a contract to tow disabled cars on a section of the highway, said he didn't record Gacy's name because the twenty-dollar towing fee was paid in cash. He identified Gacy, however, through a photograph provided by Cook County Sheriff's police who contacted him.

The garage operator said that after he was directed to the car by Tollway police, he had to rap on the window to awaken the driver. The stranded motorist acted as if he were on dope or coming off a drunk. He was unshaven and tough-looking, Kirkpatrick added. After the car was back on the pavement, Gacy drove north in the direction of his home.

Police were still searching the house when Ed Grexa got out of bed about 5:30 Friday morning, washed, had coffee and a light breakfast and left for work. By 6:45, Lillie Grexa was up and peering out the front window at a television-station news truck that had pulled up next door and parked among the clutter of official cars. She was just shaking her youngest daughter awake to tell her that "something's really wrong next door," when someone knocked.

A television reporter was standing on the stoop. "Did you hear," he inquired, "they found three bodies?" Her husband telephoned from work a few minutes later. "Did you see the news?" he asked. "They just found a body over at John's."

On Friday afternoon, Gacy was formally charged with murdering Robert Piest. Wearing a black leather jacket and rumpled trousers that looked like they had been slept in, he was escorted under heavy guard across a short walkway from the Police Headquarters to the Des Plaines Branch of Cook County Circuit Court for a bond hearing. All elevators were stopped while he was in the building, and he was walked up three flights of stairs to the courtroom of Judge Peters. At least another two dozen lawmen were scattered throughout the room. During the seven minutes Gacy was inside, he stood with his head up and his hands clasped behind his back, chattering amiably with the officers surrounding him. Peters ordered him held without bail and scheduled formal arraignment for the following Friday.

Gacy's hands were cuffed behind him at the conclusion of the hearing and he was walked to the elevator. A half dozen policemen who couldn't jam inside the elevator with him dashed down the stairs. They crowded around him, protecting him from a throng of media men and women, escorting him back across the walkway to security rooms in the police headquarters.

He continued to cooperate and talked freely to lawmen on Thursday and Friday. One detective disclosed, however, that Gacy did not sign a statement, and said notes weren't even taken of much of the conversation. Gacy was so talkative that investigators were afraid to interrupt or to take notes because of fear that he would stop.

The suspect provided the time, place, and description of the slayings but said he didn't know or couldn't recall the names of many of the victims because they were people he met in casual encounters. He said he killed them because he was afraid of retaliation or possible extortion attempts.

The first victim was stabbed to death after being picked up at the Greyhound Bus Terminal in Chicago on January 3, 1972, Gacy said. He could not remember the boy's name. But he remembered two others because they were former employees: John Butkovich, who was buried under the garage floor, and Gregory Godzik. He recalled that another victim was John Szyc, the owner of the old Plymouth Satellite that had been so mysteriously signed away and sold to Rossi. The names of the boys were withheld from the public pending official identification.

After drawing a rough diagram of his entire property indicating where bodies were buried and promising to show detectives where to find others, Gacy finally balked and stopped talking. He had rambled for hours, sometimes referring to himself in the third person, saying that the sexual and homicidal spree was committed by "Jack" or "John." He said he wanted his younger sister brought to the police station.

Investigators, meanwhile, had obtained their third and fourth search warrants of the investigation and talked a second time with Czarna, as well as to other associates of the suspect. Detectives were looking with growing suspicion at the driveway. Czarna uneasily conceded pouring concrete early in the day after the job was set up, and he told detectives of Gacy's last-minute change of mind and the overnight shuffling of the forms.

Authorities disclosed that the naked body of the bearded young man found in a marina on the Des Plaines

River south of Joliet the previous month had been identified through fingerprints as that of Frank Wayne "Dale" Landingin. Items found in the house on Summerdale Avenue indicated a link to Gacy. Wallets, driver's licenses, and other articles found in the house led police to conclude that Gacy kept souvenirs of his victims.

On December 23, Gacy spent the night under heavy guard in the lockup at the Des Plaines Police Headquarters. He dropped off to sleep at about 11 P.M., after asking officers to turn down the volume on their two-way communication radios because the noise was disturbing him.

The next day he was transferred to Cermak Memorial Hospital at the Cook County jail. Police spokesmen cited his heart condition as the reason for the move, which was accomplished by a troop of armed guards and without prior publicity. Authorities later conceded that they had planned the transfer with maximum attention to security to ensure the safety of the prisoner. No one, observed one policeman, wanted another Lee Harvey Oswald.

On December 20, the highest criminal appeals court in the state of Texas cited a technicality in overturning the murder conviction of Elmer Wayne Henley, Jr. The decision erased sentences he was serving in the three-year-long Houston homosexual sex-and-torture spree that led to the deaths of twenty-seven boys. The Texas Court of Criminal Appeals said it was forced to overturn the conviction because San Antonio State District Judge Preston H. Dial had refused a change of venue, even though there were strong indications the jury had been influenced by pretrial publicity. Henley was expected to be retried in the case, which drew tremendous international publicity as the most extensive instance of mass murder in the history of the United States at that time. The court ruling was announced the day before the first body was found at the death house on Summerdale Avenue.[3]

In California, the previous May, a new trial was also

---

[3]In June 1979 Henley was convicted for a second time of six murders in the series of homosexual torture slayings in Houston. The jury recommended six concurrent life terms.

ordered for Juan Corona, who had been convicted in 1971 of murdering twenty-five itinerant farm workers in the Yuba City area. The murders attributed to Corona, who, like Gacy, was troubled by a heart ailment, also had homosexual overtones, and the bodies of some of the victims were found with their genitals exposed. The California Court of Appeal referred to attorney Richard Hawk's handling of Corona's defense as "a farce and a mockery" in wiping out twenty-five consecutive life terms in prison for the former day-labor contractor.

9

Death House

Charlie Hill almost ran off the road when he heard on his car radio that several bodies had been found buried under John Gacy's house.

"But I felt it was true when he said he could lead police to more bodies," Hill recalled. "Knowing John, he would know how many there were and he would like the feeling of being Number One."

One of the first thoughts Gacy's first wife had when she heard about her former husband's latest entanglement with the law was about how she was going to tell the children.

Former Black Hawk County Prosecutor, David Dutton, was outraged when he heard about the murders on the Chicago outskirts. "When we had him, I felt that the best thing was to keep this man locked up," he said.

The three men who had approved Gacy's parole from prison in Iowa in 1970 were dismayed. George Paul said the occurrences at the house near Chicago were "a slaughter." The Board might not have discharged Gacy from supervised parole had members known of the disorderly conduct arrest eight months after his release from prison, Paul said. "That certainly was an error or carelessness on the part of the officials who are supposed to keep those records. We probably would have done some things differently if we had had that information."[1]

[1]Associated Press, January 12, 1979.

In Chicago, the woman who was Gacy's second wife cried.

Robert Martwick returned home from vacation a few hours after police began carrying bodies out of Gacy's house. "At no time did he indicate he was a Dr. Jekyll–Mr. Hyde or a homosexual," Martwick said. "When I read the first story about him in the newspapers, I almost collapsed."[2]

Donald Czarna snapped awake from an exhausted sleep at 3 A.M. He was sweating. Leaning over, he shook his wife awake. "Lydia," he said, "John buried a gun." Even though he was specifically asked by lawmen if his friend owned a gun, he had forgotten. It had been three years since Gacy told him of burying a gun in the rear stoop. Later that morning, Czarna telephoned the sheriff's department.

Martin Zielinski was having uncomfortable thoughts about his own mortality. He couldn't understand why he had been spared.

Early Friday morning firemen and workers from the Cook County Highway Department began cutting up the floor of Gacy's office and ripping it out with sledgehammers and crowbars to provide easier access to the crawl space. As they worked, their activity was filmed on videotape and sound recordings of the voices of evidence technicians were made for possible trial use. The camera filmed technicians as they removed bodies and painted numbers and other marks on the concrete sides of the foundation to pinpoint each burial spot.

Crowds gathered outside, drawing their shoulders up against the late December chill and staring in fascinated horror as the sound of hammering and the shrill scream of power saws reverberated inside the house. The firemen divided the floor into sections, ripping out segments so that other members of the search team could reach into the crawl space with small trenching shovels and begin sifting through the dirt.

As soon as the shovels touched bone, workmen laid

[2]"Kup's Column," *Chicago Sun-Times,* December 27, 1979.

the tools aside. Then they dug with their gloved fingers until they had removed skulls, pelvises, rib cages, and what Stein refers to as "the long bones"—or the major bones of the legs and arms. "It's like panning for gold," explained one weary technician. "You sift until you hit something hard, like a bone or a belt buckle." Water seeped into the ditches, complicating the sensitive work. Pumps were brought in but the water was not deep enough to be drawn out.

Nevertheless, two bodies were removed from the property the first day, including remains lifted from the gravesite in the garage previously marked by Gacy with spray paint. That body was encased in concrete, and methane gas from the decomposing tissue was so strong that Stein had to order a break in the work. None of the lawmen wore masks and the gas made everyone lightheaded and nauseous.

The other body was lifted from the crawl space after it was found wrapped in a plastic sheet and covered with dirt and lime. Lime hastens decomposition. Sheriff Richard J. Elrod told assembled newsmen that the remains appeared to be those of young males, and conjectured that as many as twenty bodies might be found before the investigation was closed.

Before excavation efforts could resume in earnest, a professional moving company carried furniture and personal belongings from the house and garage, transporting it in two forty-foot truck trailers to a southside Chicago warehouse. Stereo equipment, television sets, game machines, the built-in bar, clown art, a refrigerator, and three large food freezers were among the possessions removed from the house. Carpeting from the bedroom, set aside with other items for closer scrutiny when time permitted, was found to be bloodstained when it was examined a week later. The top surface had been cleaned but stains were found on the bottom and on the padding.

Stein's mind stiffened in ghastly apprehension when he first saw the lineup of food freezers. In 1957, authorities in south central Wisconsin had arrested Edward Gein, who was known to pass out chunks of fresh venison to his neighbors. It was learned that the mild-mannered semi-recluse had been robbing graves and finally murdered and butchered two women. He ate some of the flesh himself and distributed additional meat to neighbors.

The Cook County Medical Examiner breathed a sigh of relief after he had examined the meat in the freezers and determined that it was not human remains. Pictures hung throughout the house had also worried him. Most were of heads and he pondered a possible link with several investigations he had underway involving decapitated bodies. Then he learned that Gacy was a clown aficionado and realized that the suspect's interest in clowning was responsible for the many pictures of clown heads and faces in the home.

Boxes full of records were carried into the den of the seven-room house from the former living room, which Gacy had converted into an office. A guard was posted until lawmen could inspect the papers for clues to the identity of some of the bodies. Included in the mix were documents relating to Gacy's contracting business, campaign material from Democratic candidates, pornography, and cards with telephone numbers. Two color photographs of "Snags" Sipusich, nude and unconscious, were among the haul.

Even more intriguing to investigators were the photographs of Gacy with Mrs. Carter and with Mayor Bilandic found among the suspect's political mementos. When the news media learned of the pictures there was an immediate outcry with accusatory fingers pointed at the Secret Service and criticism of slipshod work in exposing the President's wife to danger from a convicted felon.

Others, when they became aware of the photograph, merely shook their heads, and marveled at the First Lady's talent for becoming linked with two men who appeared to be among the most heinous alleged mass murderers of the century. Only a few weeks before, her name had been tied to the Reverend Jim Jones, architect of the Jonestown massacre in Guyana. She had both dined with him and mailed him a friendly note.

A spokesman for the Secret Service at first announced that Gacy's criminal record hadn't turned up despite a check with Chicago police prior to Mrs. Carter's visit. The next day the statement was amended to say the Secret Service was unsure if Chicago police files had been checked.

While police were preparing to scrutinize the records, a former employee tipped them off to watch for evidence of kickbacks to contractors who referred remodeling jobs to PDM. He claimed Gacy padded his bills to finance the payoffs.

In the garage, investigators discovered huge mirrors glued to the ceiling. Rubber sexual devices were found and several prophylactics retrieved from behind the walls and kept for laboratory analysis. The garage and attached shed had been carefully insulated with plywood and drywall.

The exhumation process was conducted with painstaking care. Dr. Stein made it clear during his first public statements that the search team was faced with "camel-hair brush-work. . . . I don't want a hurry-up job to destroy any evidence," he warned. The day after the first bodies were found, he announced that he would seek help from two local medical experts to guide the investigative and exhumation teams collecting human remains, fragments of clothes and other possible evidence in the crawl space and elsewhere on the property.

Professor Charles P. Warren, a forensic anthropologist at the University of Illinois Chicago Circle campus, and Dr. Edward J. Pavlik, a forensic odontologist, were called in on the investigation. Stein explained that Warren would be looking for anything, ranging from strands of hair, teeth, and bone to clothing, jewelry, and other evidence that might turn up during close scrutiny of the death house. Blood type can be determined from hair, fingernails, and sometimes from bone.

Dr. Pavlik, a regular consultant to the Medical Examiner's Office, would work with a handful of other dental specialists and concentrate on dental records and teeth in efforts to identify victims through fillings, caps, and other dental characteristics. Teeth that were not matched with charts would be kept in a chemical solution capable of preserving them for two hundred years in case dental records were eventually located to match them with.

Under the direction of Dr. Stein and the other experts, the search team carefully catalogued each piece of potential evidence, noting the precise location where it was found. For Stein, that was standard procedure.

The son of a civil engineer in Brooklyn, Stein first became interested in legal medicine when he was a senior in high school. His family physician was a pathologist and introduced him to Charles Norris, the first medical examiner for the city of New York. Stein knew immediately that forensic pathology—utilizing medical facts and legal knowledge to determine cause of death—was the career he wanted for himself, even though his father was deeply disappointed that the young man didn't choose to follow engineering, a profession practiced in his family for generations.

But Stein had chosen his career. He was so enthusiastic that, between school terms, he voluntarily washed down the tables at the morgue. He graduated from medical school at the University of Innsbruck, Austria, in 1952, and did his graduate work in pathology. At professional meetings, through correspondence and other means, he developed friendships with other pathologists, including Dr. Lester Mooto of Guyana. Mooto was in charge of the investigation of the mass murders and suicides in Jonestown, and shortly after they occurred, he contacted Stein, who offered his assistance. The Cook County Medical Examiner had no way of knowing then that in a matter of a few weeks, he would be deeply involved in an investigation of a mass murder within his own jurisdiction that would rival the tragedy at Jonestown—if not in numbers, in savagery.

More bodies were carried from the house on Saturday and as the toll mounted, Gacy's ghastly count began to take on shocking credibility. Already sixty years old when he became Cook County's first medical examiner two years earlier, Stein was on the scene every day wearing fireman's boots, disposable coveralls, and gloves, using his fingers to help dig bodies from the foul mud and fetid odors of the crawl space with men thirty years younger than he.

Every so often one or more of the workers would stagger from the house into the fresh, frigid air outside for a brief respite away from the brooding, dark place of death. Removing the bodies from the enclosed spaces posed a tremendous health hazard. Danger from methane, hydrogen sulfide, and other noxious gases released by the decomposing bodies was great. And the protective clothing was mandatory. Even a scratch on the hand could lead to serious infection.

When the search was suspended on December 24 and 25 for the Christmas holidays, an around-the-clock guard was posted to keep the curious away and to preserve evidence.

Gacy had strung colored Christmas lights days before and they winked incongruously from across the front of the grim charnel house throughout the holidays. Lights were strung at most of the houses in the neighborhood and Christmas trees were visible through many of the windows. But the holiday was subdued and bleak. Few could forget or ignore the menacing little brick home in their midst where an unknown number of hideous murders had taken place.

Christmas was also bleak for the family of Johnny Butkovich. Mrs. Butkovich was in the bathroom when her husband cried out to her as he heard a radio report about Gacy's arrest. They had always believed that John Gacy was closely tied to the disappearance of their son, but they had held out hope that the handsome blond boy was somehow still alive. Now, there was nothing to do but wait in despair and fear for the call from police they had always hoped would not come. A few days later, they were notified that their boy's remains had been positively identified after exhumation from Gacy's garage.

The night of Gacy's arrest, someone broke into the Godzik home and stole money, leaving the entire family upset. The next day, Mrs. Godzik was sitting with her twenty-five-year-old daughter, Eugenia, when they heard on the radio that bodies had been found in the Gacy house.

In Des Plaines, Mr. and Mrs. John Szyc were disheartened when they learned that a Maine West High School ring with their son's initials had been found among the souvenirs in Gacy's home. Until that time, they had never permitted themselves to consider that he might have been the victim of violence.

James Mazzara's family became increasingly concerned as the Christmas holiday arrived and passed without word from him. They knew something was terribly wrong, and the uneasiness that his sister Annette had previously felt for him returned as dread.

A frosting of powdery new Christmas snow sparkled like fine crystal under the late December sun, contrasting with the depressed mood of the men who toiled inside when the search resumed. Before the day was over the numbing count of bodies attributed to Gacy had reached six, five taken from the house and garage and one from the river. The scene inside the house was almost indescribable in its horror. "It's like a battlefield," Dr. Stein exclaimed. "People are digging trenches, filling trenches—As they work, their faces have such a look of despair." The bodies were so decomposed, most without any flesh at all, that he realized the job ahead would be as difficult as identifying victims of an air-crash disaster.

Three of the bodies were found so close together that investigators theorized the victims may have been killed, or at least buried, on the same day. The location of two other bodies in a common grave led to similar speculation.

Gacy's map was incredibly accurate. Most of the remains were arranged in long rows lining three of the foundation walls, and others were placed diagonally inside the pattern of bodies and pointed toward the center of the crawl space. They were arranged like the spokes of a wheel. Placement in the makeshift graveyard was obviously "something that was orderly, something well thought out," Stein mused.

Several of the bodies brought from the house were wrapped in black material like tarpaper, similar to that used in roofing or other construction work. Some still had pieces of cloth caught in their mouths and throats. It appeared they had died, as Landingin had, strangled by their own underwear. The bodies were lifted carefully and an effort was made to take a bit of dirt with each one. Nevertheless, some bones snapped off fragile skeletons when they were lifted from their damp graves. One of the bodies in the crawl space was covered by cement.

Ten bodies were removed from the lime-laced tomb on the second day after Christmas and six the next day.

The number of white plastic body bags was building up at the Fishbein Institute of Forensic Medicine where Dr. Stein worked. The dapper physician with the neatly trimmed mustache and gray hair objects when people refer to his office near the Cook County Hospital as "the morgue." The morgue is merely one component of the Institute. And the Medical Examiner is sincere when he insists that his office is for the living, not for the dead. He considers his work to be the labor of a specialist, trained to investigate the causes of death so that the information may be used for the preservation of life.

Nevertheless, it was his job to work with the dead, and after a week of digging in the ghastly ossuary under the Gacy house, nearly thirty body pouches were stacked on metal trays in a frigid room referred to as "Crypt 1" in the Fishbein Institute. A refrigeration unit constantly pumped in cold air, cooling the bodies in the bags and shutting out the stringent odor of chemicals from outside. Numbers were jotted on the bags with black ink, indicating the order in which the corpses were recovered. Separate case numbers were on attached tags.

The men and women who shared Stein's profession as forensic pathologists are members of a small sophisticated profession. There are fewer than three hundred forensic pathologists in the country. They routinely exchange advice and other assistance, conferring often at professional meetings and on other occasions. Early in his investigation of the Gacy case, Stein disclosed plans to confer with the medical examiner and other authorities in Houston to compare notes on the similar instances of mass murder.

Stein wasn't thinking of himself as a member of a select profession when he emerged from Gacy's house on Friday night, December 28. "Gentlemen, I have horrible news," he announced to waiting newsmen. "Six more bodies were exhumed today." He grimly added that there was "some evidence of still other remains in the trenches along the south wall" in an area not yet excavated. The south wall was where Rossi and Cram had dug what they were told were trenches for drainage tile to solve flooding problems. No tile could be immediately observed and the ditches were filled in with soft earth. Both young men reportedly took and passed lie detector tests corroborating their statements.

The medical examiner's announcement brought the number of known dead to twenty-eight, one more than the twenty-seven boys attributed to the homosexual murder ring in Houston more than five years earlier. John Gacy had now been linked to more murders than any other individual in the history of the United States.

Parents across the country as well as in some foreign nations worried about missing sons were aware by that time that their boys might be among the bodies under the modest bungalow in Norwood Park township. Lawmen had realized early in the probe that some of the victims were likely to have been plucked from among the thousands of youthful transients drifting along the highways of America or heading for the action in Chicago and other large cities.

The telephone numbers of Operation Peace of Mind and of the National Runaway Switchboard and its Chicago affiliate, Metro-Help, were disseminated so runaways could notify their relatives that they were alive and not among the murder victims.

Sergeant Howard Anderson was supervisor of the Sheriff's Investigations North unit in Niles, and was coordinating police work in the case. His officers had begun files on fifty missing persons. Inquiries were received from parents or police agencies as distant as London, England, and Sydney, Australia. But most of the descriptions of missing youths had come from other police departments in the United States, in cities such as Pueblo, Colorado; Lincoln, Nebraska; and Whitewater, Wisconsin. A mother from Massillon, Ohio, personally brought complete medical records of her son to Anderson. The boy had been missing two years.

Detectives from the Kenosha County Sheriff's Department in Wisconsin were among the first out-of-town investigators to show up in Des Plaines in hopes of questioning Gacy about an unsolved homicide in their home area.

Carl Gailbraith, the thirteen-year-old victim, had

been found brutally stabbed to death in December 1977, a few miles due west of the city of Kenosha and just north of the Illinois-Wisconsin state line. The 100-pound, five-foot junior high school student and newspaper carrier boy was last seen alive as he walked along Illinois Route 173, a highway leading out of Antioch, Illinois.

An autopsy disclosed that an artery in his neck had been severed and he had bled to death. His neck was mutilated with six deep slashes and there were thirteen stab wounds in his back. He and his sister had been sent from their home in Chicago to live with relatives in Twin Lakes, Wisconsin, because his mother thought they would be safer there.

Detectives became suspicious of a possible tie-in with the Chicago area slayings when they learned that Gacy told detectives he had stabbed his first victim to death, and after further investigation disclosed that the contractor had visited and worked in the Paddock Lake area of Kenosha County. Unfortunately, the Kenosha County detectives were unable to talk with the suspect and left Chicago after trading information and asking local investigators to be alert for Gailbraith's name or for some other clue that might link him to the mass murders.

Police from Sangamon County, Illinois, also asked the Chicago area investigation team to query Gacy about the murder of a thirteen-year-old boy from Riverton. Robert Mann had been missing thirteen days when his body was found on July 24, a few miles east of Springfield in the backwater of the Sangamon River. He was clad only in underwear and identification was made with dental charts. His body was so badly decomposed that it was impossible to determine the cause of death.

Curiosity about a possible tie-in with Gacy was piqued when a map was found in the glove compartment of his car with the names of both Springfield and Riverton circled in red pencil. It was easily understandable why he might have circled Springfield where he worked on various jobs, but it seemed strange that he should have circled the smaller farming community of 2,100.

Near Weeki Wachee, Florida, Hernando County Sheriff's police dug up part of a vacant lot after Cook County authorities notified them that the property was owned by Gacy. Nothing suspicious was turned up by the search.

Authorities checked out other reports in Chicago of suspicious odors and strange cavities in basement floors or walls where Gacy had worked with his young construction crews on the north side, also without turning up additional bodies. The suburban contractor who had sent young men to Gacy for jobs provided a list of their names to police and they were all found to be alive. The nine-year-old prostitute whose disappearance had sparked surveillance of Gacy by police three years earlier was also scratched from the list of potential victims when he was discovered alive in California.

Anderson was disappointed at the lack of response from relatives and theorized that many parents may not have responded because they couldn't imagine their sons involved in a case with homosexual overtones. But many of the victims were snatched off the street, raped, and killed, he pointed out. "The indications are that it could have happened to anyone."

Both Anderson and Stein were asking police agencies and relatives who contacted them to provide dental X-rays, medical records—especially those showing bone injuries, and descriptions of clothing or jewelry the missing boys may have been wearing.

On Thursday, one day prior to Stein's disclosure of twenty-eight known dead, Gacy's legal counsel filed a motion in U.S. District Court to withdraw the civil-rights suit charging the Des Plaines Police Department and others with harassment. Gacy's attorneys had agreed that Stevens, with more experience in civil law, would handle noncriminal matters for Gacy. Amirante, who had been joined by co-counsel Robert Motta, would be responsible for Gacy's defense on all criminal charges.

Chief Deputy State's Attorney William Kunkle and Assistant State's Attorneys Robert R. Egan and Terry Sullivan, were designated as the team that would oppose Amirante and Motta. Months later, Carey announced that he had decided to head the prosecution team, unless the trial extended into the fall of 1980 when he expected to be campaigning for re-election.

At the house, hundreds of people continued gathering to watch the grisly parade of victims carried from the crawl space in limp body bags. Some families piled out of their cars and lined children up in the street to shoot photographs with the house in the background.

Township workers drove stakes and strung cord around Gacy's property and the property of his two immediate neighbors to keep the crowd away. The street was barricaded and additional sawhorses were loaned to other residents on the block to put across their driveways, but still the throng came, drawn by a mixture of horror and macabre curiosity.

Scores of people crowded in front of the house, staring at television camera crews and watching for signs of new activity. A solidly built woman wearing a bowling shirt with "The Maulers" emblazoned across her ample chest watched with a friend as four officers lugged a body bag to a waiting police van. The house and property should be exorcised, she muttered. "You gotta throw some salt on it and say some words to get the spirits out. My grandmother used to do that in Europe."

Her companion touched a crucifix held by a tiny gold chain around her neck and crossed herself, whispering a silent prayer.

"If Satan's among us," said an old man shaking a cane at the house, "that's where he lived."

One day a group of people climbed over ropes and stood in the Grexa yard cursing and screaming out their hate. "You live next door," one of them yelled. "You had to know what was going on."

A few days later, Gacy was indicted on seven counts by a Cook County Grand Jury in the suspected kidnapping, sexual molestation, and death of Robert Piest. The indictment charged Gacy with murdering the boy while committing the additional felonies of aggravated kidnap, deviate sexual assault, and taking indecent liberties with a child.

Curiously, with six bodies of those recovered already identified, Gacy had been charged in the death of a boy whose body had not been found.

Despite the pathetic proof of so many of Gacy's statements, weary law enforcement officers were beginning to have doubts about the credibility of his claims that he dropped Robert's body into the river.

Dragging, diving, and visual surface searches of miles of the Des Plaines River near Morris by boat and by helicopter had failed to turn up any trace of the boy's body, and suspicions were growing that he might have been buried. How else could police explain the mud that caked Gacy's clothes when he first walked into the Des Plaines Police Headquarters for questioning? A large amount of mud was also later found on his car. Yet, when lawmen checked the snowbank his car was pulled from there was no mud visible.

The nearly five hours between the time he was first interviewed in his home and the time he finally reported for questioning was much more time than he would have needed to drive to the bridge. It would have been time enough to go to a forest preserve, dig a hole, and bury the body.

Lawmen were also aware that stopping a car on a narrow, heavily traveled bridge is difficult, especially when there has been a heavy snow. And the high safety guardrails would pose additional problems in lifting a body to roll it over the side and into the river.

The river search continued but the probe also moved to open spots and areas in the forest preserves surrounding Chicago. Forest sites close to parking areas with the type of mud that had soiled Gacy's clothing and car drew special attention. Some officers made nocturnal visits to areas of the forest that were popular as lovers' lanes, seeking someone who might have seen a body being removed from a car or buried.

The Piests had asked a New Jersey psychic for help in locating the body of their son. Dorothy Allison, who works with psychometry—touching people's belongings to tune in on their vibrations—was recommended to the family by a Des Plaines policeman because she had been helpful in other police cases. She worked nearly two weeks but was unable to pinpoint the location of the boy's body. After handling his jacket, she developed hives and had to return home.

A Kenosha woman told her local newspaper of having met Gacy with Robert the previous summer when she was working as a waitress in a Des Plaines snack shop. But others discounted her story, insisting that Robert had never met Gacy prior to the day of his disappearance.

Chicago police, meanwhile, were interviewing associates and friends of Gacy's and visiting north-side Chicago bars frequented by homosexuals to put together a file on his life and activities in preparation for his anticipated trial. A list of some twenty straight and homosexual bars was found in his house. Two agents with the Illinois Department of Law Enforcement traveled to Waterloo to compile additional behavioral information.

Other officers put together a list of names of missing Chicago area youths to assist in the investigation. The names of Gregory Godzik and John Szyc were prominent on the list.

On New Year's Day, the Medical Examiner's office confirmed that positive identification had been made on the remains of Godzik, Szyc, and Rick Johnston.

One other name had been added, James "Mojo" Mazzara. On December 28, the nude body of another young man had been pulled from the Des Plaines River near the spot where Landingin was found a month earlier. Like Landingin, the victim's underwear was jammed into his throat. He was identified two days later by his fingerprints, and Assistant State's Attorney Sullivan said it was believed the death could be "definitely" linked to Gacy. Gacy had told lawmen that one of the bodies he disposed of in the river was that of a youth nicknamed "Mojo." The recovery of Mazzara's body and his identification brought the number of known victims of the murder orgy to twenty-nine, not counting the presumed death of Robert Piest. Will County Coroner Robert Tezak determined that the slight young man had died of suffocation.

With the identification of Butkovich, Godzik, Szyc, and Johnston, Stein had amazingly exhausted all the available medical and dental charts he had on missing boys.

Even though most of the remains were no more than bones, Stein and members of his staff had rapidly determined that none of the victims were females. And apparently none of them were Negroes. Gacy apparently liked slender young boys with light hair. In determining the race of the victims, pathologists paid close attention to the mouth structure. The roof of the mouth in Caucasians is more angular than that of Negroes, who have more of a horseshoe configuration and lower jaws that protrude more. The orbit of the eyes also differs according to race, with a squarish orbit for Caucasians, oval for Negroes, and circular for Orientals. There are other differences, too, such as the nose cavity in the skulls, which is wider for blacks than for whites.

The femurs, or thigh bones, were measured to determine the height of the victims, and the approximate ages were worked out by measuring the fusion plates of the long bones. The fusion plates are the site of rapid growth in the body. Stein had perfect skeletons to work with. There were no dismemberments or damage to the skulls. A few of the bodies were found with bits of clothing or cloth, some with a shoe or other item which could also possibly help in identification.

Yet, from the beginning, Stein made no promises that all the victims would be identified. Most of the bodies he had to work with were skeletons or bones only, so there could be no tattoos, scars, or fingerprints to aid his efforts. Most juveniles do not have their fingerprints on file anyway. And, of course, there was the additional problem of too few dental charts. It was conceded that the task of identification could take years.

Five years after the discovery of the horror in Houston, only twenty-one of the twenty-seven victims there had been identified. But Dr. Joseph Jachimczyk, the Medical Examiner who headed the forensic team, told newsmen that he believed the identification of all the bodies would eventually be achieved.

On January 4, some three hundred residents of the neighborhood, relatives of victims and clergymen, struggled through the snow-clogged streets and bitter cold to attend an interfaith memorial service at the St. Eugene Catholic Church a few blocks from the house where the lives of so many young men had been abruptly and violently snuffed out. People of the neighborhood were stunned by the horror in their midst. They could not understand how one man who had lived among them as a popular and trusted neighbor and friend could have committed crimes so atrocious as those of which he was accused.

Residents had been living like hermits, as if they felt a common shame merely for having shared the same street with the accused killer. Residents of the 1800 block of Summerdale Avenue couldn't even drive on their own street unless they could prove they lived there. Gawkers were parking on their lawns, blocking their driveways and keeping them imprisoned in their own homes. They were hemmed in by the disregard for privacy and property and the ghoulish disrespect of the morbidly curious. The whole affair had turned into a grueling and macabre carnival.

One resident recalled the night when television trucks were outside with floodlights illuminating the area and Sheriff's officers carried a body outside. Someone on one of the television trucks yelled, "Go back. We're not ready yet." The Sheriff's men carried the body back into the house and a few minutes later brought it out again.

The people gathered in the dimly lit church to ask how the horror unfolding before them could have happened to their neighborhood—and to their sons. They met to pray, to ask for healing, and to somehow exorcise the outrage and the shame.

Mrs. Eugenia Godzik was there, as were the Reverend Francis Buck of our Lady of Hope Parish in Rosemont, and Kenneth and Kerry Piest, the pastor, brother, and sister of the boy whose apparent abduction and murder had led to Gacy's arrest. Lillie Grexa was there, also.

Many of those present were parishioners of St. Eugene's and knew its pastor, Father Frank Shaunessy, as a personal friend. Women sobbed and men listened somberly, some allowing tears to trickle down wind-chafed cheeks, as Fathers Shaunessy and Buck and four other clergymen from area churches read prayers and led hymns.

Toward the end of the service Lillie Grexa stood and in a quivering voice, on the point of tears, moaned, "God forgive me. I take back every good thing I ever said about

John Gacy. I just feel so bad for the parents of all these children."

In Chicago, spokesmen for the homosexual community were also denouncing Gacy. At a press conference called at a Michigan Avenue hotel, spokesmen for the Illinois Gay Rights Task Force said the homosexual community was outraged by the murders. Concomitantly, they cautioned that there should be no "witch hunts" against homosexuals in the name of crime prevention.

The day before the memorial gathering at St. Eugene's, investigators had their first talk in more than a week with the man blamed for the mass murders. In two separate sessions at the Cook County Jail's Cermak Memorial Hospital, Gacy assured lawmen that the twenty-seven bodies already unearthed from his property were all there were. He also identified a seventh victim by picking the boy's picture from a *Gay Life* magazine, but the youth's name was not immediately disclosed by authorities. Prior to talking with police, Gacy huddled in a lengthy private conference with his lawyer and was advised of his right to remain silent. But he chose to talk, and Amirante was present during the questioning.

Investigators conceded that they were "fairly well convinced" that Gacy was telling the truth, but determined to continue the search as a precautionary measure.

A couple of days later, it was disclosed that four more victims had been identified, bringing the number of dead whose names were known to ten. At the Fishbein Institute, thirty-one sets of dental records supplied by families of missing young men and boys had been compared with teeth.

The newly identified victims were named as Robert Gilroy, Jon Prestidge, Michael Bonnin, and Russell Nelson. Nelson and Prestidge were the first to come from outside the Chicago area.

On January 8, the Cook County Grand Jury returned the second set of indictments against Gacy, accusing him of murdering seven young men. State's Attorney Carey announced, incidentally, that he would seek the death penalty when the suspect came to trial. He added that he would oppose any effort by defense attorneys to move the proceedings elsewhere because he was sure that Gacy could receive a fair trial in Cook County despite the widespread publicity the case had attracted.

The indictments charged Gacy with two counts of murder in each of the deaths of Butkovich, Godzik, Szyc, Johnston, Landingin, and Mazzara. The indictments contended that Gacy acted intentionally and was aware that his acts could result in murder. The remaining indictments accused him of the same two counts of murder in the slaying of Piest, as well as the additional charges of murder in the commission of a felony previously cited.

According to Illinois law, murder during the commission of another felony is a capital offense. Thus conviction on any one of the murder charges relating to Piest that were connected with second felonies, such as deviate sexual assault, could merit the death penalty.

Illinois statutes additionally provide death by electrocution for conviction of multiple murders occurring after February 1, 1978, when Governor James Thompson signed legislation creating a new capital-punishment law. Landingin, Mazzara, and Piest all vanished months after the law was signed.

According to the law, however, even after a murder conviction, the death penalty cannot be invoked until another trial is held to determine if the statute has been satisfied. Either the original jury or a new one can sit during the proceeding.

It was disclosed for the first time that three sheets of paper on which Gacy apparently wrote the first names of victims were being held as key bits of evidence. Gacy was reportedly given writing paper while he was in his cell and among the things he wrote were several first names of males followed by the names of various cities and towns. The information was considered useful both in developing the criminal case against Gacy and in learning additional identities of victims.

Another piece of written material provided by Gacy that had already been useful and was being looked on as valuable evidence was the diagram he drew to pinpoint the locations of bodies on his property.

Severely cold weather and back-to-back blizzards

that struck the Midwest, one dumping more than twenty inches of snow on the Chicago area, had hampered digging and caused equipment breakdowns. As investigators became increasingly convinced that all the bodies had been recovered from the crawl space, the work also became less tedious.

A seven-man crew of county highway department employees was helping with the excavation work. As dirt was dug out, it was tossed into a conveyor and sifted. When a sliver of bone, a clot of hair, or piece of clothing showed up, the machine was shut down and digging with the fingers was resumed.

The inside of the main house was gutted. The floorboards were gone and planks were laid over the joists with rope handrails to use for walking from the front door to the rear. The recreation room, which had been added at the rear of the house after the initial construction, did not extend over the crawl space and it was preserved from the wrecking crews until the last so they would have a place to sit and eat lunches that were brought in during the search. A couple of bar chairs and a folding chair were left for the workmen and police who continued to maintain their round-the-clock vigil.

On January 27, the bodies of John Mowery and Matthew Bowman were identified through dental records supplied by their families. Mowery's brother, Robert, said John had never worked for Gacy but he frequented the north side and may have been "in the wrong place at the wrong time."

After a mid-January break in the search caused by the bad weather, investigators prepared to seek extension of the search warrants and resume their probe of Gacy's property. Attention would be shifted from the crawl spaces, and plans were underway to rip up the rest of the garage and shed, the patio, including the barbecue pit, the driveway and front yard.

The defense opposed the extension and charged at the hearing that the warrants did not show probable cause of wrongdoing. Motta added that the house had already been gutted and said it was obvious that there were no additional bodies on the premises.

Egan responded that the warrants were valid, pointing out that twenty-seven bodies were eventually exhumed from the property. The appeal to permit immediate resumption of the search was rejected and a February hearing was scheduled on the defense motion to quash the warrants. The search couldn't continue anyway until crews had a chance to remove snow that had accumulated on the property during the past month.

Permission to resume the search was granted on February 21 as the motion to quash the existing warrants was dismissed. County Highway Department employees broke up the concrete stoop and uncovered the gun Czarna had told police about. The rusted .38-caliber revolver was sent to the Chicago Police Crime Laboratory for closer examination and ballistics tests. The owner had gone to obvious pains to conceal the weapon, and it would be checked to determine if it had been used in another crime. Additional skeleton fragments were also recovered from the garage in the same area where Butkovich's body was previously exhumed.

A workman was breaking up the patio a few days later when he peeled off the top layer of frozen earth with a giant bucket scoop at the end of a machine similar to a backhoe and was enveloped by a putrid odor. Ignoring the sudden nausea that rose in his throat, he yelled to his supervisor, "Bill, we've got another one." A few moments later the yard was full of investigators, looking down at the grave of the first corpse discovered on the property in ten weeks.

One of the workmen later admitted that they might have dug right through the body and accidently destroyed it if the frost hadn't been so deep. Faced with a combination of concrete reinforced with chicken wire, blacktop, and frost-hardened earth, they were peeling it away in layers instead of digging straight down.

The skeletal remains were wrapped in three garbage bags and had been preserved in remarkably good condition in their concrete burial crypt. Unlike the bodies previously recovered, the cadaver appeared to be that of an adult male, six feet tall or more. The shredded remains of blue jeans and shorts were still on the body. It had reposed under electric lines leading from the house to the garage.

Even more intriguing to investigators anxious to learn his identification was a small chain around his neck and a wedding band on the ring finger of his left hand. The presence of the ring meant that the scope of the investigation would, for the first time, be broadened to include missing men who were married.

The discovery prompted gloomy speculation that the toll might continue to climb, and investigators prepared to seek court permission for another meeting with Gacy to explore the possibility that there were still more bodies. But discovery also provided timely vindication for the argument authorities had pressed while seeking approval from the court to continue their search.

Exactly one week after discovery of the twenty-eighth victim on the property, still another body was removed.

It was announced almost simultaneously that the body found in the Illinois River near Morris the previous June had been identified as Timothy O'Rourke. Identification was made after a friend of O'Rourke's father had seen a newspaper story and recognized the description of the young man with the "Tim Lee" tattoo. The youth's father, Terrance O'Rourke, later explained that his son was an admirer of Bruce Lee and borrowed the Kung Fu champion's last name for the tattoo. Friends of the twenty-year-old murder victim said he frequented some of the same gay bars as Gacy.

The Des Plaines River flows into the Illinois River just west of where the bodies of Landingin and Mazzara were recovered. O'Rourke's body was apparently carried into the Illinois by the current. He had not been reported missing.

With the latest two bodies exhumed from Gacy's property and the three youths pulled from the water, the toll of dead attributed to the suburban contractor now stood at thirty-two, and the bodies of Piest and possibly one other victim were still thought to be in the Des Plaines or Illinois Rivers.

The latest victim discovered on Gacy's property was exhumed from under the recreation room. The body had lain directly below the large table where workmen ate their lunches and Sheriff's deputies read paperback books during all-night watches at the house. It was located when workmen probed in the soft dirt and uncovered a hip bone after ripping off a portion of the flooring. The skeleton was dry and fragile because the heat ducts had been installed on top of it after burial. Another driver's license and additional identification were found when a cabinet was ripped apart.

Despite the most recent discovery of bodies on the premises, the right of authorities to continue demolition of the house and property was soon challenged again.

That occurred after State's Attorney Carey filed a civil suit in Circuit Court for permission to tear down the remaining shell of Gacy's house. The State's Attorney contended that the house was "unoccupied, unsafe, dangerous, and hazardous," adding that further excavations were needed in the east and west sections.

Working in the house was dangerous because floor joists had been cut and removed, plumbing and sewage drainage were gone and four-to-six-foot holes had destroyed "the integrity" of partition footings. The county was prepared to bear the cost of demolition. Wiring was open and exposed and the crawl spaces, dug to the depth of four feet, were flooded and posing danger of fire or electrocution.

Charging that the home was a public nuisance, the suit was filed against Gacy as one-half owner, and against his mother, Marion E. Gacy, and his two sisters, Karen Kusma and Joanne E. Casper, as owners of the other half. A Chicago bank continued to hold a mortgage for several thousand dollars on the property.

Before action on the petition could be concluded, Dr. Stein released the identity of another of the victims. Billy Carroll was identified through his dental charts. He had been to the dentist once in his life and had two small fillings.

Representing the interests of Gacy's mother and sisters LeRoy Stevens threatened a damage suit if authorities went ahead with their plan to demolish the house. But a real-estate appraiser testified at the hearing that the house was a magnet for sightseers, it no longer had any worth, and it was lowering neighborhood property values. Three other expert witnesses told the court that after three months of digging under the house for bodies, the structure was dangerously unstable.

Gacy requested to attend the hearing, and it was transferred from the City Civic Center to Criminal Court because authorities believed that otherwise they could not guarantee his safety. Although he had appeared uninterested during hearings on the murder charges against him, he showed keen interest in the testimony concerning his home, frequently turning to ask questions of his lawyer.

But at the conclusion of the hearing, Housing Court Judge Richard E. Jorzak issued an order approving demolition—almost two months after permission was initially sought. In early April, the Illinois Supreme Court refused to reverse Judge Jorzak's order and within an hour the walls and roof of the house were being tumbled down. In barely a week's time, the once cozy ranch house was reduced to splinters and hauled away. A few bricks were handed out to children and adults who asked for souvenirs. Then nothing remained but an uneven plain of black dirt and ocher clay.

10 . . .

John and Jack

The day before Gacy's scheduled arraignment in Third District Circuit Court on December 29, Des Plaines police officials huddled for hours planning security for the suspect.

Thirty-five off-duty policemen were called in, many on overtime pay, to beef up the protective umbrella spread over the city's Civic Center and court complex, before Chief Alfano was satisfied that they were fully prepared.

Although the press had been told that the hearing was scheduled for 9:30 A.M., authorities in Des Plaines were privately advised that Gacy would be taken from his room at Cermak Hospital at about ten o'clock and would arrive with a heavy police escort at the Civic Center about an hour later.

By seven thirty, uniformed officers and plainclothesmen were scattered around the Civic Center, stationed at doorways with two-way radios and peering from the roofs and windowed offices of surrounding buildings. As Judge John L. White began his regular court call at nine thirty, extra bailiffs joined full-time employees using metal detectors to screen people entering the courtrooms.

But by ten thirty, despite all the security and the obvious care taken to ensure the safety of the defendant, newspeople and others who had crowded into the courtroom were exchanging whispered rumors that Gacy wouldn't show up for the hearing.

At eleven o'clock, Chief Alfano was officially notified that Gacy would not be leaving his room at Cermak Hospital. A half hour later Judge White announced that "Mr. Gacy will not appear in this courtroom because of fears for his safety."

"You don't know what could transpire over there," Judge Fitzgerald later explained, pointing out that he made the decision for security reasons. "The community is inflamed. But even more, it's the kooks who would feel that they were doing a service by blowing his head off."[1] No threats were made on Gacy's life, but Des Plaines police received religious pamphlets and letters for him in the mail from "God," as well as a note suggesting that spaceships should quit dropping people like him off on earth.

Amirante was astonished at the last-minute development, and vigorously protested continuing the hearing without his client. He complained to Judge White that Gacy had "the right to be in court." The attorney also took exception because he wasn't notified of the plans in advance and warned that he would protest to Judge Fitzgerald. But the chief judge had already determined that the hearing and consideration of motions could take place without the suspect's presence.

When the hearing finally got underway, the judge granted Amirante's petition for an order to have Gacy given a psychiatric examination to determine if the defendant was mentally capable of understanding the charges against him and of assisting in his own defense. The Cook County Psychiatric Institute was designated to conduct the examination, but White also agreed that a private psychiatrist could be selected by Amirante to make a similar study.

The judge additionally issued a gag order forbidding witnesses and public officials, including policemen, from making statements that might prejudice Gacy's right to a fair trial. Amirante complained that such massive publicity had already been disseminated on the case that it would be impossible for his client to obtain a fair trial anywhere in the country.

[1]*Chicago Sun-Times,* December 30, 1978.

A plea for dismissal of the murder charges filed in the Piest case, on the grounds that no body had been found, was continued. Members of the boy's family were watching from seats near the front of the court and when Amirante asked for dismissal, Harold Piest reached over and placed his hand comfortingly on that of his wife. After the hearing the family was escorted from the room by police officers, shielding them from reporters.

Amirante was still ruffled as he walked from the courtroom and he grumbled that it was a tragedy that this man (Gacy) could not be in court today to face the charges against him. He should have been there.

Amirante wasn't alone in his disappointment. The city of Des Plaines had spent considerable money and effort to ensure the safety of the suspect during a court appearance. To some the incident appeared to be just one more instance of Chicago politicians pushing their weight around.

The local weekly newspaper, the *Des Plaines Times,* wrote in an editorial that "Behind the scenes . . . there was talk the decision was based on the desire of downtown judges to get the arraignment and resultant publicity, rather than giving it to a suburban judge."[2] The editorial added bitterly that the State's Attorney's office had effectively left the Des Plaines Police Department out of the continuing investigation and prosecution effort.

Resentment in the community had been simmering. Residents of Des Plaines were rightfully proud of their police department and of the fine investigative work that had broken open a case that its much larger and presumably more sophisticated and better trained brother organization in Chicago had bungled, despite several encounters with the suspect. Lieutenant Kozenczak, in particular, had distinguished himself. But other members of the department had also exhibited the highest degree of proficiency in their police work, pursuing the case with relentless determination and detailed investigative methods.

Now, suddenly, it seemed to some residents of the suburb that after all their hard work, the investigators

---

[2]*Des Plaines Times,* January 11, 1979.

responsible for breaking the case were being crowded out by larger agencies anxious for the positive publicity.

When Judge Fitzgerald ruled against Gacy's appearance, partly because of the enormous security problems that would have been involved transporting him the twenty miles to Des Plaines, he also announced that the case was being moved to the Criminal Courts Building adjacent to the county jail. Tighter security could be provided for the suspect's court appearances there.

Amirante was also having problems relating to his decision to defend Gacy. First he began receiving abusive and threatening telephone calls at his home. Then he came under mild criticism in the media for representing Gacy while still a member of the Cook County Public Defender's Office. According to court-imposed guidelines, public defenders were allowed no outside work whatsoever. Amirante defended himself, explaining that he tried to contact his boss to quit his job the night he began representing Gacy. He said he couldn't get in touch with his office chief that night, however, and resigned the next morning. Spokesmen for the public defender's office indicated they were satisfied with Amirante's behavior in the affair.

Dr. Stein also found himself in the middle of a brouhaha when he ventured into sensitive areas during taping of a program scheduled for later airing on Chicago radio station WMAQ. Responding to a question about the murders, the medical examiner remarked that ". . . a sane person could have done this and could go to the (electric) chair." When excerpts of the interview were published, the comments brought an immediate outcry from Gacy's defense lawyers, and they filed for an injunction to block the broadcast. Motta complained that "sanity may be an integral part" of the trial.

The attorneys were especially incensed because the gag order had just been issued. Sheriff Elrod had met with Cook County Corrections Director Philip Hardiman and worked out guidelines for jail and hospital employees to protect Gacy from disclosures that could prejudice his case, and there was some indication that public interest was beginning to wane.

A circuit court judge rejected the injunction suit two

days before the scheduled broadcast. The program was aired Sunday night after considerable free publicity.

Gacy's defense had experienced other unwelcome publicity. Just prior to Judge White's order limiting conversations with the press, the *Chicago Tribune* published a front-page picture of Gacy in the psychiatric ward of Cermak Hospital with his arms spread and strapped to the sides of the bed by leather restraints. A sheriff's deputy was subsequently accused of smuggling the photograph from the jail complex and was fired.

Newspapers reported that Gacy was secured to his bed, except for brief exercise periods under the watchful eyes of guards, after bungling a suicide attempt. Anonymous sources were quoted as saying he crawled under his bed and wrapped a towel around his throat in an effort to strangle himself. Hardiman claimed Gacy merely fell off his bed, and said the incident wasn't classed as a suicide attempt. He refused to confirm or deny the report that Gacy was not strapped into the restraints until after the reputed tumble.

Gacy's behavior and experiences while in custody contributed to the publicity glut that continued regardless of the judge's order. Newspapers first announced that Gacy had written two notes, one to his mother and another intended for a pair of Chicago newsmen, *Chicago Sun-Times* columnist Mike Royko and television commentator Walter Jacobson.

It was reported that he wrote to his mother that he had been sick for a long time, both physically and mentally, and that if he died he wanted to be buried next to his Uncle Ray. He also reputedly listed locations where he had picked up youths. Hardiman conceded that letters were written, but he refused to confirm any other information.

Even though he was housed in an isolation ward at Cermak Hospital where he was shut off from the regular jail population, Gacy acquired the distinction of becoming the first inmate to have a twenty-four-hour guard. Hardiman conceded that not even Richard Speck was watched so closely.

As he did at Anamosa, Gacy appeared to adjust easily to his new circumstances as a prisoner. His guards addressed him as "Inmate Gacy," and he referred to them in turn as "Guard" or "Officer." He was quiet and seemed to be satisfied with his treatment except for once when his room was searched for weapons. He complained that he was being singled out for the shakedown, but quieted down when it was explained that the searches were routine for all prisoners.

Shortly after his arrival at the county jail complex, he began collecting articles about himself from newspapers and magazines, which he filed in a folder. When he wasn't clipping stories he was often playing Scrabble, chess, checkers, and other board games or watching television with two other prisoners who shared the isolation ward with him. They sometimes ate together. Both inmates, whom he befriended, were accused of murdering small boys.

Edward Wierzbicki, a part-time handyman, was being held for the murder of five-year-old Patrick Chavez. The child's naked body was found on June 6, 1978, stuffed into a garbage can behind Wierzbicki's home. Wierzbicki, who was earlier tried for the murder of his grandmother and acquitted, had a record as a child molester and was charged with Patrick's slaying.

Gacy's other prison friendship was with Allen Washington, who was being held for the murder of a three-year-old stepson. Washington had previously served a prison term for killing his twenty-three-month-old daughter when she began crying as he was feeding her. He was accused of beating the little boy to death after the child wet his pants, and dumping the body in a field, then dousing it with gasoline and igniting it.

Gacy was quartered in the hospital section of the jail after complaining of heart problems, but authorities admitted that he was kept there more for his own safety from other inmates than for treatment of illness. Gacy could be in danger from other inmates among the general population of the jail, who might see opportunities to build reputations as tough guys by murdering the celebrity prisoner. But he could also be in serious danger from other inmates who simply hated child molesters. Prisoners traditionally look down on other inmates accused of or convicted of sex crimes, and especially despise those who have sexually abused children.

The hatred for child molesters was never more dramatically displayed than during the Kingston Penitentiary riot in Ontario, Canada, in 1971. A gang of inmates waving clubs stormed into a cellblock where sexual offenders were kept and dragged thirteen of the shrieking men outside during the bloody uprising.

The terrified prisoners were tied to chairs in the center of a circular dome, and while hundreds of other inmates screamed their hatred from the tiers above them, the sex offenders were slashed with knives and beaten to bloody pulps with karate chops, clubs, and iron bars. Two child molesters died.

Brutal treatment of sex offenders by other prisoners, especially if children have been the victims, can be an expression of status. It gives a convict, who might be serving a prison term for car theft or murder, an opportunity to look down on someone considered worse than himself.

Both Albert H. DeSalvo and Juan Corona were stabbed in prison. DeSalvo, better known as the "Boston Strangler," after confessing to a murder orgy that cost the lives of thirteen women and triggered near hysteria in the Boston area in the 1960s, was slain in his infirmary cell at Walpole State Prison. He was stabbed sixteen times, six times in the heart.[3] Corona was stabbed thirty-two times at the California Medical Facility, the prison hospital at Vacaville. He survived the attack but lost his left eye. It was no accident that Gacy shared isolation with two other prisoners charged with crimes against children.

The old jail complex is notorious for its inadequacies and is the target of regular media exposés of its poor conditions. Vicious street gangs like the Black P Stone Nation, the Disciples, and Latin Kings are dominant forces inside the walls and it has been charged that they smuggle contraband, run extortion schemes, and brutalize

[3]DeSalvo later retracted his confession and was sentenced to a life term in prison after being convicted of burglary, robbery and molestation involving four women.

and rape other prisoners almost at will. Guards have been quoted as saying privately there are almost fifty serious assaults daily among the 3,600 prisoners over such things as food, selection of television shows, and sex.

One year thirty-nine inmates escaped from the troubled institution, and in 1977 a U.S. Justice Department Study by top environmental health experts criticized the jail as "unfit for further human habitation." The same year the Cook County Corrections Director was tried on charges of beating prisoners, and fired even though he was found not guilty.

In isolation with his fellow prisoners accused of child murder, Gacy was spared the brutality of living among the general jail population and found renewed interest in religion. He turned to the comfort of his faith, a not uncommon occurrence among men and women in prison. Inmates have time in jail to ponder such things as their own spirituality and they are regularly exposed to clergymen anxious to save souls. A social worker gave Gacy a Bible and a deacon gave him a second one. Not long after that, Gacy told the Catholic chaplain that he was praying, saying the rosary and reading his Bibles every day. He especially liked the Book of Psalms.

In early April he was rushed semiconscious and under heavy armed guard from his jail cell to nearby Cook County Hospital for emergency treatment. He had vomited and complained of stomach and chest pains, all symptoms of heart attack, before being taken to the hospital's intensive care unit shortly before midnight.

He had low blood sugar and had been fasting for Lent. Since February 28, he had refused all food and liquid except orange juice, coffee, and water, losing almost twenty pounds in the process. The medical staff treated him with intravenous doses of glucose, and his physician explained that the fast may have contributed to some of the symptoms of heart attack. After extensive testing, there was no conclusive evidence his illness was related to a heart ailment. (Subsequent trips to the hospital in June and July occurred and it was disclosed that he suffers from a chronic heart condition, angina pectoris.)

The same night in April when Gacy became ill, the Chicago area was raked by a killer windstorm that generated gusts up to sixty miles an hour and caused at least two deaths while inflicting damage throughout the state estimated at $10 million.

Three days later a crane operator spotted a body above the locks at the Dresden Dam in the Illinois River south of Joliet, and notified the lockmaster, Dan Callahan. That night a team from the Cook County Medical Examiner's Office, using dental charts and X-rays, identified the remains of Robert Piest. It had been almost four months since his disappearance. Callahan speculated that the heavy winds had dislodged the body.

An autopsy was performed at the Fishbein Institute and it was determined that death had been caused by suffocation. Paper towels had been jammed down the boy's throat. A few days later nearly four hundred relatives, friends, and newsmen gathered in Rosemont, squinting against the bright sun and talking softly against the intermittant roaring of jet aircraft from nearby Chicago O'Hare. Some filed inside Our Lady of Hope Church for Robert's funeral Mass. In the church, the Reverend Francis Buck expressed his sympathy to the family. "Their sense of loss will remain for some time," the minister reminded the mourners, "but they will know his life and death were not in vain." He suggested that the youth gave his life "to end these senseless killings."

In another move designated to give meaning to the short life of their son and brother, and to the lives of other victims of the mass slayings, the family announced establishment of the Robert J. Piest Foundation to "recognize and support those individuals and organizations or activities committed to helping reduce crime against children." The Piests said family members would work with a board drawing from the professions of psychology, religion, journalism, medicine, law enforcement, and child welfare to select recipients of cash awards. Several donations had already been received in their son's name and others were promised.[4]

The Piests also filed an $85-million damage suit

---

[4]The Robert J. Piest Foundation is administered by the First National Bank of Des Plaines, 701 Lee Street, Des Plaines, Illinois 60018. Account number: 097321-1.

against John Wayne Gacy, Jr., and others, including the Chicago Police Department, the Illinois Department of Corrections, and the Iowa Board of Parole. Negligence was charged on the part of the law enforcement and corrections agencies.

Marko Butkovich had filed suit earlier against Gacy and PDM Contractors, Inc., for $6 million, which he expected the murder suspect to earn through "publication and other reproduction of his narratives of his acts." Gacy is accused in the lawsuit of causing John Butkovich's death.

Rignall, represented by the same attorney as the Butkoviches, was also talking of filing a multimillion-dollar suit, possibly against both Gacy and the Chicago Police Department, arising from the abuse he said he suffered at the suspect's hands.

While funeral arrangements were being made for Robert Piest, police were announcing that the identity of another victim had been established. Randall Reffett was officially listed among the dead after authorities learned he had once been X-rayed at a Chicago hospital for a stab wound. The X-ray showed his jaw and some of his teeth. A microfilm of the X-ray was enlarged and compared with the teeth of unidentified skeletons taken from under the house, to match them with Reffett's.

A few days later Reffett's friend, Sam Dodd Stapleton, was identified as another of the victims. The bracelet permanently welded to his wrist helped in the identification.

Almost a month later, X-rays and dental charts were used to identify William "Shotgun" Kindred. Police had been told that the youth may have been picked up by Gacy near Broadway and Diversey in New Town. Mary Jo Paulus said she began crying when she read about the bodies of the young men being found in Norwood Park township.

"It was like instinct. I figured Billy's got to be under that house, too," she said. "I even called Billy's sister and even told my mother that I felt Billy was under that house."[5]

[5]*Chicago Tribune,* May 22, 1979.

Gacy's fast was over and he was transferred back to the psychiatric unit at Cermak Hospital, where he could be more carefully watched and better protected. The hospital, jail, and Criminal Courts Building were all part of the same dingy complex of adjacent buildings and it was convenient to move Gacy back and forth between his cell and the courtrooms for hearings. Flanked by armed guards, he was moved through a concrete tunnel to his hearings. It was never necessary to take him outside.

The drawn-out process of hearings that had gotten underway in Des Plaines resumed on January 10, before Chief Judge Fitzgerald in the somber Cook County Criminal Courts Building. The handbags, parcels, and persons of everyone entering the old graystone structure were searched by hand and with metal detectors.

Gacy made his first court appearance behind a high protective glass partition, heavily guarded by a half dozen white-shirted sheriff's police. Wearing a chocolate-colored sport-coat, tan slacks, and black shoes, the defendant appeared startled when he peered out at the crowded courtroom, and dropped his head, moving closer to his attorney. Twenty journalists, some busily drawing on sketch pads, had been assigned seats in the jury box. A public address system carried the proceedings into the glassed-off section.

Amirante entered not-guilty pleas for his client on the seven charges then filed in the Piest indictments and began presenting a series of motions. Fitzgerald appeared to ponder them, then remarked that the rulings should come from the judge who would hear the case. Before recessing the court moments later for a lunch break, he announced that the trial judge would be Louis B. Garippo. It was Garippo who, as a young state's attorney, had handled administrative affairs in the Richard Speck case. He was appointed to the bench in 1968 and immediately began distinguishing himself as one of the most respected trial judges, by both defense lawyers and prosecutors, in the criminal courts. Now, years after his work on the Speck case, he had been named to preside over a murder trial that promised to become even more notorious and widely publicized.

The thin, scholary Garippo was on the bench when the hearing resumed after the lunch break. Instead of walking Gacy to Garippo's courtroom as would have been done with most defendants, the judge moved to Fitzgerald's courtroom to begin hearing eleven motions presented by the feisty defense attorney, who was handling his first criminal case in private practice.

Rulings were reserved on most of the motions, including Amirante's effort to force the prosecution to disclose if it would seek the death penalty. Gacy blinked at the reference to the death penalty, in his most obvious display of emotion during the hearing.

The judge took immediate action on two motions—overruling a request that Gacy be released on bond, and repeating the order for a psychiatric examination to determine Gacy's sanity and ability to understand the proceedings and assist in his own defense.

Among the motions taken under advisement was a move by Amirante to quash the indictments on grounds that the search warrants were invalid. During subsequent hearings the motion was denied, and attorneys and the court worked through other pre-trial maneuvering. New indictments were filed on twenty-six new murder counts, bringing the total to thirty-three slayings Gacy was charged with. Amirante entered innocent pleas for his client on each count, and the case moved slowly onward, observed with little obvious emotion by a defendant who had grown a beard and was considerably thinner.

Gacy was becoming lighter in the pocketbook as well, as the costs of shaping his defense were burgeoning. With permission of the court and the prosecution, Amirante announced that some of his client's last personal possessions would be auctioned to raise funds for the defense. Among the items to be sold were the pickup truck, van, and 1979 Oldsmobile. One prospective buyer representing a museum was already said to be talking of offering fifty thousand dollars for the car. Not all the money raised from the sale would go to Gacy, however, because he still owed thousands of dollars on the vehicles.

Amirante filed a $375,000 claim against the county for the demolition of Gacy's house, and that was also being looked on as another possible source of revenue to help defray some of the rapidly mounting legal costs.

The issue of pre-trial publicity promised to continue to play a prominent role in the case. Some of the best-known murder convictions in the country have been reversed because of matters relating to pre-trial publicity. Henley's conviction in the Houston murders is one. Going further back, F. Lee Bailey won reversal of a murder conviction and exoneration in a second trial for Ohio osteopath Dr. Samuel Sheppard in 1966 by arguing that publicity had tainted the first trial. Sheppard was accused of murdering his wife.

Defense assertions that publicity in notorious criminal cases has been so overpowering that it would block fair trials for their clients are not at all uncommon. The claims can be traced to respectable judicial precedent, and extend back much further than the Sheppard case, although that is one of the best known.

In Chicago, State's Attorney Carey pointed out that Cook County has a population of more than five and one half million from which to draw prospective jurors who have not been "tainted" by publicity, to the point where they could not make a fair judgment of Gacy's guilt or innocence after a trial.

Carey, who said he would seek death in the electric chair for Gacy, continued to insist that he would oppose any change of venue to a court outside of Cook County. The State's Attorney also revealed that he planned to try Gacy first for the murder of Robert Piest. It was considered to be the case that would most readily lend itself to the death penalty because Gacy was accused of kidnapping the boy and committing various other felonies, and, as previously stated, murder in the commission of another felony is a capital offense in Illinois. Some of the felonies are related to Robert's age, which made him legally a child. Although some of the other presumed victims were also juveniles, as plans for the prosecution began shaping up, the Piest case was considered to be one of the strongest.

However the state's attorney approached prosecution, he was sure to be faced with a plethora of difficult legal problems. Despite the twenty-nine bodies found on Gacy's property and the four pulled from area waterways, despite other circumstantial evidence, and despite the suspect's admissions to entire groups of police and state's attorneys, prosecutors would nevertheless be faced with serious legal difficulties in gaining a conviction.

If the search warrants were ruled to be invalid because the trial judge or an appeal's court decided that there was not sufficient cause to believe that evidence was located on Gacy's property before they were issued, prosecution for the deaths of the young men found under Gacy's house and garage would be severely crippled. According to the Supreme Court, the prosecution cannot profit from the result of an illegal search warrant.

The confessions appeared almost certain to be challenged. They could be ruled inadmissible as evidence if a court found that Gacy was not previously advised of his legal rights not to talk, if he was not told he had a right to have a lawyer present, if he was found not to have been sane enough to understand his rights at the time of the confession, or if he was coerced into talking.

Many other problems promised to crop up along the way, but they were not all difficulties for the prosecution alone. For example, there could be negative aspects to accepting a change of venue to a more rural area where jurors would be presumably less hardened to crime and less tolerant of homosexual or bisexual behavior than are residents of the Chicago area.

Overshadowing all the legal maneuvering and alternatives, however, were plans by Gacy's attorneys to plead him innocent by reason of insanity. Nearly six months after Gacy's arrest, Amirante filed documents with the court advising that, "The defendant will rely on the state's inability to prove him guilty beyond a reasonable doubt in addition to the affirmative defense of insanity."

According to Illinois law, a person is considered not responsible for a crime if a mental disease or defect prevented him from understanding the criminal nature of what he was doing at the time the offense occurred.

At trials where the mental state of the defendant is at issue the prosecution and defense usually wind up putting psychiatrists on the stand whose testimony is diametrically opposed to each other. The testimony of two experts at such loggerheads can have a way of canceling itself out in the minds of jurors. And that can happen often. A report compiled by the American Civil Liberties Union called "The Rights of Mental Patients," states that psychiatrists and psychologists can be expected to agree only about 54 percent of the time. Even more disconcerting to those who rely on the expert opinion of such witnesses is the report's contention that psychiatric "predictions of dangerous behavior are wrong about ninety-five percent of the time."

After complying with a court order to examine Gacy, Dr. Robert A. Reifman, director of the Psychiatric Institute of the Circuit Court of Cook County, reported that the defendant was "mentally fit to stand trial." After receipt of the report and the results of additional examinations by Dr. Reifman and by the defense's psychiatric expert Dr. Richard Rappaport, Garippo announced that the ruling on Gacy's sanity would not be dealt with until the time of the trial in order to reduce pre-trial publicity.

A successful insanity defense by Gacy would mean that he could be confined to a mental institution, but could not be imprisoned or executed.

Surprisingly, considering the amount of publicity it receives, insanity is a relatively rare defense. Only about 2 percent of criminal trials before juries revolve around issues of insanity. Those that do can be dramatic. Especially when there are implications of multiple personality, which Gacy's attorney's have hinted may figure prominently in their defense.

One of the most dramatic recent examples in American legal history involved an Ohio man charged with kidnap, rape, and robbery after a series of sexual assaults of young coeds abducted from or near the Ohio State University campus.

William Stanley Milligan was arrested for the crimes but pleaded innocent because of multiple personalities which psychiatrists indicated were unaware of one another and had no control of each other. Among ten personalities identified were those of "Ragan," the twenty-three-year-old evil side of Milligan, "Adelena," an aggressive lesbian, and a three-year-old girl artist.

The history-making trial of Milligan, which was the first major felony case in which a defendant claimed innocence because of multiple personalities, ended in December when Milligan was found innocent by reason of insanity.

Franklin County Commons Pleas Court Judge Jay Flowers, hearing the case without a jury in Columbus, Ohio, remarked that "There is no alternative from the evidence presented but to find this man not guilty by reason of insanity. In a case of this type it is always difficult to determine if the defendant is faking illness. But every bit of evidence discounts that conclusion."

Another accused mass murderer diagnosed by psychiatrists as a split personality is Kenneth Bianchi, accused by Los Angeles authorities as the "Hillside strangler," responsible for a string of slayings of young women. Even under hypnosis, Bianchi claimed to know nothing about five murders he was charged with. Psychiatrists reported that as soon as he identified with "Steve Walker," the alter ego talked freely under hypnosis of the slayings. But Bianchi's insanity ploy failed and he is serving life sentences in prison after convictions for the sex slayings of ten young women in California and two women in Washington state.

As early as January, Amirante was quoted as telling journalists that Gacy drifted from one personality to another and while talking, "his voice would change completely and he would look different."[6] In the letter he wrote to his mother from his jail cell, he reportedly observed that "I should have gotten rid of Jack." Some people interpreted his reference to "Jack" as evidence of an alter ego and evil side of the good natured "John" his neighbors and friends thought they knew.

[6]*Chicago Tribune,* January 9, 1979.

11

The Trial

Thirteen months after Gacy's arrest, selection of a jury for his trial on charges of murdering thirty-three young men and boys began in Rockford, Illinois.

State's Attorney Bernard Carey had been only partly successful in his bid to keep the proceedings in Chicago.

After protracted legal maneuvering, Judge Louis B. Garippo ruled that because of extensive pre-trial publicity the jury would be selected in the industrial metropolis of 200,000 some eighty-five miles northwest of the "Windy City" near the Wisconsin border. Then the twelve jurors and four alternates would be moved back to Garippo's tightly secured courtroom in the Cook County Criminal Courts Building for the trial, and sequestered in a Chicago hotel.

The controversial State's Attorney had also dropped his plans to personally head the prosecution team, because of his desire to run for re-election, and turned the job of chief prosecutor over to his able Chief Deputy, thirty-eight-year old William J. Kunkle, Jr.

A stocky veteran of seven years with the State's Attorney's office, Kunkle was assisted by Robert R. Egan, thirty-one, and by Terry Sullivan, thirty-five, who as chief of the Third District office in Des Plaines had been in on the Gacy investigation from the beginning. Assistant State's Attorneys Lawrence Finder and James Varga backed up the team, helping with legal research, preparation of evidence, and other chores.

Plans to try Gacy individually for each murder had also been abandoned. A single proceeding would be long and costly enough. And it was to become one of the most grisly, emotion-packed, and exhausting criminal trials in American history—even though the defense admitted at the outset that Gacy had, indeed, slaughtered a dizzying number of young men and boys.

The state had amassed a massive amount of material to prove its case, including an impressive array of witnesses, Gacy's own confessions, and the most damning evidence of all, the pitiful remains of victims pulled from under his house and on his property.

The determined members of the prosecution team were also aware, however, that despite the solid evidence in their hands they were faced not so much with proving that Gacy had committed the murders, but that he was sane, that he knew what he was doing when he systematically and with premeditation tortured, sexually abused, and killed his victims. Gacy was pleading innocent by reason of insanity.

The defendant was cleanshaven, several pounds lighter than his normal weight, and nattily dressed in black loafers and a three-piece gray tweed suit, one of four new suits his attorneys had purchased for the trial, when he appeared in a third-floor courtroom in the Winnebago County Courthouse for the beginning of jury selection. He might have been mistaken for one of his attorneys if his photos hadn't been seen during the previous thirteen months by almost everyone who watches television news programs or reads newspapers and magazines.

The direction the trial would take was immediately apparent when Judge Garippo began asking each prospective juror about his or her personal views regarding the death penalty, the insanity defense, and whether he or she could suspend any opinion about homosexuality in reaching a fair verdict.

After Garippo rejected several questions the defense lawyers wanted to ask, they groused that the judge's questioning wasn't thorough enough to develop sufficient information about the prejudices of prospective jurors. Nevertheless, the first day, four jurors were selected. They were two women and two men, one the father of twin twenty-year-old sons.

Gacy appeared relaxed and jovial during the proceedings. Predictably, perhaps, he seemed to be enjoying himself and basking in the limelight. He swiveled in his chair to gawk at spectators, including a woman sketch artist he seemed particularly captivated by, chatted with his lawyers, scanned legal papers, and scribbled on a notepad.

By Thursday, four days after jury selection began, the last of the twelve jurors and four alternates was accepted. The jury consisted of seven men and five women. Three women and a man were picked as the alternates. By contrast, jury selection for Richard Speck's trial for the murder of the eight student nurses had taken six weeks.

Wearing the last of his new suits, a mint green selection, also vested, Gacy leaned toward the prosecution table after the last of the alternates was selected and taunted in a stage whisper, "You lose!"

The prosecutors ignored him.

The following Wednesday the prosecution opened its case against Gacy in the Criminal Courts Building on Chicago's south side. Upstairs, five stories above Judge Garippo's cramped sixth-floor courtroom and conveniently out of sight of the jury, the jawbones of thirty-three young men and boys were arrayed in a quiet room. They were remains of the victims. The names of only twenty-two of them were known at that time.

Within the next few days the parents, brothers and sisters, and girlfriends of those who had been identified would be taking the stand to offer testimony.

In his opening statement, Egan described in ghastly detail how Gacy stabbed his first victim to death, then garroted the thirty-two others while using a device he called his rope trick. The first victim, a young man Gacy admitted picking up at the Greyhound bus station in Chicago's downtown Loop area in January 1972, still had not been identified.

"He started his rampage in 1972 and it took him six years, until December 11, 1978," Egan advised the jury. Then, turning and pointing an accusing finger at the defendant, he declared: "He killed people like he was swatting flies." The murders, he said, were "planned, mechanical, and premeditated." In the spectators' section, Mrs. Lola Woods, the mother of victim William Kindred, began to sob audibly.

Egan spared none of the gruesome details in cataloguing the Gacy horrors. The young Assistant State's Attorney quoted the burly defendant as bragging that when Greg Godzik was working for him, the unsuspecting teenager dug his own grave.

Recounting the murder of Gacy's last victim, Robert Piest, Egan told the jury that the helpless youth was frightened to tears and was whimpering after being manacled and sexually tortured by the sadistic pederast.

"Don't cry. I'm going to show you one more trick," the prosecutor quoted Gacy as telling the terrified boy. Then Gacy stepped behind Robert, placed a rope around his neck, tied three knots in the rope, slipped a stick between two of them, and twisted the stick until the youngster died. The sadistic contractor had just performed his final rope trick. "Piest convulsed," Egan intoned, "and was dead in seconds."

Egan said that in statements to investigators Gacy recalled several of the murders in detail. The killer was described as engaging at times, occasionally laughing, although methodical in his replies to questions and accounts of the killings.

Before concluding his statement, Egan warned the jurors to be skeptical when listening to the testimony of psychiatrists expected to testify for the defense. "Use your common sense and I think you will come to the conclusion that he [Gacy] is nothing more than an evil, evil man."

Robert Motta drew a far different picture of his client, during the opening statement for the defense. He claimed that Gacy suffered from an unconscious and uncontrollable mental illness and could not be held responsible for his actions under the state's insanity law. The fact that Gacy killed over and over again was described as illustrating a "profound and incredible obsession."

The defense lawyer claimed that Gacy was helpless against an all-consuming mental disease that forced him to kill. "He sleeps with corpses. He lived in a house with bodies under it for years," Motta declared.

Continuing, he insisted that Gacy was "incapable of forming an intent because of a profound mental disease. . . . His intelligence and thought process were helpless against a consuming mental disease."

It was for this reason that Gacy immersed himself so fully in his construction business, in his political work, and in his activities as an amateur clown, Motta said. Gacy had to fill all of his time "because he knew something was happening and couldn't help it."

Motta addressed the jury for an hour, setting the stage for the testimony of four psychiatrists and other medical experts he said he and co-counsel Sam Amirante planned to call to prove their client was insane. Defense psychiatrists had already described the defendant with labels such as "pseudoneurotic, schizophrenic, paranoid, and delusional," Motta declared. "But you can't label him. He's dangerously and incomprehensibly ill."

With the conclusion of the opening statements it was time for the prosecution to begin calling the first witnesses in what was already one of the most celebrated criminal cases in Chicago history. It would also be exhaustingly long and arduous for everyone concerned, from the families of the victims to the officers of the court and the defendant himself. However long the trial might last, the jury members would earn every cent of their $16.50 per day.

As is well known, the prosecution in criminal trials presents its evidence and witnesses first because, according to American law, the state has the responsibility of proving the defendant guilty beyond a reasonable doubt. The defendant has no similar official burden of proving himself innocent beyond a reasonable doubt.

When Kunkle and his colleagues opened the state's case, they did not focus on the issue of sanity. That was an issue for the defense to bring up, and for the state to counter. The prosecution team opened by calling family members and friends of Gacy's twenty-two young murder victims whose identities were known.

Marko Butkovich was the first witness summoned to the stand, and he told the court of the last time that he saw his son, John, alive. He and his wife, Teresa, had six children, Butkovich testified. "Now we got five."

Kunkle questioned the grieving father only a few minutes, and Amirante completed cross-examination equally rapidly. Then Butkovich was excused. After Kunkle showed an eight-by-ten photograph of John Butkovich to the jury, he carefully mounted it over the boy's name on a four-by-six-foot rectangular display board.

Immediately aware of the damaging effect that the pictures of the twenty-two identified victims placed one after another on the board might have on a jury, Amirante asked for a sidebar conference with Judge Garippo and the prosecutors—a discussion held out of the hearing range of the jury. Compiling a lineup of victims in front of the jury panel, such as Kunkle was obviously intent on doing, would be inflammatory, he objected.

Garippo sustained the objection, ruling that each photo could be mounted on the board only during testimony relating to that particular victim. The names on the board, each under a black rectangle where the photos were briefly mounted, would be permitted to remain.

Dolores Vance, the mother of Darryl Samson, was next. She recounted how she walked the streets nights looking for her missing eighteen-year-old son. "I got blisters on the bottom of my feet this big," she said, making a quarter-sized circle of her thumb and forefinger. "I burned up four cars looking."

Then Bessie Stapleton was called to testify about her son, Samuel Todd. When Egan asked her to identify the charm bracelet found on the boy's remains, she took it in her hand, confirmed that it was his, and cried out, "God, why?" She collapsed and lurched forward in the witness box, with her head on the railing.

Garippo ordered the jury from the room, and as they were filing out, court aides took the distraught woman by the arms and began helping her to a door. But she slumped again, and bailiffs and deputies picked her up and carried her outside the marbled and wood paneled courtroom.

As the agonizing but necessary ordeal continued, Myrtle Reffett testified about her son, Randall, believed to have been one of the two boys, along with Samuel Todd, that Gacy killed on the same night. Gacy had referred to the twin killings, in a statement to investigators, as "the double."

The State's Attorneys shared the questioning, one of them working with one witness, then passing the questioning to a teammate. Shirley Stein, the mother of Michael Bonnin, was questioned by Varga. Mrs. Stein said her family searched for her son in Wisconsin and Colorado, before his fishing license was found in Gacy's house.

Esther Johnson told of the terrible aftermath of the day she drove her son, Rick, to the Aragon Ballroom. Greg Godzik's mother and sister, both named Eugenia, each testified. So did his sweetheart, Judy Patterson. Violet Carroll recounted her last goodbye to Billy. And Rosemary Szyk identified her son John's ring.

Roger Sahs, forty, who had met John Prestidge in a bar and opened his home to the Michigan youth, was the last witness called during the first day of testimony. He told of parting with the victim after sharing coffee in a restaurant near Bughouse Square. Sahs said he put his young friend's picture in a gay magazine, with a notice listing him as missing, but never saw him again.

The grim procession continued through the next day, with the parents and friends of the twelve other known victims called one by one to the stand to add their sorrowful last recollections of the victims to the awful litany. William Kindred's girlfriend, Mary Jo Paulus, had been hurt in a car accident a few days earlier and was brought from her hospital bed to testify. She was pushed into the courtroom wearing a neck brace and in a wheelchair. Speaking barely above a whisper, and with difficulty, she identified a medallion recovered from among Gacy's belongings as one she had given to her former fiance.

Motta was cross-examining her when she interrupted and pleaded, "I would like Mr. Gacy to please stop staring at me." No one responded to the request, and Gacy's expression never changed.

Donita Ganzon wept as she testified about her relationship with Timothy O'Rourke, and during cross-examination the willowy transsexual found herself on the defensive against probing questions about her sex change. And still others were called.

Finally, Elizabeth Piest told of the terrible night of December 11, 1978. Although she sobbed softly when she was asked to identify her son's parka, there was no need for the fire department rescue crew the prosecution team had arranged to have standing by in case of a collapse or breakdown. The defense waived cross-examination.

The next day, Saturday, the state turned to details surrounding the investigation of her son's sudden disappearance from the pharmacy. As the trial moved on in the ensuing days, Gacy's friends, business associates, neighbors, and young men and boys who had lived with him, worked for him, and had sexual or violent encounters with him—and survived—testified.

The policemen who had dogged his steps, following his every move for days after he was linked to Robert Piest, and before his arrest, recounted the wild car chases and the defendant's sudden mood swings from angered quarry to genial host.

Des Plaines police detective David Hachmeister recalled that a few days before Gacy's arrest, the suspect was talking with two surveillance officers about his activities as a performing clown when he remarked: "You know . . . clowns can get away with murder!"

Assistant State's Attorney Finder demonstrated to the court how Gacy had once showed off his rope trick. Gacy was in jail when he agreed to demonstrate for Finder how he tied and tightened the ropes or cord that he used to strangle his victims. Finder said that Gacy instructed him to stick his hand through the bars and to pretend that his wrist was his neck. Then the prisoner fished a rosary from his pocket, looped it around Finder's wrist, and tied three knots. Finally, he stuck a pen between the second and third knots—and twisted. As the victim struggled, or convulsed, the garrote tightened. Consequently, Gacy explained, the victims "killed themselves."

The effect as Finder repeated the experiment on Kunkle's wrist in front of the jury and the judge—who had moved down from the bench for a closer look—was electric.

By the time Dr. Robert J. Stein, the doughty Cook County Medical Examiner, was called, the clamor for seats at the trial was already beginning to slacken. Dozens of people had been turned away during the first few days, but it was now possible to walk into the courtroom a few minutes before the trial and find a vacant seat. Soon there would even be vacancies among the fifty seats especially set aside for the press. And before the trial ended only family members of victims, reporters, a few curious individuals who looked suspiciously like men dressed up in women's clothing, and hard-core courtroom groupies with time on their hands and a preference for the real-life drama of a famous criminal trial to the bed-hopping antics of television's melodramatic daytime soaps were finding seats in the spectators' section.

And it *was* real life drama!

Two-and-a-half weeks after opening its case, and after calling some sixty witnesses, the state rested.

Amirante and Motta were facing enormous odds in their effort to save their client from life in prison, or the death penalty, and they knew it. It would be an uphill battle.

The defense opened with an expected move for a directed verdict of not guilty, a routine maneuver that was denied by Judge Garippo. Then the first witness was called, a surprise to many courtroom observers who would have expected him to testify for the prosecution. Jeffrey Rignall took the stand. Rignall was fidgety, and clearly still suffering damaging effects to his physical and emotional health, but he was determined to have his say about the man who had attacked and tortured him so savagely.

Amirante wanted to know if the witness believed that Gacy had the ability to appreciate the criminality of his acts and to conduct himself according to the law.

"No," Rignall replied.

"How did you reach that opinion?"

"By the beastly and animalistic ways he attacked me."

During cross-examination by Kunkle, Rignall cried. Then he vomited. Judge Garippo called a recess as the young man was led from the courtroom, crying hysterically. Gacy watched impassively, apparently unmoved, from the defense table a few feet away.

Witnesses continued to parade to the stand, as Amirante and Motta worked to build a case for their client's insanity.

227 . . .

Lillie Grexa was called and talked glowingly of her relationship with Gacy, whom she had known as a good neighbor and close friend. But during cross-examination she declared, "There is no way I'm going to say that John is crazy. He is a very brilliant man." It was not a statement helpful to the defense.

Finally, it was the turn of the medical establishment. Thomas Eliseo, a clinical psychologist from Rockford, was called. Eliseo had examined Gacy for five-and-a-half hours shortly after it was decided to select the jury from the broad-shouldered city to the north of Chicago.

Questioned by Motta, the psychologist reported that his examination indicated Gacy was very bright, so intelligent in fact that he would probably rank among the top 10 percent of the population. Eliseo added, however, that he considered the defendant to be a borderline schizophrenic, "a person who on the surface looks normal but has all kinds of neurotic, antisocial, psychotic illnesses."

At last, the defense case had been stated. Other experts called by the defense would provide similar if not exactly matching testimony. But once all the psychiatric and behavioral mumbo jumbo was stripped away and the professional jargon reduced to plain talk, the message would be essentially the same: In layman's terms, John Wayne Gacy, Jr., was crazy—at least during the terrible periods when he snuffed out the lives of his known victims. The defense attorneys were determined to prove that their client had been helpless in the grip of an uncontrollable compulsion to sexually abuse, torture, and murder, either continuously during the six-year period of the killings or periodically while thirty-three young men died.

Under Motta's careful questioning, Eliseio advised that it was his conclusion that Gacy suffered from paranoid schizophrenia during the period that the killings took place. The condition prevented Gacy from behaving in accordance with the law, and he did not recognize the criminality of his acts while they were occurring, the psychologist testified.

"That does not mean he was psychotic overtly all of the time," the witness stressed, "but the condition was there. . . ."

The professional testimony was interrupted after Eliseo's appearance by several other witnesses, including the defendant's former wife, Carole Lofgren; his mother, Mrs. Marion Gacy; and his sister, Mrs. Karen Kuzma.

Questioned by Amirante, Mrs. Lofgren told the court that the John Gacy she had read about in the newspapers, which depicted him as a depraved sadist and sex killer, was not the same man she had known as a husband. "I feel sorry for him. My heart goes out to him," she said. Then she broke down in tears. At the defense table, Gacy also placed his hand to his eyes, bowed his head, and wept. It was the first emotion he had betrayed since the beginning of the trial. Judge Garippo called a recess as two guards assisted the defendant, wiping at tear-reddened eyes, from the courtroom.

Whispers rippled through the spectators' area as Gacy's seventy-two-year-old mother hobbled down the long aisle, pushing her walker ahead of her, to testify on February 25, the first day of the fourth week of the trial. During her grueling appearance the defendant's mother described him as a good and loving son. Tearfully, she recounted his deep love for his father, and how that love was constantly rejected and frustrated by the elder Gacy's authoritarianism and drunken brutality. "He seemed to be after John all the time," she said. "He always called him 'Stupid.'"

One time her husband picked the boy up "and threw him against the stove," she said. At other times her husband beat the children with a razor strop. At the conclusion of her testimony, Judge Garippo called a recess, and as Gacy was being led from the courtroom, the old lady reached out her arms and mother and son hugged each other.

Mrs. Kuzma also characterized "the brother that I knew" as "always sweet, loving, understanding, generous." But she also recalled the stormy relationship between her father and the rest of the family. He beat her brother, she said, and once threatened to kill him, branding him as a coward.

By mid-week, the emotional testimony from the women who had loved the defendant, and from childhood friends, had been concluded and the defense once more turned to the professionals they were banking on to prove that their client was unable to control the dark forces that compelled him to torture and kill.

Dr. Lawrence Z. Freedman, a University of Chicago psychiatrist, announced that Gacy was a pseudo-neurotic paranoid-schizophrenic. And he traced the defendant's mental illness to his traumatic childhood, especially the brutality of his father.

Clinical psychologist Robert Traisman testified that he had administered the Rorschach Ink Blot Test to Gacy and discovered that he was "a paranoid schizophrenic who had homosexual conflicts, marked feelings of masculine inadequacy, a man who had a lack of empathy, a lack of feeling for other people, an individual with an alarming lack of emotional control or ego control when under stress, who had strong potentials for emotional or ego disintegration and expressions of very hostile, dangerous impulses, either to others or to himself."

Yet, when asked during cross-examination if he believed that Gacy was aware of the criminality of certain acts he performed, and of their morality or lack of morality, Traisman replied that Gacy understood the nature of his criminal acts and might even be aware of their rightness or wrongness. But even if he was aware, the psychologist said, Gacy might not have been able to control his actions.

Dr. Richard Rappaport, a Chicago-area psychiatrist and veteran professional witness, had conducted sixty-five hours of interviews with the defendant and poured over an impressive array of additional consultations and tests he had ordered, by the time he was called on to testify. Based on these talks, tests, and Gacy's own medical records, Dr. Rappaport had previously determined that the defendant had no critical physical illness and no evidence of organic brain disease.

And although concluding that Gacy was, indeed, insane at the time the alleged crimes occurred, it was Dr. Rappaport who struck hardest of the defense witnesses at the contention that the defendant was suffering from multiple personality. The name Jack Hanley, which Gacy sometimes used, was merely a ploy to prevent his identification, the psychiatrist declared.

In court, Rappaport said Gacy exhibited psychosexual disorders including fetishism (his preoccupation with women's underwear), sadism, homosexuality, and necrophilia. The psychiatrist testified that during the period he was conducting the examination, Gacy was probably not psychotic. The defense had concluded its case.

The state opened its rebuttal of the insanity defense by calling witnesses who had known Gacy in Iowa, including victims of his sexual abuse, in efforts to prove that he was sane at the time of his sodomy conviction. If this could be accomplished, it would taint or discredit the previous testimony of defense witnesses characterizing the defendant as suffering from a longtime mental illness or condition.

The prosecution's first medical witness was Dr. Leonard L. Heston, professor of psychiatry, who had examined Gacy in Iowa. Although his examination of the defendant prior to the sodomy conviction indicated he was an antisocial personality, Dr. Heston said, he believed Gacy to be sane at the time the offense occurred.

Testimony the next day was highlighted by the appearance of Robert Donnelly, a twenty-one-year-old college student who painfully recounted a night of horror when he was abducted at gunpoint by Gacy on December 30, 1977.

Donnelly said he had left a friend's house late at night and was walking to a bus stop when a spotlight was trained on him by a man driving what appeared to be an unmarked police car. A burly man wearing a short black leather jacket like policemen wear got out, demanded to see his identification, then pulled a gun and ordered, "Get in this car or I'm going to blow you away." In tears, the witness testified that his hands were cuffed behind his back and he was forced to lie on the floor of the front seat as the car roared away.

He told a harrowing tale of gross sexual abuse and psychological terror that occurred when his kidnapper choked him with a rope, shoved his head under water in a bathtub until he passed out, played Russian roulette with him, and raped him until he lost consciousness. At one point Judge Garippo had to call a recess when the distraught witness cried, "This is hell! This is hell!" as he described how Gacy had abused him with a dildo.

One time, Donnelly said, he regained consciousness to find himself gagged, with his ankles bound. Gacy sexually tortured him until he lost consciousness once more. The distraught witness said the next time he revived, he begged his tormentor to kill him because of the excruciating pain.

Donnelly testified that Gacy finally released him in an alley in the Loop and warned him against going to the police because he wouldn't be believed. He reported the kidnapping and night of torture to the police anyway. But Gacy was right. They didn't believe him.

After the rape victim's graphic testimony, the prosecutors again turned to expert medical witnesses and called Dr. Arthur Hartman, chief psychologist of the Psychiatric Institute of the Cook County Circuit Court. Dr. Hartman said his investigation, which included twelve interviews, had shown there was no sign of mental disturbance or mental disease in the defendant. There was, however, a "psychopathic or antisocial personality with sexual deviation," and minor symptoms of paranoid hysterical reactions. He said he believed Gacy understood the criminality of his actions.

Dr. Robert A. Reifman next advised that he didn't believe it was possible for an individual to have thirty-three instances of temporary insanity. Gacy, he told the jury, suffered from a personality disorder, not a mental disease.

"There is no doubt in my mind that when he came in for his interview he was trying to fake a multiple personality," said the psychiatrist about his meeting with the defendant shortly after Gacy's arrest. "He told me he had four personalities: John Gacy, the clown; John Gacy, the politician; John Gacy, the contractor; and a fellow named Jack Hanley."

Dr. Reifman said he quickly saw through the ruse, because although Gacy claimed the crimes were committed while Hanley was in control, Gacy was able to recall a considerable amount of information about them. Research into legitimate cases of multiple personality indicates that one personality does not recall events that occurred while another personality was in control.

Richard Rogers, a clinical psychologist, told the jury that he had diagnosed Gacy as obsessive-compulsive. He said that Gacy had probably experienced "sexual sadism," but was aware of the criminality of his behavior and was able to conform to society's rules if he wished.

Dr. James Cavanaugh, Jr., director of the Isaac Ray Center of the Rush-Presbyterian-St. Luke's Medical Center in Chicago, where he supervised a program dealing with criminals who were mentally ill, also diagnosed Gacy as having a mixed personality disorder.

Then, under questioning by Kunkle, Cavanaugh was asked: "Is it possible to guarantee a person found not guilty by reason of insanity, and then committed to a mental hospital . . . will remain there for the rest of his life?"

"Absolutely impossible," the witness declared.

Cavanaugh had begun to elaborate when Motta objected. But the damage had been done. It seemed unlikely that there was a single juror whose mind didn't flash at least for a moment or two on an image of John Wayne Gacy being released in a few years from a mental hospital to begin his depraved cruising, torturing, and murdering all over again. A defense call for a mistrial was denied.

Moving into the next phase of the trial the following day, Amirante and Motta called still more medical experts, in their attempt at rebuttal of the state's case. Dr. Tobias Brocher, a psychiatrist associated with the famed Menninger Foundation in Kansas, told the jury that his study of Gacy showed the defendant to be a borderline toward a schizophrenic process.

Another psychiatrist, Dr. Helen Morrison, agreed with other experts that Gacy had a high IQ, but claimed he hadn't developed emotionally past the infant stage. She diagnosed him as suffering from mixed psychosis as far back as 1958. Under cross-examination by Egan, she said that it was her opinion Gacy would have murdered the Piest boy even if there was a uniformed police officer in the home with him at the time.

233 . . .

That day, outside the hearing of the jury, Gacy made a statement to the court, citing his reluctance to testify. The confessed multiple killer would not exercise his right to take the stand in his own defense.

The trial was winding down, and the state had a last chance before the beginning of summations to rebut the testimony of the defense's final witnesses. Dr. Jan Fawcett, chairman of the Department of Psychiatry at Rush-Presbyterian-St. Luke's, was called to the stand. Fawcett said he did not believe Gacy to be suffering from a mental disease and, likewise, that his mental condition did not conform to the standards of the Illinois insanity defense qualifications. He said he had seen no indication of psychosis in the defendant.

A final witness testified, then Kunkle advised the court that the state was resting its case. Amirante told the court that he and his colleague, Motta, had also concluded their defense of the defendant. Summations would begin in the morning, with Sullivan speaking first for the prosecution, then Amirante for the defense, and finally back to Kunkle for the prosecution.

The evidence board was still set up and numerous other exhibits cluttered the courtroom as the defendant, officers of the court, and spectators assembled the next day to begin the final phase of the trial before the jury was instructed to begin deliberations. One of the most grim reminders of the horror that had raged across Chicago's north side and near northern suburbs was the trap door to the crawl space under Gacy's house where so many of the victims had been buried. It had been reassembled in the well of the courtroom with the opening plainly visible, a grim reminder of the limp bodies that had once been dumped or shoved inside.

Sullivan talked, shouted, and accused for nearly four hours, stalking back and forth before the jury, reminding them of the young lives that had been cut short, while tracing Gacy's cunning, manipulative behavior both before and after becoming a suspect in the Piest disappearance. The lanky Assistant State's Attorney repeatedly recalled testimony and evidence to illustrate that Gacy's careful planning and his intent to rape, torture, and kill were the conscious acts of a sane, though depraved man.

Amirante's closing argument for the defense was equally emotional. Admitting that his client had committed evil acts, he insisted, however, that Gacy was not an evil man. Instead, the lawyer declared, the defendant was a man driven by "perverted obsessions and compulsions he could not control."

Amirante quoted from Robert Lewis Stevenson's famous novel *The Strange Case of Dr. Jekyll and Mr. Hyde,* while painting Gacy as the personification of evil—insane evil. He even recounted the shameful witchcraft trials in Salem, Massachusetts, nearly three hundred years ago, as he pleaded with the jury to avoid deciding their verdict on emotional grounds.

Gacy was insane, Amirante insisted, and should be spared the death penalty so that he could be studied and society could learn from him in an effort to understand the mad forces that impelled him to hurt and kill. The jury, he said, must find Gacy not guilty by reason of insanity.

In his closing argument, Kunkle dismissed Amirante's plea to spare Gacy's life so that he could be studied. Noting the years of appeals and protracted legal maneuvering that were ahead if Gacy was convicted, the veteran State's Attorney pointed out that there would be plenty of time for study even with a verdict of guilty.

Kunkle insisted that Gacy knew exactly what he was doing when he planned and carried out his ghastly executions. And he knew what he was doing when he covered up the evidence.

Striding to the display board, Kunkle began plucking off the photographs of the identified victims, one by one, with calculated, cold fury until he held them all in his beefy hand.

"Don't show sympathy!," he boomed. "Don't show sympathy! Show justice! Show the same sympathy and pity that this man showed when he took these lives and put them there."

Whirling, Kunkle hurled the sheaf of photos into the open mouth of the crawl space hatch. Startled gasps of surprise and shock filled the otherwise silent courtroom.

The Chief Deputy State's Attorney's closing act was as dramatically effective as if it had been scripted in Hollywood; and it dwarfed the courtroom histrionics of his predecessors.

The remainder of Kunkle's argument was anticlimactic. The state had completed its case and there was nothing more that could be done to influence the jury's verdict. More than a hundred witnesses had testified during the nearly five weeks of the grueling trial, before Judge Garippo ordered the courtroom locked while he delivered instructions to the jury. Shortly after lunch, the twelve jurors were left to make their decision.

According to Illinois law, verdicts on each of the thirty-five indictments had to be unanimous. There were three possible findings: guilty, not guilty, or not guilty by reason of insanity.

Less than two hours later, an amazingly short time for deliberation after a murder trial—especially such a trial as this—Judge Garippo was notified that verdicts had been reached.

Attorneys, officers of the court, and spectators hurried back to the courtroom. The end of the drama was at hand, and they waited, hushed and expectant, as the judge entered and solemnly took his seat at the bench. Before the jury was ushered in, Garippo warned against any unusual or emotional behavior that could influence the panel members in case they had to be reconvened. Gacy sat upright at the defense table, stone-faced, to await the verdicts.

The courtroom remained quiet as the jury members filed in and took their seats. After ascertaining that the thirty-five indictments had been properly signed, Garippo instructed jury foreman Ronald L. Beaver, thirty, a Rockford factory worker, to pass them to the bailiff, who in turn would pass them to the clerk for reading.

Standing to the right of the judge, facing the spectators, and speaking in a clear resonant voice, the clerk read: "We, the jury, find the defendant, John Wayne Gacy, guilty of the murder of Robert Piest."

"We, the jury, find the defendant, John Wayne Gacy, guilty of indecent liberties with a child upon Robert Piest."

The clerk continued on, reading the jury's finding of guilty in the deviate sexual assault of Robert Piest, of guilty in the murder of John Butkovich, and of guilty in the remaining thirty-one murder indictments. The ex-contractor had just been convicted of committing more murders than anyone in American history.

As he was led from the courtroom, Gacy smirked and winked at a deputy sheriff.

On March 13, four days before St. Patrick's Day, Gacy's thirty-eighth birthday, court was reconvened for sentencing. The state asked the death penalty in the twelve murders known to have occurred since the current Illinois statute on capital punishment became effective in 1977.

The defense submitted two motions to have the statute declared unconstitutional. The motions were denied. Then Amirante argued that the string of murders began before the statute became law, and thus were part of a continuing ritual. The feisty defense lawyer next claimed that his client had been denied his right to be committed prior to trial. None of the maneuvers worked.

Amirante also argued that the jury should be dismissed because, based on the short time members deliberated, they obviously had been predisposed to the finding of guilty. And if that was true, he reasoned, then their minds could already be made up on the question of the death penalty as well. That argument, too, was denied, precluding the dreary prospect of assuming the arduous task of selecting a brand-new jury to deliberate over the punishment phase of the trial.

Amirante and his colleague, Motta, were now faced with a choice: of conducting the death penalty hearing before the jury that had just returned thirty-five guilty verdicts against their client or of leaving sentencing solely up to the judge. They opted for the jury. If only one of the twelve members of the panel voted against the death penalty, Gacy would be spared execution in the electric chair.

Garippo again instructed the jury. Sullivan delivered the opening statement during this, the final phase of the proceedings. Once more, the blond, blue-eyed attorney retraced the horror and pain that Gacy had inflicted on his victims, both those he allowed to live as well as those he killed. Was there anyone, he asked, for whom the death penalty was more appropriate?

Despite the jury's refusal to return a verdict of innocent by reason of insanity, the defense wasn't giving up on their contention that Gacy's bestial crimes were impelled by deep psychological and emotional disturbances that were beyond his control.

Motta told the jury that the question now before them was whether or not the conditions that ruled Gacy's mind and actions were sufficient to justify sparing him from execution. And he admonished the jurors that if they did, indeed, return the death penalty, "when you put your name on the verdict, you pull the switch."

Kunkle objected vigorously. The objection was sustained. But the words could not be retracted nor erased from the memory of the jurors.

Motta pleaded with the jury to allow his client to live: "I ask you to let him exist in a six-by-ten cell for the rest of his life."

Egan, speaking for the prosecution, assured the jurors that if they voted for the death penalty—as they should—in fact it would not be they who would be responsible for Gacy's execution. It was Gacy who earned execution and sentenced himself to death by his own actions, Egan declared.

It was Amirante's turn next, and he echoed Motta's plea to spare the life of their client. Gacy belonged in a mental institution for the rest of his life, the lawyer insisted.

"Only God," he said, "can judge his blackened soul."

At last it was Kunkle's turn for rebuttal. Victory has healing powers, and the Chief Deputy looked as fresh as he had on the first day of the trial, when he arose from his chair at the prosecution table and strode purposefully to the front of the jury box. He reminded the jurors that Gacy had been convicted of not one, but thirty-three dreadful murders. He scoffed at the idea of Gacy's so-called emotional disturbance as a mitigating factor.

Describing Gacy as a "competent, skillful torturer and killer," who revelled in his God-like power of life and death over his victims, Kunkle warned: "If you allow this evil man to walk this Earth, then God help us all."

The chief prosecutor characterized the convicted killer as a liar and con man who slaughtered his victims remorselessly and should be made to pay for his crimes. "John Gacy learned to kill, kept on killing, and knew he was killing," Kunkle told the jury.

"If this is not an appropriate case for the death penalty, then there is no death penalty in Illinois. This is a case that cries out, not only with the voices of thirty-three dead, but the voices of thirty-three families, but yes, the voices of every single citizen of this state, and that voice says, 'John Gacy, enough! Enough!' "

Garippo instructed the jury for the last time. He explained that if the panel decided for imprisonment, Gacy would be sentenced to from twenty to forty years for each offense. Significantly, he added that prisoners usually serve only about half the term specified.

This time the jury deliberated just slightly more than two hours before sending a message to the judge that a verdict had been reached.

Gacy was called before the bench and stood between his two lawyers as the clerk read the verdict:

"We, the jury, unanimously conclude that the defendant, John Wayne Gacy, attained the age of eighteen years at the time of the murders, and has been convicted of intentionally murdering the following individuals:

"Matthew H. Bowman, Robert Gilroy, John Mowery, Russell O. Nelson, Robert Winch, Tommy Bolin, David Paul Talsma, William Kindred, Timothy O'-Rourke, Frank Landingin, James Mazzara, and Robert Piest.

"That these murders occurred after June 21, 1977.

"We, the jury, unanimously conclude that the court shall sentence the defendant, John Wayne Gacy, to death!"

Epilogue

Before all the bodies were pulled from the dark tomb under John Gacy's home, the Chicago Police Department was developing plans for an improved computer system to trace missing persons. Two top police officials were named to head the program, which will make it possible for investigators to match up common denominators in missing-persons cases that are connected. There was also some indication that the new system would comply with recommendations by Carey and Dr. Stein to computerize area-wide data extending well beyond the city limits of Chicago.

During a ceremony at the Des Plaines Civic Center, a grateful and proud community presented awards and commendations for a job well done to police and civilian employees, including communications clerks and secretaries, who worked on the investigation. "I submit to you that lives of persons unknown were in fact saved because of the professional manner in which this case was handled," Chief Alfano told the assembled officers and civilians. "Who knows how many more victims there might have been." Lieutenant Kozenczak was moved to command of the department's Patrol Division and was expected to be promoted to the rank of captain.

Jeffrey Rignall's medical bills had burgeoned to fifteen thousand dollars by early 1979, and he was talking of filing bankruptcy.

Dr. Stein and his staff continued their ghastly task, attempting to learn the names of nearly half the victims who were still unidentified. Parents of the boys and young men whose names were known buried their dead.

Neighbors on Summerdale Avenue complained that the empty lot where Gacy's house once stood was left littered with rocks, pieces of fencing, and other trash. The site was damned as an eyesore, a threat to surrounding property values, and a danger to children.

Others, including parents of some of the victims and much of the media, were looking around for someone to blame. It was difficult to understand how so many murders could occur in one place, apparently at the hands of one man, over such a long period of time. Even more puzzling was how it could happen under the nose of what was ostensibly one of the largest, most sophisticated, best-equipped, and well-trained police departments in the country. Chicago police were publicly criticized for negligence, and named in lawsuits.

Some people focused their anger on homosexuals, confirming the worst fears of some of Chicago's large gay community. The killer may have been afraid of being exposed as a homosexual, as he reputedly claimed, if some of the young men and boys he raped went to their parents or to police. But rape is a crime, regardless of the sex of the perpetrator and the victim, gay spokesmen maintained. They pointed out that not all homosexuals commit murder, just as all heterosexuals don't commit monstrous crimes against children. The boys and young men who died in the cozy little home near Chicago O'Hare International were the victims of a sadist and pederast who happened to be homosexual.

Blame was leveled at the Iowa Board of Parole. The Board was named in at least one lawsuit arising from the mass murders. But sex criminals walk out of American prisons every day. And John Gacy was one of those people who thrived and did well in the tightly confined area of the prison where he was under rigid control, and his behavior was exemplary. Based on existing standards of judgment, he appeared to have earned parole.

During the eighteen months he was in custody, there was no attempt to cure him or to modify his sexual behavior in anticipation of the day he would be freed. This was neglected, even though both the judge and prosecutor responsible for sending him to prison recognized his potential for violence and aberrant behavior that indicated he could continue to be a threat to young men and boys.

Perhaps some day future generations will look back with uncomprehending horror on the twentieth-century practice of freeing known sex criminals before they have been cured. But in today's society, the Iowa correctional system is little different than those in most other states.

It has been estimated at various times that sex offenders make up anywhere from 10 to 25 percent of the population of most prisons. Yet very little is done to alter the behavior of the sexually dangerous, and, except for the most heinous sex murderers, they are freed time and time again. After the horror in suburban Chicago was discovered, psychiatrists and behavioral scientists attempted to bring the actions of mass killers into focus. Dr. Marvin Ziporyn, an authority on mass murder who was interviewed on Chicago's local ABC television outlet, said the killings on Summerdale Avenue appeared to be classic. "He had the love of power that we all have and he almost has gone berserk, gone wild, gone out of control," Ziporyn said of the murderer, "because he has killed and tasted flesh."[1] Ziporyn continued that, having killed once, a murderer might be surprised at how easy the act is, and be pleased with his ability and power to make life-and-death decisions.

Other behaviorists pointed out that for sexual acts to be fully gratifying for some individuals, they must be tied to aggression and violence.

But Lawrence Z. Freedman, professor of psychiatry at the University of Chicago, observed: "Mass killings in this country are usually not related to sexual activity . . . The most common mass murders are committed by killers frustrated with society and venting their frustrations against a general populace by killing strangers." He added, revealingly, that "persons who commit mass murders often wish to be liked and admired."[2]

There has been a tendency by behaviorists pondering

---

[1] WLS-TV—Channel Seven, February 14, 1979.
[2] *Chicago Tribune,* December 26, 1978.

factors that cause people to become criminals to blame society as the villain. This can make reformers feel very good, but it is counterproductive because it merely provides the lawless with ready-made excuses for their actions by tracing the genesis of their criminality to fathers, mothers, broken homes, poverty, or some other individual or condition. It seems that no one ever thinks of blaming the criminal himself. Nevertheless, it seems possible that some people are so vicious and devoid of feeling for others that they become thieves, murderers, and rapists merely because they choose to.

Certainly more could be done to protect society from sex criminals. Many sex crimes could be prevented if once offenders were caught they were either executed, sentenced to long-term imprisonment, or provided with effective treatment and rehabilitation—depending on the severity of their crimes and their ability to respond to therapy.

All the approaches have been attacked at one time or another by civil libertarians as, among other things, violating the U.S. Constitution by inflicting cruel and unusual punishment.

The death penalty has been repeatedly assaulted on both constitutional and humanitarian grounds as illegal and barbaric. When John A. Spenkelink was electrocuted in Florida in early 1979, protestors sang civil-rights songs outside the prison and screamed that society had no right to take his life, even though he was a killer with a long criminal record. No one marched outside the house on Summerdale Avenue or protested violation of the rights of the boys and young men who were murdered and buried there or discarded in Chicago-area waterways like so many sheets of soiled tissue.

It is also cruel punishment to make someone spend his life locked behind bars without freedom of movement or association. But who deserves the pity? The individual who has proven he is unfit to walk freely in society because he is dangerous to others, or potential victims who have caused injury to no one?

Castration or treatment with such large doses of female hormones that the sex drive is virtually obliterated might also lessen the dangers from sex offenders. But these approaches can be ruled out for humane reasons too.

There is so much concern for the civil liberties of sex criminals that it is almost illegal to try to protect women or children from them. Emphasis has too often been centered on helping the child molester or rapist, when common sense should dictate that efforts be concentrated on protecting the public. Unfortunately, the law does not deal in common sense.

A complete overhaul of society's approach to dealing with the sex criminals among us is needed. This includes judicial and correctional attitudes as well as initiation of bold new approaches to treatment. There is no reason why the tremendous power of the law cannot be focused on the more effective detection and apprehension of people who sexually prey on others who are weaker than them as well as on treatment and rehabilitation.

When treatment is provided for sex offenders, individual counseling and group therapy has frequently been resorted to. But it doesn't work very well. Sexual aberration, like narcotics addiction, is one of the most difficult medical and behavioral problems to cure.

Narcotics addicts usually drift from one treatment program to another until they finally overdose and die, if they don't first lose their lives by some other means. Sex offenders charm their therapists, confess that they have been bad boys, and walk out of mental hospitals and prisons by the thousands every year, looking for new victims.

Only a few states make serious attempts to provide treatment for sex offenders that have any chance of seriously altering their behavior before they are freed from custody. And some states that do have special programs for the sexually dangerous, bar murderers from participation. But murderers are not necessarily barred from parole.

Illinois has a single treatment program for sex offenders at Menard Psychiatric Center, which is voluntary and handles about twenty prisoners at a time. There is a small waiting list.

Only a handful of states have separate institutions for the study and treatment of sex offenders. There are an enlightened few states, however, that are making significant efforts to deal with the problem. And a few brave and imaginative behaviorists have devised innovative and promising programs utilizing aversion therapy to modify the behavior of sex criminals and other violent felons. Not surprisingly, they have been attacked by civil libertarians and government agencies more concerned with safeguarding the civil rights of men with long records of sadistic abuse, than with protecting the persons and lives of innocent victims.

Aversion therapy is basically an attempt to change behavior or to cure by punishment. Electric shock and drugs that cause nausea or vomiting or brief periods of muscle paralysis and interruption of breathing have at times been employed as essential components of the treatment programs.

Programs utilizing the muscle-relaxing drug were pioneered at The California Medical Facility at Vacaville and at the Atascadero State Hospital. Electric-shock aversion was also used on homosexuals and child molesters at Atascadero. Both programs were halted after a flurry of bad publicity and outraged cries of brainwashing and legal torture.

A nausea-producing drug was used in a program at the Iowa Security Medical Facility at Oakdale near Iowa City, before the courts ruled that the activities were unconstitutional.

At the Connecticut Correctional Institution at Somers, child molesters were reportedly cured after twelve weeks of treatment. The process involved the administration of electrical shocks on the inner thighs as the convicted sex criminals watched series of pictures of naked children. The treatment was reinforced with hypnosis, which was used to associate sexual thoughts of children with things the patients feared such as snakes or heights. The American Civil Liberties Union joined with three convicts, suing the prison and claiming that paroles were denied if the child molester didn't participate.

The Wisconsin Correctional Institution at Fox Lake also instituted a voluntary program of aversion therapy for child molesters, employing electric shock treatment. Prisoners are alternately shown slides of children and of adult women in G-strings or provocative clothing. If the inmates hesitate too long over the slides of children before switching to pictures of adult women they are given electrical shocks. The treatment modalities may appear to be extreme. But so are the costs in lives and emotional trauma for the victims of sex criminals.

No one, of course, has a miracle cure that will suddenly eradicate sex crimes as totally as smallpox. Sex crimes can be reduced materially, however, by providing effective treatment or long-term incarceration for men and boys who have already run into trouble with the law because of sexual misbehavior and assaults on others.

But it is too late for new laws, shock treatment, or nausea-inducing drugs for someone who has murdered thirty-three young men and boys. For this person, there can be only two intelligent alternatives: life in prison—or execution.

Gacy is serving twenty-one life terms, with no provisions for parole, for the murders of the young men believed to have been slain before Illinois' current death penalty became law. Five years after his trial, the lengthy appeals process was still dragging its dreary way through the state and federal courts as new attorneys who were representing him continued efforts to prevent twelve death sentences from being carried out.

In June 1984, the Illinois Supreme Court upheld both the convictions and death sentences, rejecting an appeal based on grounds that Gacy was insane at the time of the slayings.

In March 1985, the U. S. Supreme Court voted six to two, denying an appeal on Gacy's behalf, claiming the Illinois death penalty law violates the U. S. Constitution's bar against cruel and unusual punishment. The only dissents against the unsigned order came from Justices Thurgood Marshall and William Brennan, liberals, who are both known for their opposition to the death penalty. The appeal questioned only the constitutionality of the Illinois death penalty, leaving Gacy's attorneys free to raise new issues before the county, state and federal courts. Gacy's fight for life returned again to the lower courts for a new round of appeals.

If and when the will of the people is finally carried out, Gacy will not die in the electric chair as originally ordered by Garippo. Since his conviction, the Illinois death penalty law has been changed to provide for execution by lethal injection instead of electrocution.

And no one will be drafted from among the hundreds of citizens from across the United States and overseas who wrote to prison and court authorities volunteering to personally execute the pug-faced killer. Letters were received from a surprising cross section of people, including housewives, a clergyman, a funeral director, a born-again Christian, a policeman, a prison inmate, and a jobless Austrian who said he needed the money from the executioners' fee. Eleven letters were received from volunteers in England, which does not have the death penalty for murderers.

While awaiting a conclusion of the appeals process, Gacy is expected to remain on death row at the maximum security Menard Correctional Center some 300 miles south of Chicago. He was the first inmate to occupy the state's new death row facility there. Even with his execution however, the story of his crimes will not be over. Families will still grieve. And several bodies will apparently continue to lie unclaimed in Chicago area cemeteries as the last unidentified victims of the notorious sex slayer.

By the summer of 1985, the identities of nine of the young men pulled from shallow graves on Gacy's property were still unknown. The last two previous identifications were made five years earlier, in March 1980, when the use of dental and radiology records made it possible to name Kenneth Parker, sixteen, and Michael Marino, fourteen, as victims. Missing persons reports were filed by relatives of both boys on October 25, 1976, and investigators said the youths may have been killed at about the same time because they were buddies, and shared a common grave in the crawlspace.

In June 1981, Coroner Stein conferred with the Funeral Directors' Association of Greater Chicago and arranged to hold non-sectarian services and burial in separate cemeteries for the unclaimed victims. The Association donated coffins, tombstones and other expenses.

"Of course, we were hoping that someone would show up at the services, some relative, some friend," Stein later confided to the author. "But no one did. Just journalists and policemen."

About the Author

Clifford Linedecker is a former daily newspaper journalist with eighteen years experience on the *Philadelphia Inquirer*, *Rochester* (N.Y.) *Times-Union*, *Fort Wayne News-Sentinel*, and several other Indiana newspapers. He is an experienced investigative reporter who has covered police and the courts on each of the papers where he was employed. He is a former articles editor for National Features Syndicate in Chicago, and for "County Rambler" magazine. He is the author of numerous true crime titles, including *The Man Who Killed Boys*, *Night Stalker*, *Killer Kids*, *Blood in the Sand*, and *Deadly White Female*.